Power of...
GeoWorks
ENSEMBLE

**ARNOLD SHULMAN
EDITH SHULMAN**

MIS: *PRESS*

A Subsidiary of
Henry Holt and Co., Inc.

Copyright © 1991 by Management Information Source, Inc.
a subsidiary of Henry Holt and Company, Inc.
115 West 18th Street
New York, New York 10011

All rights reserved. Reproduction or use of editorial or pictorial content in any manner is prohibited without express permission. No patent liability is assumed with respect to the use of the information contained herein. While every precaution has been taken in the preparation of this book, the publisher assumes no responsibility for errors or omissions. Neither is any liability assumed for damages resulting from the use of the information contained herein.

First Edition—1991

ISBN 1-55828-167-3

Printed in the United States of America
10 9 8 7 6 5 4 3 2 1

MIS:Press books are available at special discounts for bulk purchases for sales promotions, premiums, fund-raising, or educational use. Special editions or book excerpts can also be created to specification.

For details contact:

    Special Sales Director
    MIS:Press
    a subsidiary of Henry Holt and Company, Inc.
    115 West 18th Street
    New York, New York 10011

TRADEMARKS

Cakewalk is a trademark of Twelve Tone Systems, Inc.
Finale is a trademark of Coda Music Software, a Wenger Company
GEOS, GeoWorks, GeoWorks Ensemble, Ensemble, GeoComm, GeoDex, GeoDraw, GeoManager, GeoPlanner, and GeoWrite are trademarks of GeoWorks Corporation
IBM is a trademark of IBM Corporation
MS-DOS is a trademark of Microsoft Corporation
The Norton Utilites is a trademark of Symantec Corporation
PC Tools is a trademark of Central Point Software, Inc.
PostScript is a trademark of Adobe Systems, Inc.
Sprint is a trademark of Borland International, Inc.
URW Roman, URW Sans, URW SymbolPS, and URW Mono are trademarks of URW, GmbH.

Note:

The GeoWorks Ensemble software contains Nimbus Q from Digital Typeface Corporation and typefaces from URW, GmbH. Certain images and backgrounds are copyrighted works of Comstock, Inc.

Dedication

In memory of Uncle Albert.

Acknowledgments

First of all, we would like to thank the staff at GeoWorks who were especially helpful in spite of the multitude of tasks involved with launching a new program. We particularly appreciate the help Matthew Loveless gave us. He always took time to answer questions and listen to comments.

A special thanks to America Online for their cooperation and assistance in writing that section of the book.

We would like to thank the staff at MIS:Press for their excellent editorial and layout work. In particular we would like to acknowledge the editorial work of Walt Garnett. His many suggestions, comments, and careful attention to details is greatly appreciated. We would also like to thank the editors Vicky Stevens and Jeri Marler for their contributions to the book. In addition, we would also like to thank Jay Cosnett for the book layout and graphic artwork.

Contents

INTRODUCTION 1
About this Book 2
Additional Information 3
CHAPTER 1: INSTALLING GEOWORKS ENSEMBLE 5
Configuring GeoWorks Ensemble 10
    Selecting the Monitor 10
    Selecting a Different Monitor 10
    Selecting the Mouse 11
    Selecting the Printer 11
    Entering Your Serial Number 12
Summary 12
CHAPTER 2: THE APPLIANCES 13
Running GeoWorks Ensemble 14
Accessing the Appliances 15
Moving Around in GeoWorks Ensemble 16
    Mouse Pointers 16
        Arrow pointer 16
        Hourglass pointer 16
        Circle/Slash pointer 16
        I-beam pointer 16
    Mouse Buttons 17
        Pointing and clicking 17
        Multiple-clicking 17
        Scrolling 17
        Dragging 18

Contents

Using the Appliances 18
    Planner 18
    Address Book 21
    Banner 22
    Solitaire 25
    Calculator 26
    Notepad 28
Summary 29
CHAPTER 3: THE GEOWORKS ENSEMBLE PROFESSIONAL WORKSPACE ... 31
Moving Around the Professional Workspace 32
    Mouse Menu Selection 32
    Keyboard Commands for Menus 32
    Mnemonic Commands for Menus 33
    Hotkey Commands for Menus 33
        Pinning a menu 34
Using the Menu Maps 34
Accessing the GeoDraw Window 34
    Control Button 35
    Express Menu Button 36
    Title Bar 36
    Minimize Button 37
    Minimize/Maximize Restore Button 37
    Menu Bar 37
    Exit 37
Creating and Saving Documents (Files) 38
DOS and GEOS Files 38
    DOS Document File Names and Icons 38
    About Subdirectories 39
    Importing and Exporting DOS/GEOS Files 40
    Exercise 3-1 40
        Opening the GeoComm application 42
        Opening the GeoWrite application 44
        Moving around subdirectories 45
        Importing a DOS file into GeoWrite 46
        Saving a GEOS document as a DOS document 46
        Verifying the DOS file export 48
Summary 48

Contents

CHAPTER 4: GEOMANAGER	49
The GeoManager Screen	50
Control Line	52
Control Button	52
Express Button	54
Title Bar	57
Maximize/Restore Button	58
Minimize Button	58
Menu Bar	59
File Menu	59
Tree Menu	69
View Menu	72
Options Menu	75
Disk Menu	76
Window Menu	79
Information Bar	81
Main Display Window	81
Wastebasket	82
Full-Sized/Overlapping Buttons	82
World Button	82
Document Button	82
Drive Buttons	83
Summary	83
CHAPTER 5: THE PREFERENCES APPLICATION	85
Accessing the Preferences Application	86
Look and Feel	86
Font Size	87
Document Safeguarding	87
Sound	88
Opening Screen	88
OK, Reset, and Cancel	88
Date & Time	89
Date	89
Time	89
OK, Reset, and Cancel	89
Background	90
Selecting a Background	90
Display options	90
Inserting New Backgrounds	91

Contents

Printer	92
Install New	92
Parallel port	92
Serial port	93
Edit	93
Delete	93
Test	94
Close	94
Computer	94
None	95
Expanded Memory	95
Extended Memory	95
Managed Extended Memory	95
Interrupt Level options	95
Video	96
Type of Video Adapter	96
Automatic Screen Blanking	96
Mouse	97
Double Click Time	97
Mouse Acceleration	97
Type of Mouse	97
Modem	98
PC/GEOS	99
Summary	99
CHAPTER 6: THE GEOWRITE APPLICATION	101
Starting GeoWrite	102
Application Window Elements	104
The Menu Bar	104
Ruler Bar	104
Left margin and indent	105
Right margin	105
Tabs	105
Ruler settings	105
Selection Line	106
Paging arrows	106
Tabs	106
Justification Settings	108
Line Spacing Settings	108
Main Text Window	108
Headers and Footers	109

Contents

    Typing Mode 109
        Insertion mode 109
        Overwrite mode 109
    Selecting and Editing Text with the Mouse 110
    Keyboard Editing and Typing Cursor Movement 112
Summary 114
CHAPTER 7: GEOWRITE MENUS 115
File Menu 116
Edit Menu 125
View Menu 127
Options Menu 128
Paragraph Menu 130
Fonts Menu 139
Sizes Menu 140
Styles Menu 144
Window 146
Summary 148
CHAPTER 8: GEOWRITE OPERATIONS AND TUTORIAL 149
Accessing GeoWrite 150
Exercise 1 150
    Create and Save a Document 150
    Setting Options 151
    Setting a Center Tab 151
    Selecting Text 152
    Changing Font of Existing Text 153
    Changing Font Size of Existing Text 153
    Changing Text Styles of Existing Text 154
    Closing Pinned Menus 154
    Removing Text Highlighting 155
    Creating a Blank Line 155
    Changing Font, Size, and Style for New Text 155
    Typing Text 156
    Making a Header 157
    Changing Header Size 158
    Inserting a Graphic Image in the Document 159
    Saving the Document 161
Exercise 2 162
    Creating a Table 162
    Creating a Page Break 162
    Setting the Table Margins 163
    Drawing Vertical Lines with a Left Tab Marker 163
    Setting Decimal Tabs 164

Contents

    Entering the Table Text 164
    Underlining Table Entries 166
    Continuing Table Text Entry 166
    Removing Tab Markers 166
    Drawing a Border Around the Table 167
    Copying the Table within the Document 168
    Respacing a Table 169
    Saving the Document 169
Exercise 3 170
    Creating a First-line Indent Paragraph 171
    Creating an Indented Paragraph 171
    Creating a First-line Outdent Paragraph 171
    Saving the Document 171
Summary 171
CHAPTER 9: THE GEODRAW APPLICATION 173
Accessing the GeoDraw Application 174
File Menu 174
    Import… 174
Edit Menu 176
    Fuse Objects 177
    Defuse Object 178
View Menu 178
    Correct for Aspect Ratio 179
Options Menu 179
    Document Size 179
    Drag As Rect 180
        Dragging with left mouse button 180
        Dragging with right mouse button 180
    Drag As Outline 180
    Show Tool Box 180
Modify Menu 181
    Nudge 181
    Flip Horizontal 182
    Flip Vertical 183
    Rotate 45° Left 183
    Rotate 45° Right 183
    Line Properties… 184
    Area Properties 185
    Text Properties 186
Arrange Menu 188
    Bring To Front 188
    Send To Back 189

Move Forward	189
Move Backward	189
Text Menu	189
Justification	190
Text Properties	191
Window Menu	191
Overlapping (Ctrl+F5)	192
Full-Sized (Ctrl+F10)	192
Page Listing and Page Selection	192
Tool Box	192
Arrow Pointer Tool	193
Text Tool	193
Line Tool	195
Connect Line Tool	196
Rotate Pointer	196
Rectangle Tool	197
Circle Tool	197
Polygon Tool	197
Summary	198
CHAPTER 10: THE GEOPLANNER APPLICATION	199
Using GeoPlanner	200
Selected Year	201
Current Time	201
Selected Day and Date	201
Calendar	201
Schedule of Events	202
Scheduling an Event	202
Viewing Scheduled Events	203
Viewing Scheduled Events for Several Days	203
The Menu Bar	203
File Menu	204
Edit Menu	206
View Menu	208
Options Menu	209
Quick Menu	212
Utilities Menu	213
Summary	216
CHAPTER 11: THE CALCULATOR APPLICATION	217
Using the Calculator	218
Delete	219
Parentheses (Standard Configuration)	219
Clear	220

Contents

    Error 220
    Order of Operations (Standard Configuration) 220
    Memory Use 221
The Calculator Menu Bar 222
    File Menu 222
        Exit (F3) 222
    Edit Menu 222
    Options Menu 223
Summary 227
CHAPTER 12: THE NOTEPAD APPLICATION 229
Accessing the Notepad Application 230
Using Notepad for Notes 231
Using Notebook as a DOS Text Editor 232
The Notepad Menus 232
    File Menu 232
    Edit Menu 236
    Sizes Menu 236
Summary 237
CHAPTER 13: THE SCRAPBOOK APPLICATION 239
Accessing the Scrapbook 240
The Scrapbook Window 240
The Menu Bar 242
    File Menu 242
    Edit Menu 242
Changing the Default Scrapbook 244
Opening More Than One Scrapbook at a Time 245
Cutting or Copying Between Scrapbooks 246
Summary 247
CHAPTER 14: THE GEODEX APPLICATION 249
Accessing the GeoDex Application 250
The GeoDex Window 250
    Next 251
    Previous 251
    New 251
    Quick Dial 254
    GeoPlanner 254
The Menu Bar 255
    File Menu 255
    Edit Menu 255
    View Menu 256

Contents

Option	258
Prefix Option	258
Area Code Option	258
Dialing a Phone Number	259
Summary	259
CHAPTER 15: AMERICA ONLINE	261
America Online Installation	262
The Menu Bar	263
Help Menu	264
File Menu	266
Edit Menu	269
Go To Menu	269
Mail Menu	272
Members Menu	277
Window Menu	278
Summary	279
CHAPTER 16: THE GEOCOMM APPLICATION	281
Accessing the GeoComm Application	282
File Menu	284
Edit Menu	289
View Menu	291
Options Menu	292
Protocol Settings	293
Terminal Settings	296
Modem Settings	298
Show Line Status	299
Dial Menu	300
Scripts	300
Quick Dial	307
Hang Up	308
Summary	308
CHAPTER 17: THE SOLITAIRE APPLICATION	309
Card Layout	310
Playing the Game	310
The Solitaire Application	312
Game Menu	312
Options Menu	312
Summary	314

xiii

Contents

CHAPTER: 18 THE DOS PROGRAMS APPLICATION 315
Accessing the DOS Programs Application 316
The DOS Programs Window 316
Options Menu 317
    Create New Button 317
    Change Button Settings 320
    Delete Button 321
Creating and Using Batch Files 321
    Create Batch File 321
    Edit Batch File 323
Summary 323
APPENDIX: MENU MAP 325
Express and Control Buttons 326
Professional Applications 327
INDEX 345

Introduction

GeoWorks Ensemble is an exciting new multitasking graphical environment for all IBM and compatible PCs. The GeoWorks applications all utilize the same user interface and they all can share information.

GeoWorks Ensemble has the flexibility to adjust to the user's level of expertise. The Appliances section is friendly enough for novices to "get their feet wet" before going on to more advanced functions. The Professional mode is suited for the user who needs the power and convenience of integrated, graphical applications. Finally, the DOS programs facility lets you assign icons to all your favorite DOS programs.

Introduction

When you first enter GeoWorks Ensemble, you are asked which of the three GeoWorks environments you wish to use: Appliances, Professional, or DOS.

Appliances contain basic versions of the GeoWorks programs. These are intended to acquaint the new user with GeoWorks Ensemble with a minimum of fuss. The programs in this area are remarkably simple to use, but still produce fine and satisfying results.

The Professional work space provides a collection of applications which rival the power of stand-alone programs. It includes GeoWrite, a powerful word processor/ desktop publisher with a "what-you-see-is-what-you-get" display, advanced font technology, sophisticated formatting capabilities and the ability to insert graphics into your documents. GeoDraw is a versatile drawing package which allows you to create complex images, fuse and scale objects, rotate images and scale them to any size. Among the other features are a calendar, address book, and a file manager. The Professional work space allows for multitasking — you can run as many applications at a time as you wish.

Lastly, DOS program mode allows you to easily exit GeoWorks Ensemble and load a DOS program by simply clicking a button. When you are ready to return, just exit the DOS program and you are returned to GeoWorks Ensemble exactly where you left it.

About this Book

This book re-creates the working environment of your computer screen by picturing each pull-down menu in the order in which it would be encountered in GeoWorks Ensemble. Topics are addressed in the same sequence they follow in GeoWorks Ensemble, and each command is discussed, menu by menu. A complete set of menu maps give the user a graphic overview of the structure of GeoWorks Ensemble and the relationship between its applications, and also external programs.

Chapter 2 covers the use of the Appliances in detail. These programs are specifically designed for the novice user, and they are simplified versions of some of the applications found in the Professional work space.

Chapters 3 through 17 deal with the applications found in the Professional work space. They cover each of the programs thoroughly, showing every menu and discussing the use of each command. All the special features found in the Professional mode are described as well as the interaction of the various programs.

Finally, Chapter 18 deals with DOS programs. You are shown how to assign icons to your DOS programs as well as how to create your own batch files without having to leave GeoWorks Ensemble.

For the beginning user, this book serves as a step-by-step guide to using the features of GeoWorks Ensemble. Each application is discussed detail — what it does, how to use its features and how it relates to other GeoWorks Ensemble programs. This book explains the use and function of every command and provides easy to understand examples. The basic procedures such as moving and resizing screens, selecting, copying, or moving, objects, and working with multiple documents, are covered in detail.

The experienced computer user will find the book an easy way to become familiar with the fine points of the GeoWorks Ensemble Professional applications as well as a handy reference for checking on specific commands. The format of the book makes finding specific information from any menu extremely simple.

Additional Information

When references are made to keys of the PC keyboard, such as Enter or Return, this book will use key-like icons, such as [Enter↵]. If the keys need to represent a key combination, such as holding down the Alt key while pressing the F10 function key, it will be indicated as follows: [alt]-[F10]. [Ctrl]-[alt]-[delete] (which reboots your computer) would mean to hold down the Control key, and hold down the Alt key, and while holding down these two keys, press the Delete key.

Introduction

Throughout the book there will be sections that require special attention. The following icons will be used to mark these sections.

Indicates that you should take note of the information. This symbol may indicate a helpful hint or a special condition.

Indicates that you can perform an action more quickly by using shortcut keys or by following the suggestion in the text.

Indicates cautionary information or warnings. This symbol often provides a warning that you may lose data if you incorrectly perform an action.

Indicates a serious warning. Data may be lost or the system may hang-up or crash. A misuse of these functions may seriously jeopardize your data, disk, or system operation.

Indicates a particularly useful feature or usage. This is also used to indicate an exceptional suggestion for a procedure or process.

Chapter 1

Installing GeoWorks Ensemble

Before you can use GeoWorks Ensemble Version 1.0, you must install it on your hard drive, using the GeoWorks Ensemble automated installation program. The installation program creates a subdirectory on your hard drive, copies files from the floppy disks, then steps you through configuring GeoWorks Ensemble for your computer system. During the installation and setup program you will need to:

- Tell GeoWorks Ensemble where to install the program files
- Decide whether GeoWorks Ensemble should modify two system files on your hard drive — the AUTOEXEC.BAT and CONFIG.SYS files — so they will work correctly with GeoWorks Ensemble
- Tell GeoWorks Ensemble what kind of monitor, mouse, and printer are connected to your computer.

1 Installing GeoWorks Ensemble

The GeoWorks Ensemble package includes a set of seven installation disks. If you do not have all of the disks, contact the manufacturer. The automated installation procedure takes you through the installation steps and helps you make the necessary choices. The following steps describe the installation procedure.

1. Insert Disk 1 into drive A: (or Drive B:) and close the drive door.

2. Go to the drive A: DOS prompt, **A>** (or B: prompt, **B>**) by typing:

    A: (or B:) [Enter⏎]

At the DOS prompt, type:

    SETUP [Enter⏎]

3. The program displays a screen similar to the one shown in Figure 1-1. The screen states that you will be asked to answer some questions about your computer. Press [Enter⏎] to continue.

In this and all other steps, pressing [esc] takes you back to the previous screen; pressing [F3] takes you back to the DOS prompt.

```
              GEOWORKS     ENSEMBLE    SETUP
You will answer a series of questions about your computer
and the kind of equipment connected to it.  Your answers
to these questions will affect how GeoWorks Ensemble works
with your computer.

Don't worry if you don't know the best answers to some
of the questions.  In most cases where the installation
program can't tell what the best answer is, a harmless
answer will be highlighted.

You will have the opportunity to test the choices you've
made.  If something is wrong, you can make a different
choice and test it, too.




Press ENTER to continue.
Press ESC to return to the previous screen.
Press F3 to quit the installation program.
```

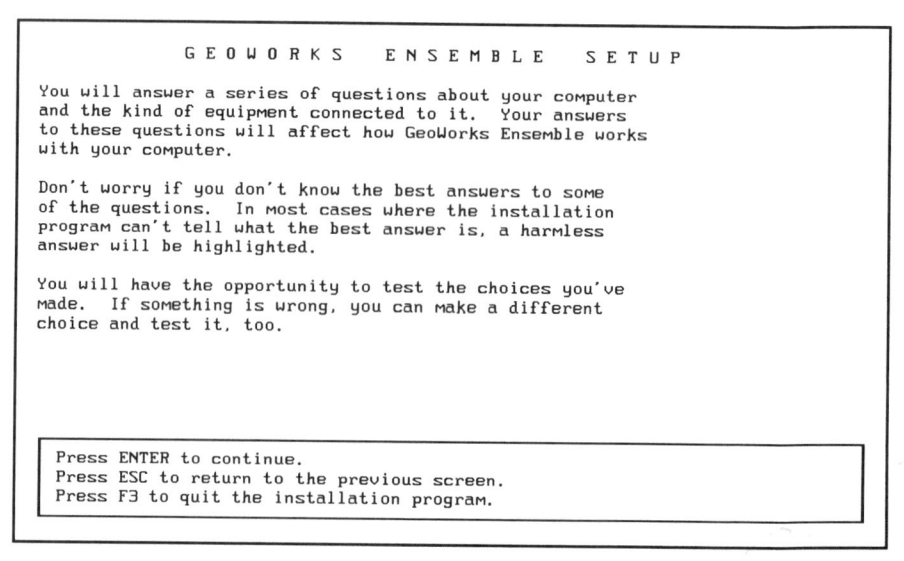

Figure 1-1 — GeoWorks Ensemble Installation Message.

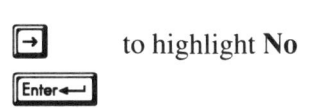

Installing GeoWorks Ensemble 1

4. Press [Enter] to continue. The program displays a notice stating SETUP will install GeoWorks Ensemble in the drive and directory shown (C:\GEOWORKS). To accept the default drive and directory — also called the path — press [Enter].

If you want to install GeoWorks on a different drive (for example, drive D:) or in a different subdirectory (for example, \GEO), press [←BkSp] to delete as much of the path as necessary, then type the new path: D:\GEO. Press [Enter] to accept the new path.

5. The program displays a screen similar to Figure 1-2, asking if you want to be able to start GeoWorks Ensemble from any DOS prompt. If so, GeoWorks Ensemble must add a statement to your computer's AUTOEXEC.BAT file. Press [Enter] to select Yes. GeoWorks Ensemble modifies the AUTOEXEC.BAT file. After the installation is completed, you can start GeoWorks Ensemble from any directory by typing:

    GCGEOS (or GEOS) [Enter]

If you do not want GeoWorks Ensemble to modify the AUTOEXEC.BAT file, press:

[→]   to highlight **No**

[Enter]

7

1   Installing GeoWorks Ensemble

```
              G E O W O R K S    E N S E M B L E    S E T U P
Would you like to be able to start GeoWorks Ensemble no matter
what directory you are currently working in?

If you say "Yes", the path in your AUTOEXEC.BAT file will be changed
to contain "D:\GEOWORKS".  A copy of the original file will be
kept in D:\GEOWORKS\SYSTEM\AUTOEXEC.OLD.

(Changes to the AUTOEXEC.BAT file don't take effect until the next
time you restart your machine.)

Options:
   Yes
   No



   Press ENTER if the highlighted answer is OK.
   Press ESC to return to the previous screen.
   Press the UP and DOWN arrows to change the answer.
   Press F3 to quit the installation program.
```

Figure 1-2 — Message Screen for Adding Ensemble to the AUTOEXEC.BAT File.

6. Press [Enter⏎] to start the installation. You will see a notice that the AUTOEXEC.BAT and CONFIG.SYS files must be changed and asking if it is OK to make the changes automatically. You can elect to proceed with the changes or choose to examine the changes first. If you select the automatic changes, you proceed to the next step and the installation begins.

7. GeoWorks Ensemble copies the first disk to the drive and directory you specified earlier. The program keeps you informed of the progress of the procedure, and displays a notice similar to Figure 1-3 when you need to insert the next disk.

Installing GeoWorks Ensemble 1

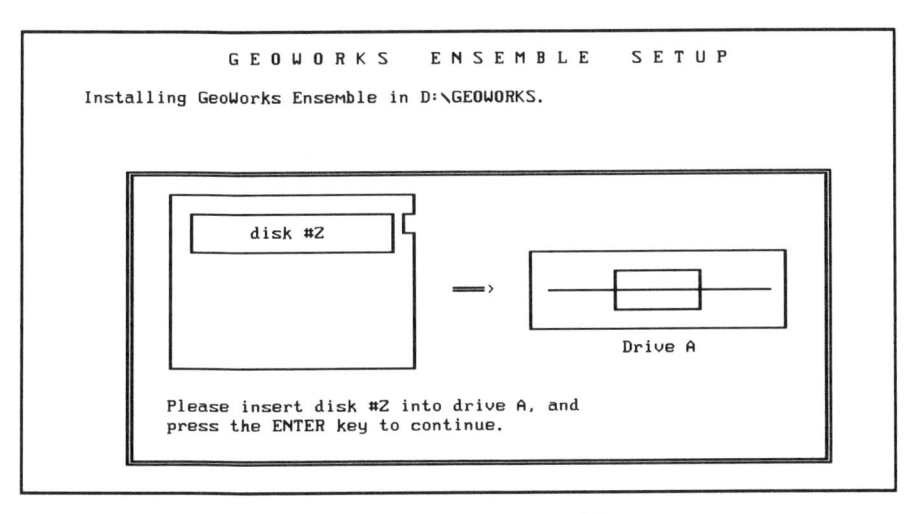

```
      G E O W O R K S    E N S E M B L E    S E T U P
Installing GeoWorks Ensemble in D:\GEOWORKS.


        ┌─────────────────────┐
        │  ┌──────────────┐   │
        │  │   disk #2    │   │
        │  └──────────────┘   │        ┌──────────────────┐
        │                     │   =>   │    ┌────────┐    │
        │                     │        │    └────────┘    │
        │                     │        └──────────────────┘
        │                     │              Drive A
        └─────────────────────┘

        Please insert disk #2 into drive A, and
        press the ENTER key to continue.
```

Figure 1-3 — Insert Next Disk Screen.

8. Insert the next disk and press [Enter←] to continue. After all the disks have been copied, the program flashes an "Installation Complete" message. Remove the disk from the floppy drive. You now have a choice.

   - If GeoWorks Ensemble modified the AUTOEXEC.BAT or CONFIG.SYS file, you must reboot the computer for the changes to take effect. To reboot, press [Ctrl]-[alt]-[delete].

   - If GeoWorks Ensemble did not modify the AUTOEXEC.BAT or CONFIG.SYS file, or you want to run GeoWorks Ensemble before rebooting your computer, press [Enter←]. Remember, after exiting GeoWorks Ensemble, you must reboot the computer for any modifications to take effect.

   - You can press [F3] to return to the DOS prompt.

1 Installing GeoWorks Ensemble

Configuring GeoWorks Ensemble

The first time you run GeoWorks Ensemble you will be asked to select the monitor, mouse and printer settings for your computer. To start GeoWorks from the DOS prompt, type:

    PCGEOS [Enter←]

The program displays a notice stating that on the next few screens you will verify that your display, mouse, and printer work properly with GeoWorks Ensemble.

Selecting the Monitor

The SETUP program displays the monitor (video display device) it senses is connected to your computer. To accept this choice for your monitor, press [Enter←]. A test screen with four arrows at the corners is displayed. These arrows should be sharp and clear. If not, you need to select a different monitor.

If you do not want to accept the SETUP choice, or if the test screen is not sharp, press [F10] to make another choice.

Selecting a Different Monitor

If you press [F10], the Setup program displays a list of monitor choices. Use the [↑] and [↓] or [PgUp] and [PgDn] to scroll through the list. When your choice is highlighted, press [Enter←] to select it.

Note: You can move quickly through the list by typing the first letter of your selection. The highlight bar jumps to the first name beginning with this letter. This can be repeated as necessary until your selection is highlighted. Once highlighted, you can select it by pressing [Enter←].

When you select a different monitor, the next screen states GeoWorks Ensemble must be restarted before it can use the new monitor. After you restart, the program returns you to the test screen with the four arrows. If you cannot see the arrows clearly, press [F10]. GeoWorks Ensemble reloads the original monitor. Select another monitor, restart the program and check your selection. When you are satisfied with the appearance of the test screen, press [Enter←] to continue.

Installing GeoWorks Ensemble 1

Selecting the Mouse

Now you can specify your mouse type. The program displays a list of choices, with the default choice, No Idea, highlighted. Select the default if you do not know the type mouse you have, or scroll through the list to highlight your choice. To select your highlighted choice, press [Enter←].

If you have named a mouse, the next screen shows the type of mouse you selected (serial or parallel) and prompts you for the port to which it is connected. The available ports are shown with the most likely port highlighted. If you aren't sure which port is correct, press [Enter←] to accept the default. Otherwise, highlight your selection, then press [Enter←].

The program displays a mouse test window. Move the mouse cursor (which looks like an arrow) to the test box. Click (press and release) the left mouse button. If the mouse type and port are selected correctly, a beep sounds and the test box flashes. If not (or if no mouse cursor appears), you may have:

- Selected the wrong mouse from the list. Press [F10] to make a new choice.
- Chosen the wrong port. Press [esc] to change your selection.
- Selected No Idea when asked which kind of mouse you have, and the default mouse settings do not work. If you know your mouse software is already installed and the mouse works correctly with other software, read your mouse software documentation to determine the correct selection. Then press [F10] to make the change.

If you have not installed the mouse software yet, press [F3] to go to the DOS prompt. Install the mouse driver (software). Return to the SETUP program by typing:

GEOS [Enter←]

Selecting the Printer

The next screen prompts you to specify your printer type. Scroll through the displayed list to highlight your printer type (or highlight None, if appropriate). Press [Enter←] to select your choice. If you select None, the SETUP is complete. If you specify a printer, the program displays a list of serial and parallel ports. Highlight the one to which your printer is connected, then press [Enter←].

11

1 Installing GeoWorks Ensemble

The program displays the printer test window. Turn on your printer. Click the mouse button in the test box. If the printer type and port are set correctly, you will print a test page. If nothing prints, you may have:

- Chosen the wrong port. Press [esc] to choose a different port.

If you printed a test page but it doesn't look right, you may have:

- Specified the wrong printer model. Press [F10] to select the correct model from the list.

When the test is successful, press [Enter←] to continue.

You have successfully configured GeoWorks Ensemble for your computer. Congratulations!

Entering Your Serial Number

You are now asked to type your 16 digit serial number (see your Customer Support Handbook). After you type the number, highlight OK and press [Enter←]. Geoworks Ensemble displays the main screen. If you do not want to enter the number at this time, you can highlight Enter Later and press [Enter←] to begin the GeoWorks Ensemble program.

Summary

In Chapter 1 you learned how to install GeoWorks Ensemble on your hard drive and how to configure the program for your computer.

Chapter 2

The Appliances

GeoWorks Ensemble offers six handy, easy-to-use applications called appliances. Appliances are simplified versions of programs in the Professional Workspace. Use the appliances to get acquainted with GeoWorks Ensemble: make notes (Notepad), plan your schedule (Planner), organize names and addresses (Address Book), do quick calculations (Calculator), create large banners (Banner), and play a challenging game in your free time (Solitaire). As you use them, you will become familiar with moving around the screen and performing basic operations.

This chapter describes:

- How to start GeoWorks Ensemble from the DOS prompt
- How to use the six items included in the Appliances section
- How to move around the program using the mouse.

2 The Appliances

Running GeoWorks Ensemble

To run GeoWorks Ensemble from the C> DOS prompt, type:

    GEOS [Enter↵]

If you get the message "Bad command or file name", the GeoWorks subdirectory may not be in your AUTOEXEC.BAT file path statement. Change your default subdirectory to the subdirectory in which you installed GeoWorks Ensemble by typing:

    CD \GEOWORKS [Enter↵] or the subdirectory you specified during the install program

Then run GeoWorks Ensemble by typing the run command:

    GEOS [Enter↵]

The GeoWorks Ensemble program displays the Welcome screen shown in Figure 2-1.

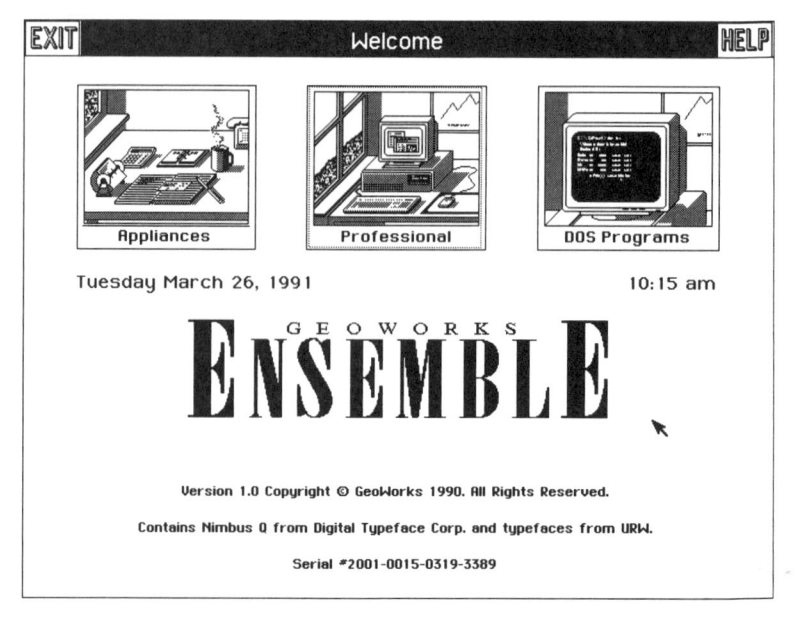

Figure 2-1 — The GeoWorks Ensemble Welcome Screen.

The Appliances 2

Accessing the Appliances

From the Welcome screen you can directly access EXIT, HELP, Appliances, Professional, and DOS Programs. The last three items are the main work areas of the program.

At the top left of the Welcome screen is the EXIT button, one of the ways you can exit the program. Selecting the EXIT button displays a prompt asking if you really want to leave GeoWorks Ensemble. Selecting Yes returns you to the DOS prompt. Selecting No returns you to the Welcome screen.

At the top right of the Welcome screen is the HELP button. Selecting the HELP button displays help screens which briefly describe features or operations — a quick way to refresh your memory.

The center portion of the Welcome screen displays three panels: Appliances, Professional, and DOS Programs. Clicking on a panel accesses the features within the program area. For example, clicking on the Appliances panel selects it and displays the window shown in Figure 2-2.

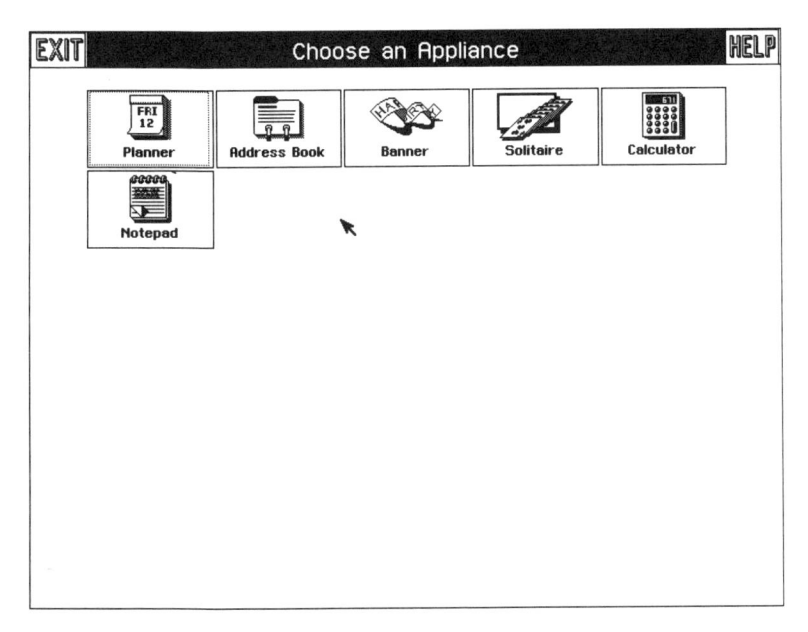

Figure 2-2 — The Choose an Appliance Window.

2 The Appliances

From the Appliances screen you can access the EXIT and HELP buttons, and the six applications: Planner, Address Book, Banner, Solitaire, Calculator, and Notepad.

Moving Around in GeoWorks Ensemble

Except when entering text from the keyboard, you can use a mouse for all operations in GeoWorks Ensemble. In the Appliances section you can use the mouse to select appliances, access help screens, use the features of an appliance, cut, copy and move text, and exit the appliance. You can use the mouse in the same way to move about in the Professional Workspace and the DOS Programs sections of GeoWorks Ensemble.

Mouse Pointers

As you move the mouse around the screen you see a pointer that corresponds to the motion of the mouse. Depending on what is occurring, the pointer takes one of four shapes:

Arrow pointer

The normal mouse pointer.

Hourglass pointer

It indicates that an operation is in progress and you must wait for the operation to complete.

Circle/Slash pointer

If you move the pointer outside the active area of the screen, the pointer changes to this shape.

I-beam pointer

It indicates the position of the text cursor for entering text from the keyboard.

Mouse Buttons

You perform actions with the left and right mouse buttons. Use the left button for most functions; if a button is not specified, use the left one. Use the right mouse button to move things around on the screen in a procedure called direct manipulation. This book always specifies the right mouse button whenever it is required for an operation.

Pointing and clicking

To select an item, move the mouse pointer around the screen until it is on the item you want (such as an icon, a selection button or a menu option), then press and release (click) the left button. The selected item is highlighted.

Multiple-clicking

Items such as appliance icons require a second click to execute the option. You can select and execute an item in one step by double-clicking. Position the pointer on the item and then rapidly press and release the left button twice. It may take a little practice, but once you master this, you can go on to triple-clicking, quadruple-clicking and even quintuple-clicking. (You will use these multiple-clicks to select text in the Professional Workspace Applications. See Chapter 3.)

Scrolling

Use scroll bars when the contents of a window are wider or longer than the window itself. A window has two scroll bars: vertical one at the right of the window and a horizontal one at the bottom. If you move the mouse pointer to one of the end arrows on a scroll bar and click on it, the window information moves in small steps in the opposite direction of the arrow. For example, when you click on a down arrow, the window text scrolls up, revealing text that was below the window. When you click on a left arrow button, the window text scrolls to the right, revealing text that was to the left of the window.

In text documents, the document scrolls one line or column at a time. With other items, each click moves the display a specific amount. To scroll continuously, press and hold the mouse button on one of the end arrows.

2 The Appliances

To scroll one complete window at a time, move the pointer to the dark area of a scroll bar (the paging area) and click. To scroll continuously one window at a time, press and hold the mouse button on the paging area.

To scroll to a specific location, move the pointer to the light colored section of a scroll bar (the slider). This area indicates the part of the document currently visible in the window relative to the entire document. Press and hold the mouse button and drag the slider to the desired position on the bar, scrolling the document. Continue until you reach the part of the document you want to see.

Dragging

Pressing and holding a mouse button while moving the mouse at the same time is called dragging. Drag using the left mouse button to highlight text in the appliances. (Use a left-button drag in the Professional Workspace to browse menus, choose commands and to move and resize windows.) If you press and hold the right mouse button when dragging, you can move items around on the screen.

Using the Appliances

At the Choose an Appliance window (Figure 2-2), click on one of the six appliance icons to select the appliance you want to run. For help using the active appliance, click on the HELP button. To quit the appliance and return to the Choose an Appliance window, click on the EXIT button.

Select Exit from the Choose an Appliance window to return to the Welcome window.

Planner

Select the Planner icon from the Choose an Appliance window to display the screen shown in Figure 2-3. Planner is a combination desk calendar and date book.

The Appliances 2

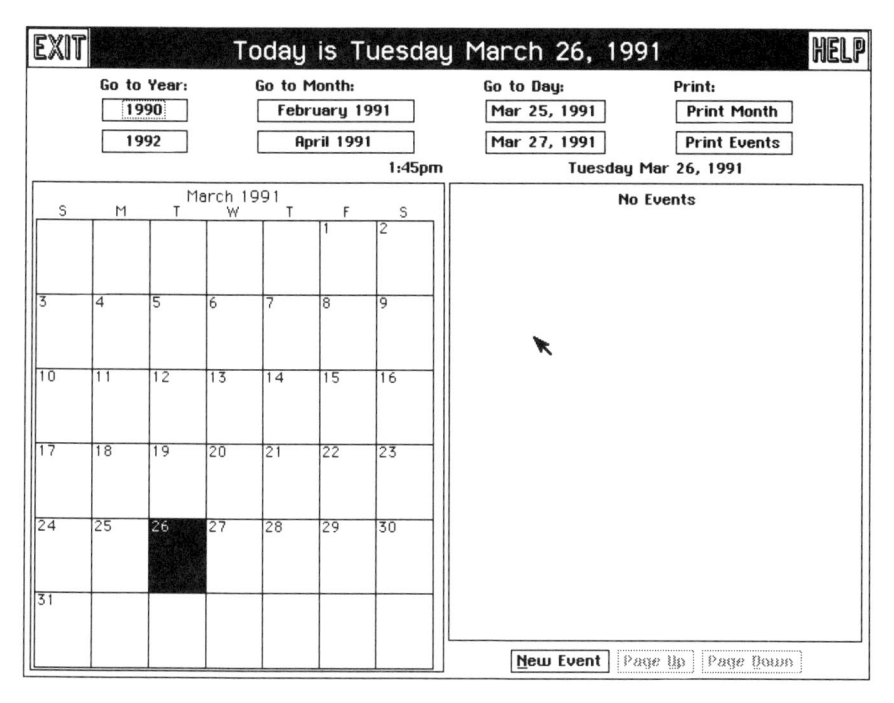

Figure 2-3 — The Planner Appliance Window.

The Planner screen

At the top of the screen Planner displays the current day of the week and date. To the left is a calendar page for a whole month. Each time you activate Planner it displays the current month, with the current day outlined and highlighted. Above the calendar is the current time. The right panel contains any scheduled events for the highlighted day. Above the events panel is the day and date corresponding to the highlighted day in the calendar. Above the calendar and events list are four items: Go to Year, Go to Month, Go to Day, and Print.

Go to Year

The two Go to Year buttons display the year preceding and the year following the currently displayed year. For example, if the displayed year is 1995, the top button would read 1994 and the bottom button would read 1996. Click on a year button to change the calendar display to the selected year.

2   The Appliances

Go to Month/Day

The Month and Day items work the same way. For example, each click on the Next Day button advances it one day. The day highlighted on the calendar page changes accordingly (although the current day remains outlined until you move to another month). Click on the preceding or following month buttons to change the displayed month.

Print

This option offers you two choices: you can print a monthly calendar or a schedule.

Events

At the bottom of the screen is the New Event button. Click on this button to enter a time block in the events panel. You can change the default time of 8:00 a.m. by typing the time you want. To enter a note about the event, use the mouse to move the text cursor (I-beam pointer) to the right of the time and type the note.

You can keep entering time blocks by clicking the New Event button, changing the times to suit your schedule. When you have more than one page of events, the Page Up and Page Down buttons become active. Click on these to scroll your schedule.

You can make entries for any date(s) you want by clicking the Go to Year, Month and Day buttons until you have the date you want. A small triangle in the lower right corner of a day's box on the calendar indicates a scheduled event. Clicking on that day in the calendar brings up its list of events.

Click on the EXIT button to return to the Choose an Appliance screen.

The Appliances 2

Address Book

Select Address Book from the Choose an Appliance window to display the screen shown in Figure 2-4.

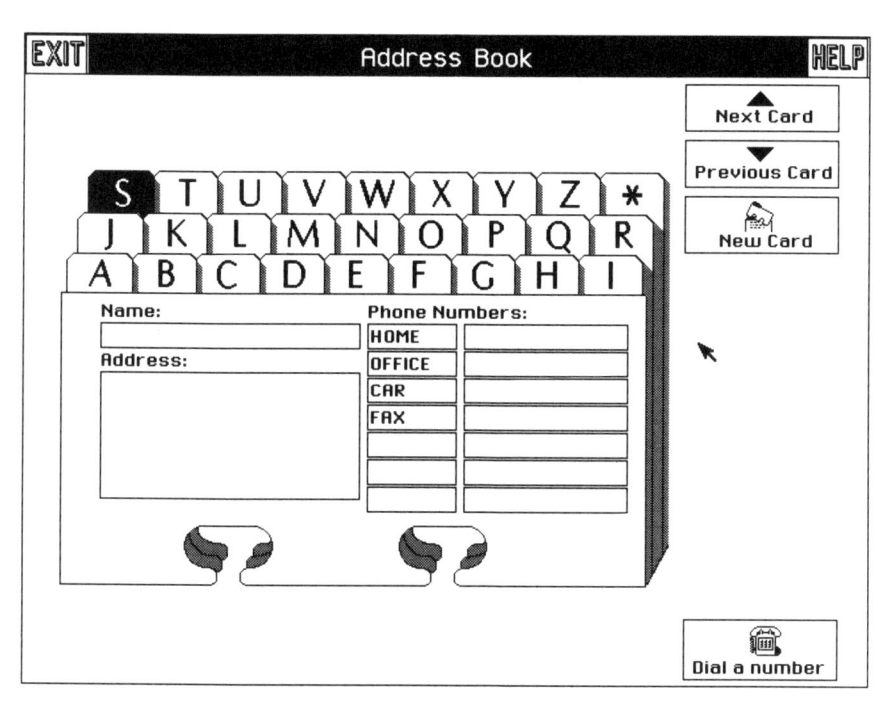

Figure 2-4 — The Address Book Screen.

The Address Book is similar to a card file with a separate card for each name and address, sorted alphabetically by the first word in the name box. If you want to sort alphabetically by last names, enter the last name first in the name box.

Beneath the name is the address box. To the right of the address is a box for entering phone numbers — you can include home, office, car and fax numbers. You can create other phone number categories by entering them in a blank phone box.

Click on a letter at the top of the Address Book window to bring up the first card sorted by that letter. Flip backward or forward through the cards by clicking on the Next Card and Previous Card buttons at the far right of the window.

2 The Appliances

You can create a new card by clicking on the New Card button. Enter the information you want and the new card becomes part of the card file. If you have a modem connected to your computer, you can dial the currently-displayed phone number on the selected card by clicking the Dial a Number button. For a detailed discussion of Address Book features, see Chapter 13.

Click on the EXIT button to return to the Choose an Appliance screen.

Banner

Select the Banner appliance from the Choose an Appliance window to display the screen shown in Figure 2-5.

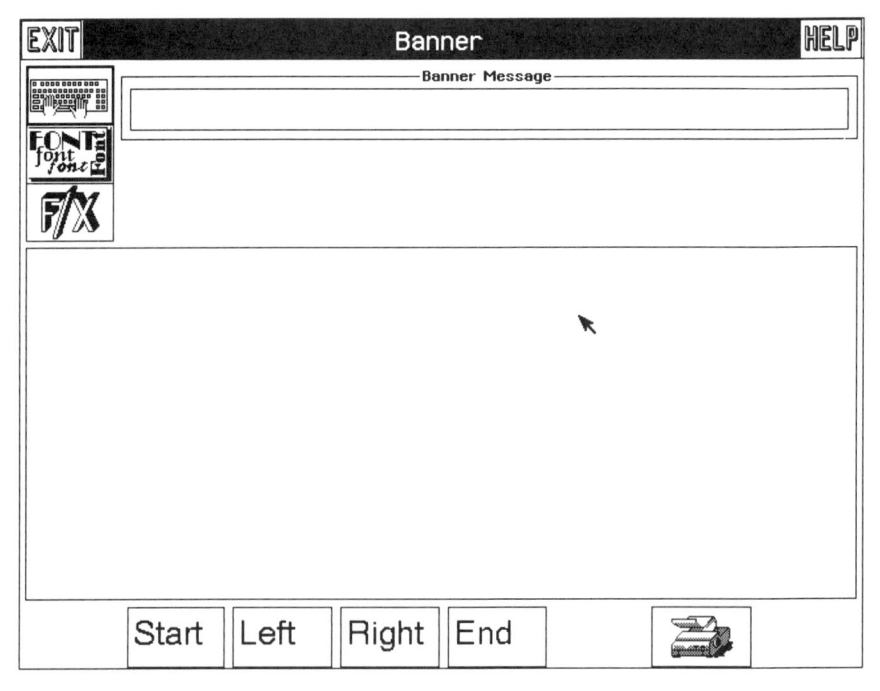

Figure 2-5 — The Banner Screen.

With this appliance you can create banners up to 100 feet long with a choice of 9 fonts, 4 text styles, 5 special effects and 4 border styles. At the top left of the Banner window are three boxes: Type, Font, and F/X.

Type

Click on the Type box. Begin typing in the banner text window at the blinking text cursor. As you type, the text is also displayed in the bottom portion of the window as it will appear in print. Note that each square in this display represents an 8 1/2 x 11 inch page. The dots at the top and bottom represent the line feed holes in the paper and do not appear in the banner print out. Figure 2-6 illustrates how the window appears as you create a banner.

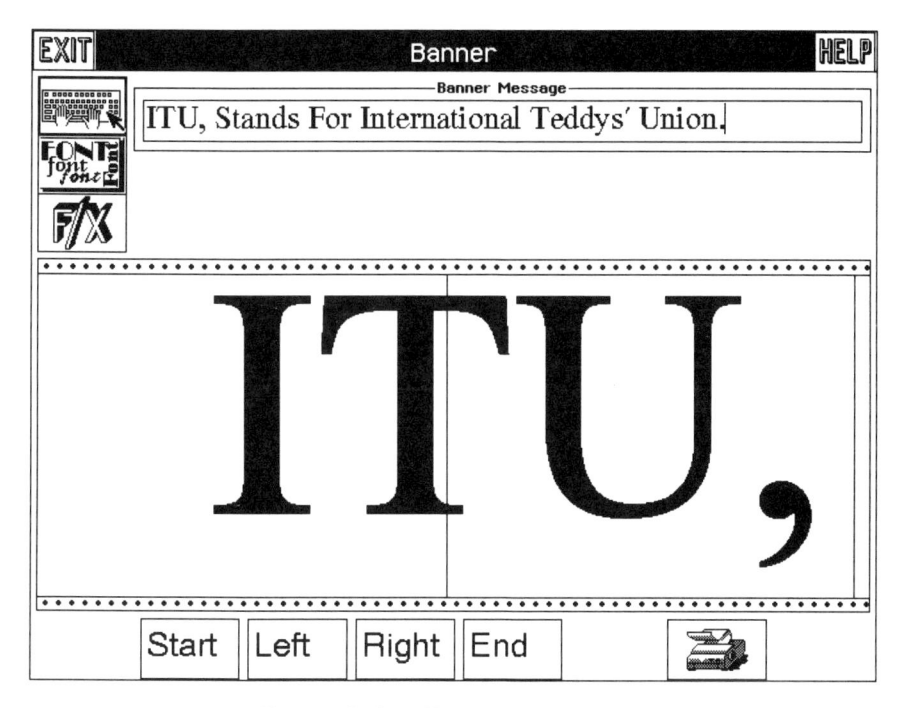

Figure 2-6 — Typing Banner Text.

If you choose double-height letters, each letter occupies two boxes (or pieces of paper) as shown in Figure 2-7.

2 The Appliances

Figure 2-7 — Typing a Double-Height Banner.

When you are finished entering the text, you are ready to select the font type and size you want for your banner text.

Font

Click on the Font box in the upper left corner of your screen to display a box containing 9 font choices. Click the font you want to try. The banner text at the bottom changes to reflect your choice. Keep trying fonts until you see one you like. Now you are ready to select the special effects you want on your banner.

F/X

Click on the F/X box to display a box with three columns of choices as shown in Figure 2-7. You can select any or all of the items in the left column: Bold, Italic, Underline, or Double Height letters. You can choose only one option at a time from the middle column: No Effects, Small Shadow, Large Shadow, Fog, or 3D

Effect. You can choose only one option at a time from the right column: No Border, Thin Border, Thick Border, or Double Border. The banner text display changes with the effects you choose.

Moving around the banner

At the bottom of your screen are four direction buttons you use to view banner text too long to fit on the screen. To see the Start or End of the text, click on those buttons. Click on the Right or Left button to scroll the banner text.

Printing the banner

At the bottom right of the appliance window is a Print button. Click this to print the banner.

Click on the EXIT button to return to the Choose an Appliance screen.

Solitaire

If you're looking for a bit of diversion, select Solitaire from the Choose an Appliance window to play the solitaire game Klondike. Unfortunately, it does not let you cheat! Otherwise, play it using the standard game rules. When you select a card to move, the program displays all the acceptable destination cards in reverse video. You can not move a card if there is no appropriate destination. See Chapter 16 for more on the Solitaire game.

Click on the EXIT button to return to the Choose an Appliance screen.

2 The Appliances

Calculator

Select Calculator from the Choose an Appliance window to display the screen shown in Figure 2-8.

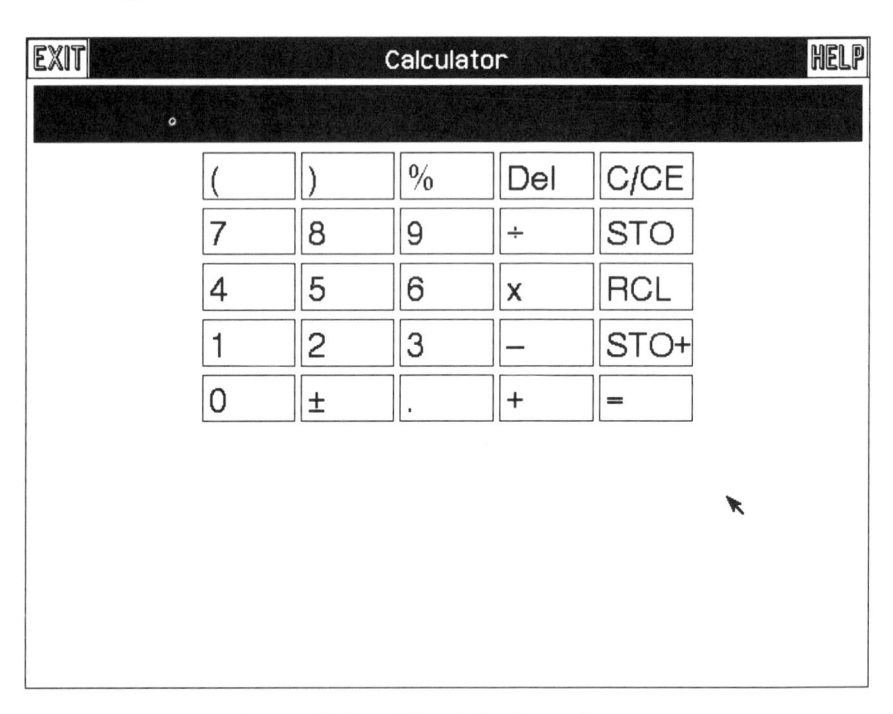

Figure 2-8 — The Calculator Screen.

This appliance is a handy on-screen calculator that performs standard computations. For example, suppose you want to multiply 5 x 3. Click on the 5 button to enter that number. Next, click on the x (times) button. Then click on the 3 button. Finally, click on the = (equal) button for the answer.

To store the displayed number, and overwriting any previously stored value, click the STO button. Click the STO+ button if you want to add the displayed number to the stored value without overwriting it. Clicking the RCL button recalls (displays) the stored value.

The Appliances 2

To subtract a number from the stored value, you must change the number (to be subtracted) into a negative, using $\boxed{\pm}$. Then use $\boxed{\text{STO+}}$ to to add the negative number to the stored value — adding a negative to a positive is the same as subtracting.

Clicking the $\boxed{\text{Del}}$ button removes digits from a displayed number, one digit at a time. Clicking the $\boxed{\%}$ button divides the displayed number by 100.

Clicking the $\boxed{\text{C/CE}}$ button clears the displayed number. To clear the storage memory, click $\boxed{0}$ (zero) and then click $\boxed{\text{STO}}$ (stores zero).

You can perform an operation such as 5x(3+4), by using the parentheses $\boxed{(}$ and $\boxed{)}$ buttons. Try it yourself:

    Step 1. Click $\boxed{5}$
    Step 2. Click $\boxed{x}$
    Step 3. Click $\boxed{(}$
    Step 4. Click $\boxed{3}$
    Step 5. Click $\boxed{+}$
    Step 6. Click $\boxed{4}$
    Step 7. Click $\boxed{)}$
    Step 8. Click $\boxed{=}$

Your answer should be 35. For a more detailed discussion of the Calculator see Chapter 10.

Click on the EXIT button to return to the Choose an Appliance screen.

2 The Appliances

Notepad

Select Notepad from the Choose an Appliance screen to display the screen shown in Figure 2-9. Use Notepad to save, recall and print notes.

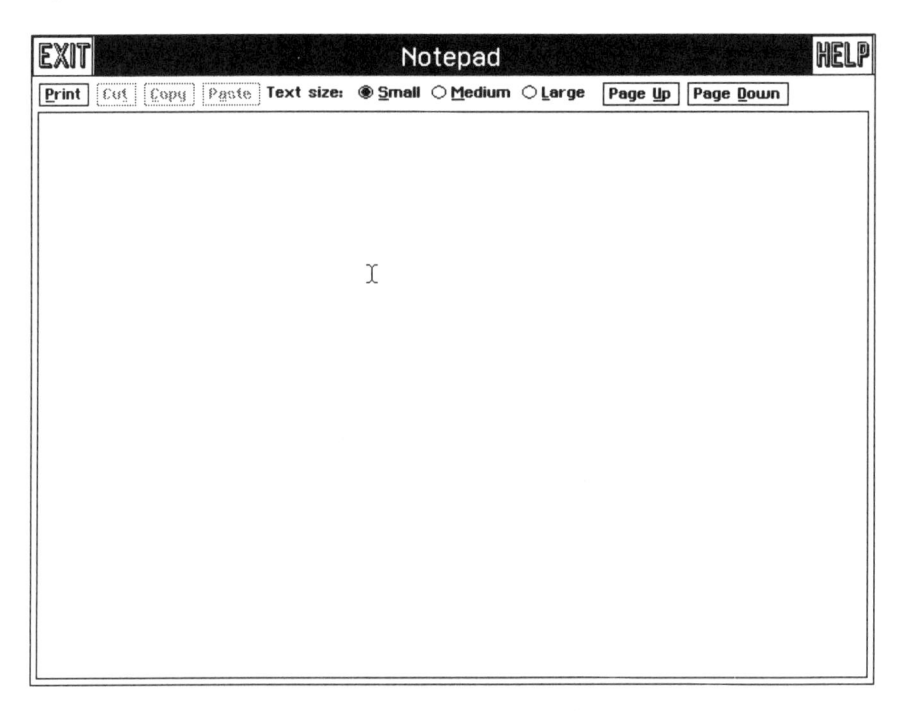

Figure 2-9 — The Notepad Screen.

The program displays automatically the last note saved on the Notepad.

Entering text in a note

Enter text by typing it in the note area. Text automatically wraps to the next line as you type. Press [Enter↵] only when you want to begin a new paragraph. Use [←BkSp] to delete the character to the left of the cursor, or [delete] to delete the character on the right. You can remove a block of text by using Cut (see below).

The blinking I-beam pointer (text cursor) indicates where the next character will be placed. To reposition the text cursor, move the mouse cursor to the new location, then click the left mouse button. Notes longer than one page activate the scroll bar buttons.

Printing a note

Click the print button in the upper left of the appliance window to print your note.

Using cut, copy, and paste

You can cut text out of the note, copy text, and paste it where you want. Select the text to cut or copy by pressing and holding the left mouse button on the first character of the text, then dragging the mouse cursor to the last character you want to include. Release the button. The selected text displays in reverse video (highlighted). Click on the Move or Copy button in the edit box at the top of the window. Cut removes the selected text from the Notepad and moves it to the clipboard. Copy puts a copy of the selected text on the clipboard. Position the mouse cursor where you want to insert the text now on the clipboard, then click the left mouse button to reposition the text cursor. Select Paste in the edit box to move the clipboard text to the text cursor location.

Changing text size

You can change the size of the letters in the note display window by clicking one of the Text Size buttons: Small, Medium or Large. Changing the display, however, does not affect the size of the printed note characters.

Summary

In Chapter 2 you learned how to move around the GeoWorks Ensemble program, and how to use the six applications in the Appliances section.

Chapter 3

The GeoWorks Ensemble Professional Workspace

The Professional Workspace, a more advanced section of the GeoWorks Ensemble program, contains 13 applications (programs designed to perform a particular function). These are among the many things you can do in the Professional Workspace:

- Make notes
- Schedule appointments
- Write and edit lengthy documents
- Make drawings and insert them into documents.

Some of the applications are similar to the appliances, but they are more advanced and more powerful.

3 The GeoWorks Ensemble Professional Workspace

Moving Around the Professional Workspace

See Chapter 2 for a discussion about using the mouse in GeoWorks Ensemble. In the Professional Workspace you can use the mouse, keyboard commands and hotkeys to access menus and make menu selections. Take a quick look at the Menu Maps in Appendix A. Note that next to many menu items in the Professional Workspace Applications are keyboard commands — hotkeys such as [alt]-[F5] or [Ctrl]-[L] — that provide quick access to the item. A hotkey is also displayed next to its item in the pull-down menus in the Professional Workspace.

Mouse Menu Selection

There are two methods for selecting items from a menu, the click or the drag method.

Click item selection

Move the mouse cursor on the menu you want to select. Click the left mouse button to display the menu. Move the mouse cursor to the desired menu item and click the left mouse button again to select the menu item and close the menu.

Drag item selection

Move the mouse cursor to the menu you want to select. Press and hold the left mouse button while you drag the highlighting to the desired menu item. Release the left mouse button to select the menu item and close the menu.

Keyboard Commands for Menus

To access menus and make menu selections from the keyboard:

1. Press [alt] to highlight the first menu across the top of the active window.
2. Press [←] or [→] to move along the menu bar.
3. Press [↓], [space], or [Enter↵] to display the highlighted menu. If you want to move to a different menu, press [←] or [→].

The GeoWorks Ensemble Professional Workspace 3

4. Press ⬆ and ⬇ to highlight the item you want in the pull-down menu. Three dots following the item name indicate that the option opens a dialog box. A cascade menu (a submenu of the highlighted option) is indicated by a right facing arrow next to the item. To access a cascade menu press ➡, then use ⬆ ⬇ to highlight a submenu item. Press ⬅ to close the cascade menu and return to the previous menu.

5. Press ⬇, [space] or [Enter↵] to select a menu item and close the menu. Press [esc] to close the menu without making a selection.

6. To access the Control menu or Express menu use ⬅ or ➡ to move the highlight off the Menu Bar and position it on the Control Button or Express Button, displaying its menu. Make your selection from the Control menu or Express menu in the same way as on other menus.

Mnemonic Commands for Menus

When a menu name includes an underlined character, you can use the character to select the option from the keyboard. The character can be a letter or number. Follow these steps to access a Menu Bar menu using the mnemonic method:

1. Press [alt] and hold it down while you press the letter key (mnemonic) associated with that menu. For example, in all Professional Workspace applications, the letter F is the mnemonic for the File menu. To select the File menu, press [alt]-[F].

2. After a menu is open, select menu items by pressing the mnemonic key alone. For example, to select the New option in the File menu, press [N].

Hotkey Commands for Menus

You can instantly access some menu items, bypassing the menus, using hotkeys (also called keyboard accelerators). Hotkey combinations are displayed in the Menu Maps (see Appendix A) and beside the corresponding option in the pull-down menus. For example, suppose you have copied text to the clipboard in the Notepad application. You reposition your text cursor where you want to insert the copied text. Now, instead of using the mouse or the mnemonic keys to access the Paste option in the Edit menu, you could simply use the Paste hotkey combination: [⇧ Shift]-[Ins]. The Paste hotkey is the same in all applications that let you cut or copy and paste text.

3 The GeoWorks Ensemble Professional Workspace

Pinning a menu

The first option in each pull-down menu is a pin symbol. Select the pin option to keep the menu open after you make a selection. The menu display changes to include a Title Bar and Control Button. Although you can select the pin option using keyboard commands, you must subsequently use the mouse to make a selection within a pinned menu.

Moving a pinned menu

To move a pinned menu, press and hold the left mouse button over the menu Title Bar while dragging the menu to its new location. Release the left mouse button to relocate the menu. (As you drag the menu, the mouse cursor changes to two small perpendicular arrows with arrowheads at each of the four ends.)

Closing a pinned menu

To close and unpin a menu, double-click on the Control button in the upper left corner of the menu. The menu unpins and closes.

Using the Menu Maps

Menu Maps (see Appendix A) indicate available hotkeys and mnemonic keys. If a menu item brings up a cascade menu, the Menu Map displays a right facing arrow. If an item brings up a dialog box, the Menu Map displays three dots following the item.

Accessing the GeoDraw Window

Windows in GeoWorks Ensemble are rectangular areas of the screen in which information is displayed. You can move windows around the screen, stack them up like sheets of paper or overlap them. You can change the size of a window so that it fills the screen or displays only a line or two, or you can reduce the window to an icon.

This section gives you an overview of the GeoDraw application window; other application windows are quite similar.

The GeoWorks Ensemble Professional Workspace 3

Select the Professional panel from the Welcome screen, displaying the GeoManager screen. Select the GeoDraw icon, displaying the window shown in Figure 3-1.

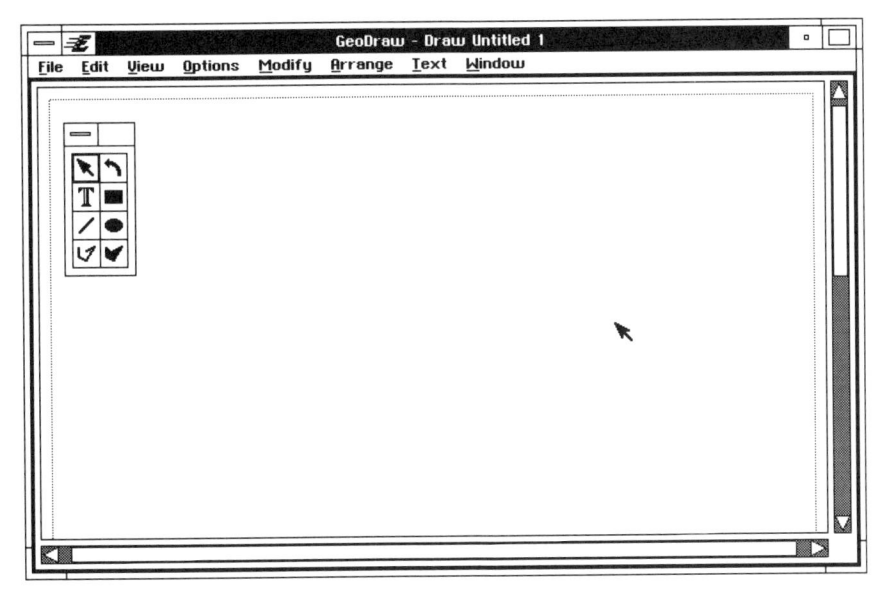

Figure 3-1 — The GeoDraw Window.

Descriptions of GeoDraw window items follow. You can use the Menu Maps at any time to see the overall relationship of the items contained in this application.

Control Button

The Control Button is a small rectangular button with a horizontal bar in it located in the upper left corner of the window. Double-clicking the left mouse button on the Control Button exits the application and returns you to the GeoManager window.

A single click on the Control Button displays the Control menu. You cannot access a dimmed menu item until some specific action activates it. Do not bother trying to access a dimmed item — it cannot be done.

When you display the GeoDraw Control menu immediately after starting the application, the only available options are Minimize, Maximize, and Close; all other options are dimmed.

35

3 The GeoWorks Ensemble Professional Workspace

Select Minimize to reduce the application to an icon placed at the bottom of the screen. Restore it by double-clicking on the icon.

Select Close to close the application and return to the GeoManager screen.

Select Maximize to expand a window so it fills the entire screen. Any Minimized icons at the bottom of the screen will be covered by a Maximized window. To restore a Maximized window to its original size, select Restore from the Control menu.

Express Menu Button

The Express menu button is to the right of the Control button. The Express menu, which is generally the same on all application windows, lets you move around GeoWorks Ensemble without closing an application. For example, when you select GeoManager from the GeoDraw Express menu you go directly to the GeoManager screen. The GeoDraw application — now an icon at the bottom of the screen — is still active, waiting in the background for you to return to it. You could open another application, then use the Express menu to leave it open (as an icon) and return to the GeoManager screen.

The Express menu lists open applications, indicating them with a filled circle to the left of the item. To return to an open application, select it from the Express menu or double-click on the application icon at the bottom of the screen. If you try to select an already-open application from the GeoManager screen, GeoManager tells you it is already open. You may have to close or minimize a window that covers the icon.

The Express menu does not display applications not currently open. To open an application using the Express menu, select Startup. Then select the application you want from the displayed list.

Title Bar   GeoDraw - Draw Untitled 1

The Title Bar is centered in the top line of the window. The Title Bar displays the application name and the name of the current document.

36

Minimize Button

Near the top right corner of the application window is the Minimize button. This rectangular button always has a small square in it. Selecting the Minimize button reduces the application window to an icon. It is the same as selecting the Minimize option in the Control menu.

Some applications, such as GeoDraw and GeoWrite, let you open several documents within the application, each with its own window. Document windows can be minimized or maximized in the way application windows can be. You can not open multiple copies of an application itself. For example, you can open the America Online application only once.

Minimize/Maximize Restore Button

In the top right corner of the application window is the rectangular Minimize/Maximize Restore button.

The Minimize/Maximize Restore button is empty when the window display is less than the full screen. Selecting an empty Minimize/Maximize Restore button maximizes the application window so it fills the screen. Remember, a maximized window covers any icons at the bottom of the screen. When the application window is maximized, the Minimize/Maximize Restore button has a small triangle in it. Selecting the button with a triangle in it reduces the application window size to less than the full screen, uncovering icons at the bottom of the screen.

Menu Bar

The second line of an application window (in this case the GeoDraw window) contains the Menu Bar. In GeoDraw the Menu Bar shows eight menu options: File, Edit, View, Options, Modify, Arrange, Text, and Window.

Exit

Close GeoDraw and return to GeoManager screen by selecting the Close option from the GeoDraw File menu.

3 The GeoWorks Ensemble Professional Workspace

Creating and Saving Documents (Files)

Most applications in the Professional Workspace create an untitled document when you first start the application. You can also create an untitled document by selecting New from the application File menu. As you work in a document, your data is stored in temporary memory in your computer. Any data not saved to the hard disk or a floppy disk will be lost when you close the application or exit GeoWorks Ensemble. To save your work, select Save from the File menu. If the document is untitled, you will be asked to give it a name. You can save the document in any subdirectory (and drive) you want, although you may find it most convenient to save it in the GeoWorks DOCUMENT subdirectory.

As a precaution, GeoWorks Ensemble periodically copies your work to disk to keep it safe. Use the Preferences application to specify the time interval between saves. If you make changes to a document and then decide you don't want those changes, you can go back to the last saved version by selecting Revert from the File menu.

DOS and GEOS Files

Depending on the application, GeoWorks Ensemble creates one of two kinds of documents. Most GeoWorks Ensemble applications work with and create DOS documents. A notable exception is the GeoWrite application which creates GEOS documents. GEOS and DOS documents are not compatible.

DOS Document File Names and Icons

A DOS file name is always 1-to-8 characters (with no spaces). It may be followed by a period and an extension of 1-to-3 characters. For example: COVERLTR.DOC is a valid DOS file name. A DOS document icon is a small file box with the word DOS on it. Below the document icon is its file name. GEOS file names are up to 32 characters long (including punctuation and spaces). For example: Resume.Cover.Letter is a valid GEOS file name. GEOS document icons display a symbol representing the originating application. Below the document icon is its file name.

About Subdirectories

Think of a directory as a folder which can hold files and other directories. The directory which contains a subdirectory is called the parent directory. GeoWorks Ensemble uses a folder icon to represent a subdirectory. The root directory (\), which is the primary or topmost directory level, does not have a name. All subdirectories on a disk branch from the root directory.

GeoWorks Ensemble uses two main directories, WORLD and DOCUMENT. The WORLD directory stores applications (programs you can run), and the DOCUMENT directory stores data files. In order to locate a directory or a file, you have to specify the path, i.e., the drive and a list of directories, and/or subdirectories that lead to the item. For example, suppose that on your C: drive you have a subdirectory called DOCUMENT under the root directory. Under the DOCUMENT directory is a subdirectory called TREES. In the TREES subdirectory is a file called SPRUCE. The path to the SPRUCE file is:

```
C:\DOCUMENT\TREES\SPRUCE
```

You must include a colon after the drive letter and a backslash (\) between each level in the path name.

To select this same file graphically, choose the DOCUMENT icon, then choose the TREES folder. The contents of the TREES subdirectory will be displayed (including the SPRUCE file). Note that the full path to the TREES directory is indicated next to the directory button.

If you are in a DOS application, the subdirectory file display shows only DOS documents, even if GEOS documents are also stored in the subdirectory. If you are in a GEOS application, the subdirectory file display shows only GEOS documents, even if a DOS document is stored in the subdirectory.

3 The GeoWorks Ensemble Professional Workspace

Importing and Exporting DOS/GEOS Files

You cannot directly retrieve a DOS document into a GEOS application document (or vice versa). Using special import/export options within applications, however, you can share data between document types. The following exercise will teach you how to import and export DOS and GEOS documents. In it, you will:

- Exit GeoWorks Ensemble and return to the DOS prompt (if you are currently running the program).
- Run GeoWorks Ensemble from the DOS prompt.
- Open GeoComm (which uses DOS documents) and verify the names of two GeoComm script files.
- Open GeoWrite (which uses GEOS documents) and import a GeoComm script DOS document, converting it to a GEOS file.
- Save the new GEOS document, then export and save the same document as a DOS file.

Exercise 3-1

Note: The purpose of this exercise is to exchange file types between applications. To accomplish this, you will be asked to perform actions you may not fully understand. These will be fully explained in later chapters, but for now, please take them on faith.

1. If you are currently running the GeoWorks Ensemble program, select Exit to DOS from the Express menu. You will return to the DOS prompt. Or, if you would rather not exit, close any open applications and return to the GeoManager screen. Skip to Step 4.

2. Run the GeoWorks Ensemble program. At the DOS prompt, type:

    GEOS [Enter⏎]

    GeoWorks Ensemble displays the Welcome window.

3. Select the Professional icon by clicking on it once.

The GeoWorks Ensemble Professional Workspace 3

Note: If this is the first time you have run GeoWorks Ensemble, the program will display the GeoManager window showing all the applications available in the Professional Workspace. Proceed to Step 4.

If you previously used the Professional Workspace, then the program displays the window you were in when you exited GeoWorks Ensemble. Close any open applications except GeoManager by activating the application window and selecting Close from the Control menu.

4. At the bottom center of the GeoManager screen is a World button — an icon with a globe in it. Select the World button to be certain the GeoManager screen is displaying application icons. If the World button was not already active, your screen will change to the display shown in Figure 3-2. If the World button was already active, your display was already similar to Figure 3-2.

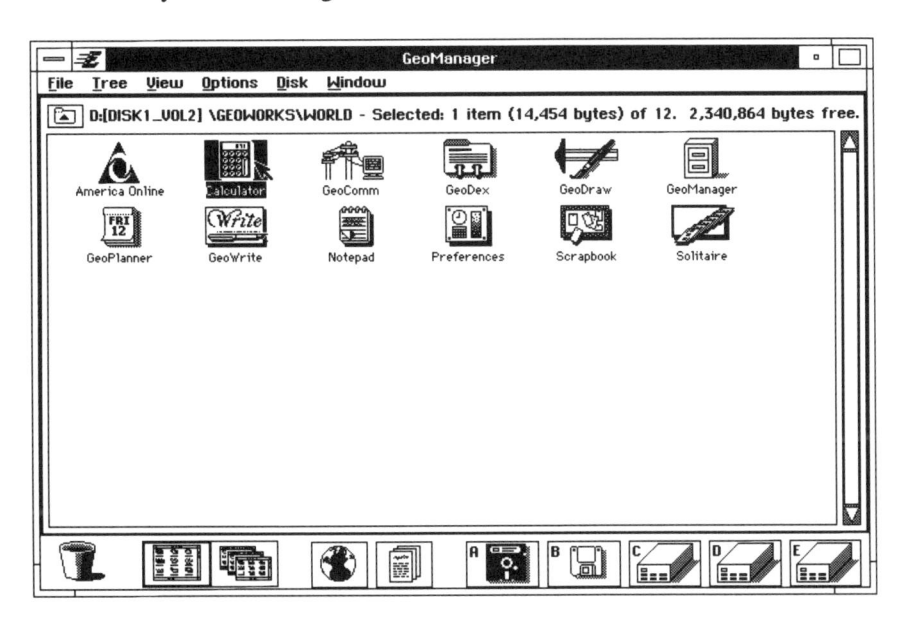

Figure 3-2 — The GeoManager World Display Window.

5. The Document button is located just to the right of the World button. Select the Document button to display a screen similar to Figure 3-3.

41

3 The GeoWorks Ensemble Professional Workspace

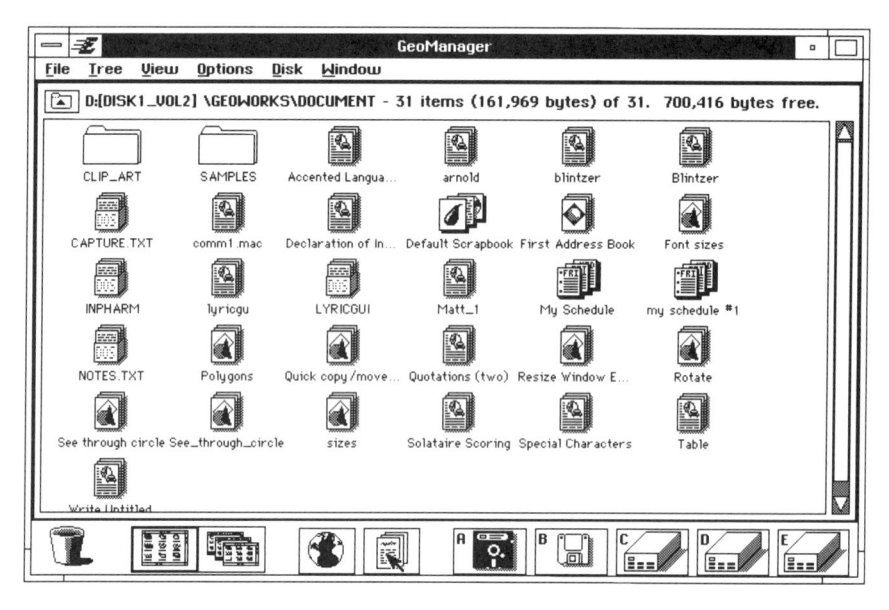

Figure 3-3 — The GeoManager Document Display Window.

SHORTCUT You will practice this shortcut later: to open a document from the Document window, click on a document icon, then select Open from the GeoManager File menu. GeoWorks Ensemble opens the application in which the document was created and opens the document itself, ready for you to use.

6. Select the World button again to return to a display similar to Figure 3-2.

The World directory displays applications (programs you can run); the Document directory displays subdirectories and files.

Opening the GeoComm application

Next you will open the GeoComm application. You already know that you could simply double-click on the GeoComm icon to open the application, so let's try another method: the Express menu.

1. Select the Express button (the ![button] button at the top of the GeoManager screen) to display the screen shown in Figure 3-4.

The GeoWorks Ensemble Professional Workspace 3

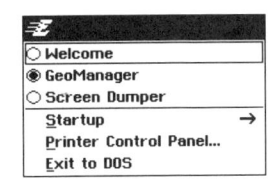

Figure 3-4 — The Express Menu.

2. Select Startup on the Express menu. The Startup menu lists all the Professional Workspace applications.
3. Select GeoComm from the Startup menu to open the GeoComm application.
4. Select Dial from the GeoComm application window.
5. Select Scripts from the Dial menu. The Scripts dialog box displays two files (DOS documents): COMPU.MAC and GENIE.MAC. Figure 3-5 shows the Dial menu and the Scripts dialog box with two script files available for selection.

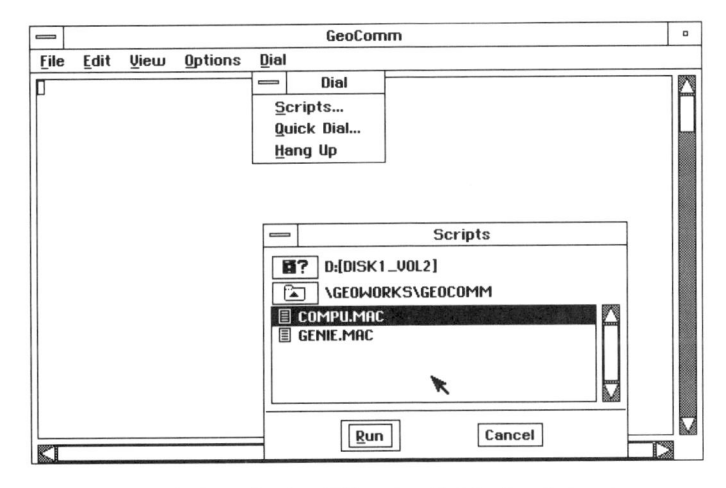

Figure 3-5 — Script Files Available for Selection.

Note: Script files (DOS documents) must have the extension .MAC as part of the file name. A script file without the extension will not display in the Scripts dialog box.

43

3 The GeoWorks Ensemble Professional Workspace

Opening the GeoWrite application

The next few steps illustrate how to open the GeoWrite application, leaving the GeoComm application open as an icon.

1. Select Cancel to close the Scripts dialog box.

2. Select the Minimize button (the rectangular button with a small box in it, top right) to keep GeoComm open but reduce it to an icon as shown at the bottom left of Figure 3-6.

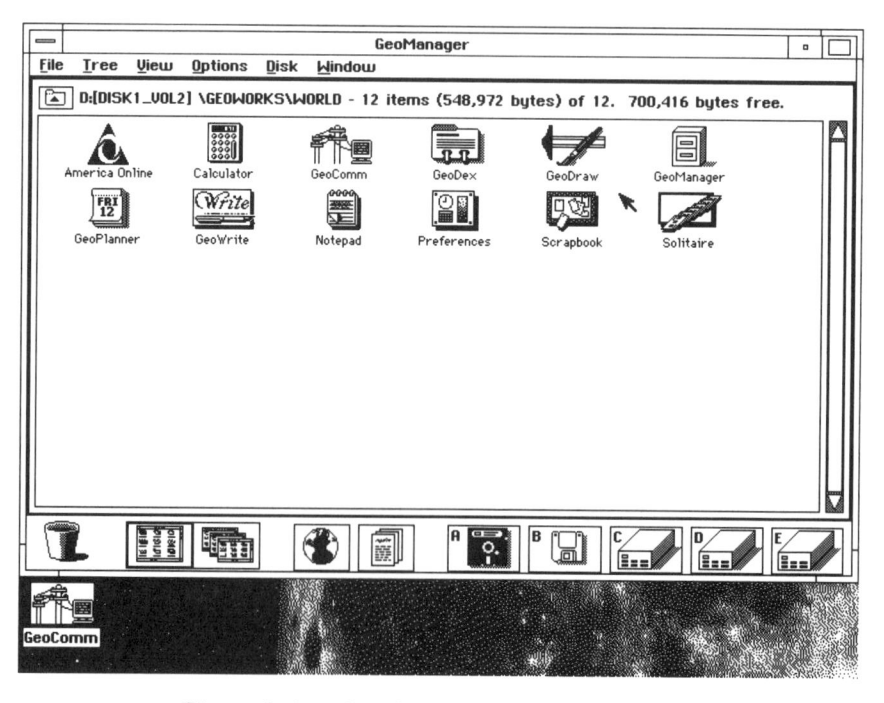

Figure 3-6 — GeoComm Reduced to an Icon.

3. Double-click on the GeoWrite icon to open the application.

4. Select the File menu.

5. Select Insert From Text File from the File menu to display the Insert From Text File dialog box. Figure 3-7 shows a pinned File menu and the Insert From Text File dialog box.

The GeoWorks Ensemble Professional Workspace 3

Use the Insert From Text File option to import a DOS file into GeoWrite. The command converts a copy of the original DOS file into a GEOS file; the DOS file remains unchanged.

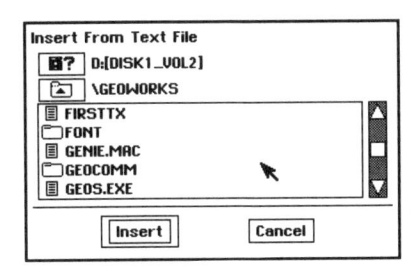

```
Insert From Text File
  ?   D:[DISK1_VOL2]
  ⬆   \GEOWORKS
  ▤ FIRSTTX
  ▢ FONT
  ▤ GENIE.MAC
  ▢ GEOCOMM
  ▤ GEOS.EXE

     [ Insert ]   [ Cancel ]
```

Figure 3-7 — The Insert From Text File Dialog Box.

Don't worry if the files listed in your dialog box are different from Figure 3-7. You may not have the same saved files on your hard disk.

Moving around subdirectories

Now you will learn about subdirectories and how to move around them in GeoWorks Ensemble. The first button in the Insert From Text File dialog box is the Drive button. Beside it is the current drive designation. (In Figure 3-7, D: is the current drive.) Below the Drive button is the Move Up One Directory Level button. Beside the Move Up One Directory Level button is an information line displaying the path to the current subdirectory. It should read \GEOWORKS. The listing in the panel below the buttons displays the subdirectories (file folders) and files in the current subdirectory.

1. Click on the Move Up One Directory Level button. The current drive ROOT directory — always identified by a \ (backslash) — becomes the current directory. The files in the root directory and subdirectories under the root directory are now shown in the panel.

2. Double-click on the GEOWORKS subdirectory line in the panel. The current subdirectory now changes to \GEOWORKS. The GEOWORKS subdirectory contents are again displayed in the panel.

3. Double-click on the GEOCOMM subdirectory line in the panel. The current subdirectory now changes to \GEOWORKS\GEOCOMM and the subdirectory contents are displayed in the panel — the same two file names you saw from within the GeoComm application: COMPU.MAC and GENIE.MAC.

Note: Because these are DOS documents, you would not find them listed if you tried to open them using the Open command in the GeoWrite File menu. GeoWrite would show that the \GEOWORKS\GEOCOMM subdirectory is empty because it does not recognize DOS files.

Importing a DOS file into GeoWrite

Now you will import a DOS document into GeoWrite and save it as a GEOS document and a DOS document.

1. Highlight the document named COMPU.MAC in the Insert From Text File dialog box.

2. Click the Insert button (below the list of files) to import the highlighted file into GeoWrite. The Import From Text dialog box closes. The program displays page 2 of the 2-page file COMPU.MAC in the GeoWrite window. The Title Bar displays the file name: Write Untitled 1. The displayed document is a GEOS file.

Saving a GEOS document as a DOS document

Now you will export a GEOS document, saving it as a DOS file in the \GEOCOMM subdirectory.

1. Select Save As Text File from the File menu, displaying the Save to Text File dialog box. The path information line reads \GEOWORKS. Note: Use the Save As Text File option on the File menu to export a GEOS document as a DOS file. The original GEOS file remains unchanged.

2. Double-click on the GEOCOMM line in the panel. The information line now reads \GEOWORKS\GEOCOMM.

The GeoWorks Ensemble Professional Workspace 3

3. Move the mouse cursor to the File Name box and click the left mouse button to activate the text cursor.

4. Type MYCOMM.MAC. Remember: if you create a GeoComm script file in GeoWrite then save it as a DOS file in the \GEOWORKS\GEOCOMM subdirectory, you must use the .MAC extension. In any case, when saving a GEOS file as a DOS text file, you must use the DOS file naming convention described earlier in this chapter.

5. Click the Save button to save the DOS file in the \GEOWORKS\GEOCOMM directory with the file name MYCOMM.MAC. The Save As Text File dialog box closes and you return to the GeoWrite application window.

6. Select Save (or Save As) from the GeoWrite File menu to display the Select Directory and Enter New File name dialog box.

7. Move the mouse cursor into the File name box and click the left mouse button to activate the text cursor.

8. Type the file name:

    MY COMM SCRIPT FILE `Enter⏎`

The program saves the file to the \GEOWORKS\DOCUMENT directory with the file name MY COMM SCRIPT FILE and closes the dialog box. The Title Bar (top line of the GeoWrite application window) displays the new file name.

When saving a GEOS file in GeoWrite, follow the GEOS file naming conventions described earlier in this chapter.

3 The GeoWorks Ensemble Professional Workspace

Verifying the DOS file export

Now you will return to the GeoComm application to make sure the exported file is there.

1. Verify that the MYCOMM.MAC file was saved correctly to the \GEOWORKS\GEOCOMM subdirectory. Select GeoComm from the Express menu to return to the already-open GeoComm application.

2. Select Scripts from the Dial menu. You now see three script files; one of them is MYCOMM.MAC.

Summary

In Chapter 3 you learned:

- How to move around the Professional Workspace using the mouse, keyboard commands, and hotkeys.
- The basic features of an application window.
- The difference between DOS documents and GEOS documents and how to recognize them by their icons and file names.
- The basics of subdirectory structure.
- How to import a DOS document into a GEOS application.
- How to export a GEOS document to a DOS application
- How to save DOS and GEOS documents.

You also reviewed the ways to open an application in the Professional Workspace.

Take a few moments to review the several ways to open an application in the Professional Workspace:

- Double-click on the application icon in the GeoManager screen.
- Select Startup from the Express menu, then select the application name.
- Click on a document icon (in the Document directory display), then select Open from the GeoManager File menu.

Chapter 4

GeoManager

The GeoManager Application is the nerve center of the GeoWorks Professional Workspace. In GeoManager you can perform file and disk management functions easily without having to remember any DOS commands. Specifically, you can:

- Open GEOS applications and documents, as well as DOS programs (non-GeoWorks Ensemble programs) and batch files.

- View the directory structure of a disk as a directory tree. You can expand or shrink branches of the tree to view more or less detail.

- View the contents of a directory by name, size, or date and time of last modification.

- Open and view more than one directory at a time.

- Perform disk management tasks such as formatting, copying, and renaming disks.

- Copy and move both files and directories by using the mouse to highlight and then drag them to other disks and directories.

- Delete files and directories by using the mouse to highlight them and then drag them to the Wastebasket.

4 GeoManager

The GeoManager Screen

When you start GeoWorks Ensemble, it displays the Welcome screen (shown in Figure 2-1). Click the Professional icon to display the GeoManager screen (Figure 4-1).

Note: When you exit the Professional Workspace, GeoWorks Ensemble remembers what programs were open and what documents were on your screen. The next time you run Professional Workspace, GeoWorks Ensemble restores the screen to the way it was when you exited. If you have been using the Professional Workspace, your screens may vary somewhat from the Figures in this book. Don't worry. Any differences will not significantly impact your ability to follow the discussions in this book.

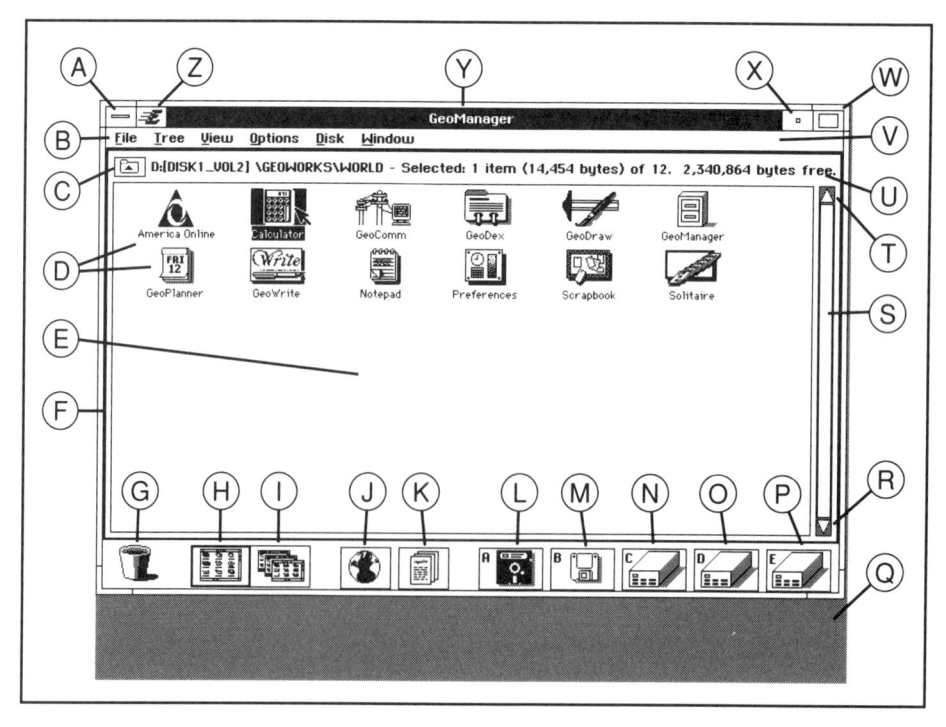

Figure 4-1 — Important GeoManager Screen Features.

GeoManager 4

A. Control button.
B. Menus.
C. Directory button.
D. Icons.
E. Window.
F. Resize border (has 8 sections).
G. Wastebasket.
H. View directories as full sized windows.
I. View directories as overlapping windows.
J. WORLD directory button.
K. DOCUMENT directory button.
L. Floppy disk (5-1/4").
M. Floppy disk (3-1/2").
N. Hard disk drive C.
O. Hard disk drive D.
P. Hard disk drive E.
Q. Workspace background (disappears when window is maximized).
R. Scroll arrow.
S. Scroll bar.
T. Scroll arrow.
U. Information bar.
V. Menu bar.
W. Maximize button: enlarges the window to fill the screen (changes to Restore when button is used).
X. Minimize button: reduces the window to an icon button.
Y. Title bar (active) — Hightlighted when active. Center of Title bar shows application name and document name and page (if available).
Z. Express menu button.

51

4 GeoManager

Control Line

The top line of the GeoManager screen is divided into five sections (from left to right): the Control Button, the Express Button, the Title Bar, the Minimize Button, and the Maximize/Restore Button.

Control Button

The small rectangular box with the bar through it on the extreme left is the Control button (see Figure 4-1, A). All application windows and most menu windows also have a Control button. It's function is always the same: to access the Control menu (with a single click), or to immediately close the application window (with a double-click). The Control menu is shown in Figure 4-2.

The Control button is most often used to close an application. You can close an application two ways using the Control button. One way is to double-click on it, closing the application immediately. The second method requires two steps:

1. Single click on the Control button to display the Control menu
2. Select Close from the Control menu.

You can also accomplish the second method by locating the pointer on the Control button, pressing and holding the mouse button to open the Control menu, then dragging the mouse down to the Close item and releasing the mouse button.

Caution: Anytime GeoManager is the only application open (as it is in this example), using the Control button to close the GeoManager screen will leave you on the Background screen with no icon or menu to select. If you find yourself stranded in this way, you can:

- Press [F2] to return to the Welcome screen, then select the EXIT button to return to the DOS prompt. From here, you can run GeoWorks Ensemble again. (You will not be able to select the Professional box because GeoManager is still running.)
- Press [Ctrl]-[alt]-[delete] to exit to the DOS prompt. (This does not re-boot your computer, it simply drops you back to the DOS prompt.) You could also use the reset button if your computer has one (this will re-boot your computer).

GeoManager 4

Note: Any time GeoWorks exits abnormally it will present you with a Reset screen the next time it is started. This screen will give you the choice to start PC/GEOS normally (the Welcome window) or to restart the Professional workspace.

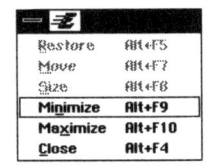

Figure 4-2 — The GeoManager Control Menu.

You cannot access dimmed options in the Control menu (or any other menu). The options remain dimmed until you perform specific functions. For example, the Restore option is dimmed unless you Maximize the window. (Restore returns the window to its previous size.)

Beside each menu option is a shortcut command you can use from the keyboard instead of using the Control menu. Every option in the Control menu has a corresponding shortcut command. Not all options in all menus have shortcuts.

Restore (Alt+F5)

Restore is unavailable until you Maximize the window. Select Restore to return the window to its original size.

Move (Alt+F7)

Move is unavailable until you select an application window you want to reposition.

Size (Alt+F8)

Size is unavailable until you select and application window you want to resize.

Minimize (Alt+F9)

Minimize reduces the window to an icon at the bottom of the screen.

Maximize (Alt+F10)

Maximize expands the window to fill the entire screen. When you select Maximize, Restore becomes active.

4 GeoManager

Close (Alt+F4)

Select Close to exit an application window.

Express Button

The Express button is immediately to the right of the Control button (see Figure 4-1, Z). It always has the same function: to display the Express menu shown in Figure 4-3. (Your Express menu may differ from the Figure depending on what applications you have open at the moment.)

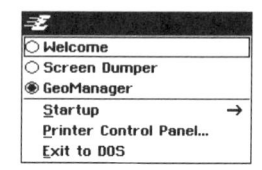

```
○ Welcome
○ Screen Dumper
● GeoManager
  Startup              →
  Printer Control Panel...
  Exit to DOS
```

Figure 4-3 — The Express Menu.

When you run more than one application at a time (which you will soon learn to do), the Express button moves to the active application window — you always have access to the Express button within an application.

Note: Sometimes when you move from one application window to another, the Express button and Title Bar may not be visible. Simply click the mouse cursor anywhere in the application window to display the Express button and Title Bar.

The Express menu is divided into three item groups: Welcome, Reopen an Application, and Go To a New Application.

Welcome (F2)

When you select Welcome from the Express menu, both the Express menu and the GeoManager screen close and you return to the GeoWorks Welcome screen. Or you can press [F2] from the GeoManager screen to close GeoManager and return to the Welcome screen without using the Express menu.

Reopen an application

The middle section of the Express menu gives you instant access to any application that is already open. As the number of open applications increases, the Express menu lengthens to include those applications. You can quickly switch to any open application by selecting it from the Express menu.

Note: You can open multiple applications and move among them easily within the Professional Workspace. Only one application window is active at a time — whichever one you are working in at the moment. Every open application has either a window or an icon visible on the Professional Workspace screen.

When you select an application from the Express menu, the Express menu closes and the selected application becomes the active window. To switch from one application to another, open the Express menu and click on the desired application program. The current program becomes inactive and the selected program becomes the active window, overlapping other windows on the screen. The active window Title Bar is highlighted; an inactive window Title Bar is dimmed.

Applications which do not create documents, such a GeoManager and America Online, will not allow more than one open window at a time for that application.

Applications which create documents, such as GeoWrite or GeoPlanner, allow many open windows for the same application. For example, you could open multiple GeoWrite windows, each displaying a different GeoWrite document. Creating several documents from within the same window does not create separate windows for each document. To create separate windows you must open the application from GeoManager each time.

The Express menu lists every open application window in the order it was created. The only way to distinguish among multiple GeoWrite applications in the Express menu is to remember the order in which you created them.

4 GeoManager

Startup

Select the Startup option when you want to open an application. The program displays a cascade menu similar to Figure 4-4 showing the available applications.

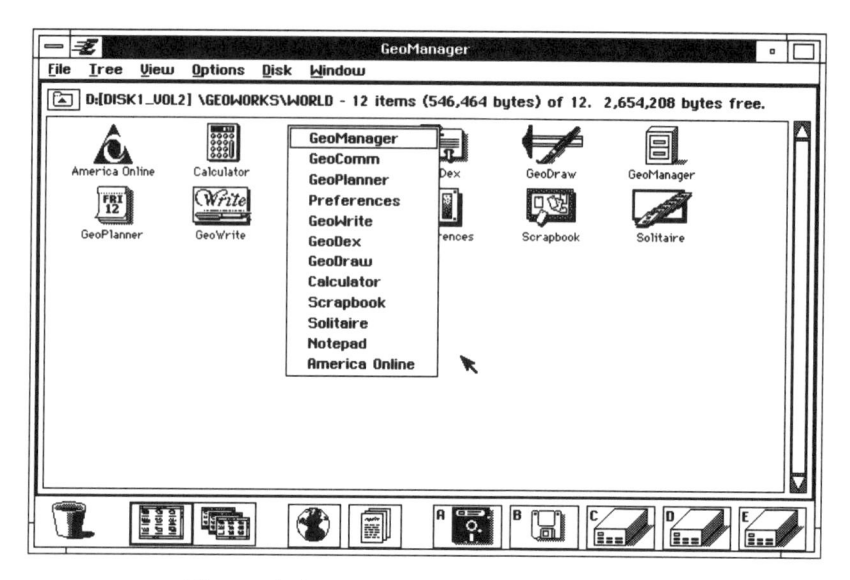

Figure 4-4 — The Startup Cascade Menu.

Clicking on the application you want opens an application window, which becomes the active window. The Express menu adds the new application to its list of open applications. You can start as many applications as you want in the Professional Workspace.

Printer Control option

Selecting the Printer Control option from the Express menu displays a dialog box telling you which printer is currently selected, which document is currently printing, and whether any documents are waiting to print. Select Close from the Printer Control dialog box to return to the screen from which you accessed the Express menu.

GeoManager 4

Exit to DOS

Selecting the Exit to DOS option closes both the active window and the Express menu, returning you directly to the DOS prompt.

Another slightly longer way to exit to DOS is to select Welcome from the Express menu (or tap [F2]) to return to the Welcome screen. Then click the EXIT button to return to the DOS prompt. No matter which method you use, when you return to the Professional Workspace the next time, it will be exactly as it was just before you selected Exit to DOS.

Title Bar

The center portion of the top line of a window is the Title Bar (see Figure 4-1, Y) which identifies the window's application. Applications which create documents, such as GeoWrite and GeoComm, will also display a document name in the Title Bar.

Relocating a window

You can relocate an active window by placing the mouse cursor over the Title Bar, then pressing and holding the left mouse button. The mouse cursor changes to a small cursor with four arrowheads, one pointing up, one down, one left and one right. As long as you hold down the left mouse button you can drag the window around the screen. Release the mouse button to "set down" the window in its new location. Moving and resizing windows allows you to arrange the workspace to suit your preferences.

Resizing a window

The outer edge of most windows is divided into eight resizing sections: each corner of the window and the sides between the corners. You cannot resize a window if it doesn't have these resizing sections. Moving the mouse cursor onto any of these sections changes the mouse cursor appearance. The appearance of the cursor depends on the section of the resizing border it is on. Its new shape indicates the border(s) you can resize.

4 GeoManager

Press and hold the left mouse button to display an outline of the window. Drag the window edge in the direction of the mouse pointer to change the outline size (larger or smaller). Release the mouse button when the window is the size you want. You will not be able to shrink a window beyond its minimum size.

Maximize/Restore Button

Use the far right button on the top line of the GeoManager window (or any window) to maximize the display, expanding the window to fill the screen. The Maximize button turns into the Restore button. (see Figure 4-1, W)

To return the screen to its previous smaller size so you can see the background, icons and other windows, click on the Restore button. The Restore button turns into the Maximize button.

Note: You can also select Restore from the Control menu.

Minimize Button

Use the Minimize button (second from the right — a small button with a small square in it) to reduce a window to an icon. The icon will be labeled with the application name. It will remain open but its contents will not be displayed (see Figure 4-1, X).

Note: You can also Minimize an application to an icon by selecting Minimize from the Control menu.

Repositioning an icon

Place the mouse cursor on the icon you want to reposition, then press and hold the left mouse button while you drag the icon to its new location. Release the left mouse button.

Unshrinking an icon

To restore a window from an icon, double-click the left mouse button on the icon.

Menu Bar

The GeoManager Menu Bar, the second line at the top of the window (see Figure 4-1, V), contains six options: File, Tree, View, Options, Disk and Window.

File Menu

Select File to display the File menu shown in Figure 4-5.

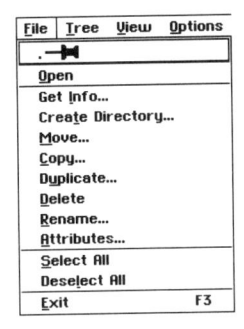

Figure 4-5 — The GeoManager File Menu.

The File Menu contains the following menu items:

Pin

Select the pin symbol to keep the menu open after you have made your selection from it. Once a menu is pinned, you can relocate it wherever you want.

4 GeoManager

Open

Before you can open a file, you must be in the DOCUMENT directory. Click on the Document button at the bottom of the GeoManager window to display documents and subdirectories in a window similar to Figure 4-6.

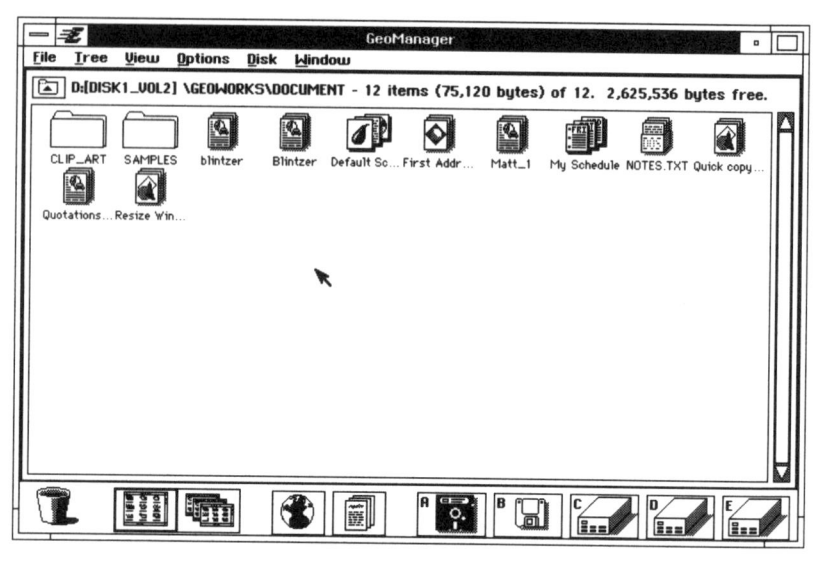

Figure 4-6 — A Typical Documents and Subdirectories Display.

The first two items in the DOCUMENT directory in Figure 4-6 are subdirectories (folder icons) labeled CLIP_ART and SAMPLE. The remaining icons in Figure 4-6 represent DOS and GEOS documents.

Click on a document icon, then select Open from the File menu. (You can also double-click on a document icon to select it directly from the GeoManager window.) If you selected a GEOS document, the program displays the document in an application window. If you selected a DOS document, GeoManager alerts you that the file cannot be opened.

GeoManager 4

Get Info

Click on a document icon to highlight it. Select Get Info from the File menu to display the Get Info dialog box. Figure 4-7 shows a typical GEOS document Get Info dialog box (with a pinned File menu in the background).

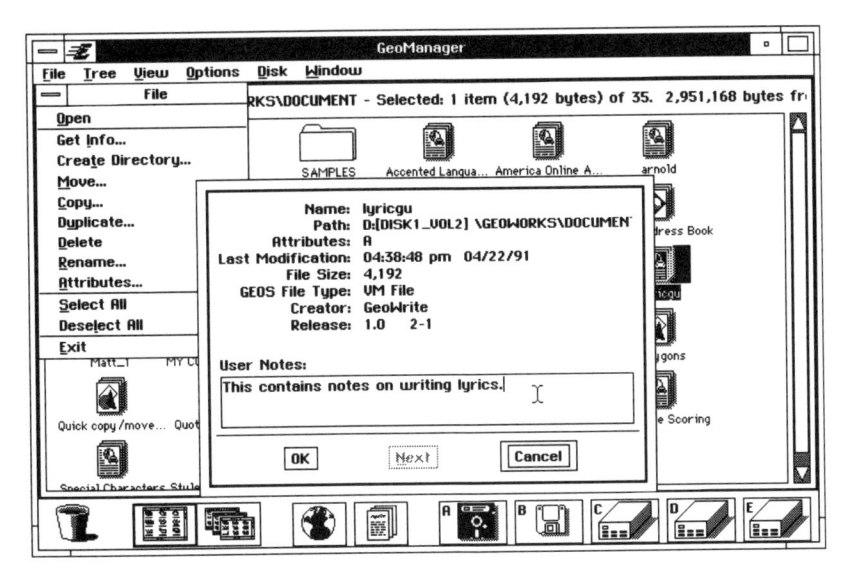

Figure 4-7 — Get Info Dialog Box Display for a GEOS Document.

If the read-only attribute is not set, you can enter and edit text in the User Notes box as shown in Figure 4-7. Click the OK button to save the notes with the file. If you selected more than one document, click the Next button to display the next selected document. Click the Cancel button to close the dialog box.

Figure 4-8 shows the Get Info Dialog Box for a DOS document.

61

4 GeoManager

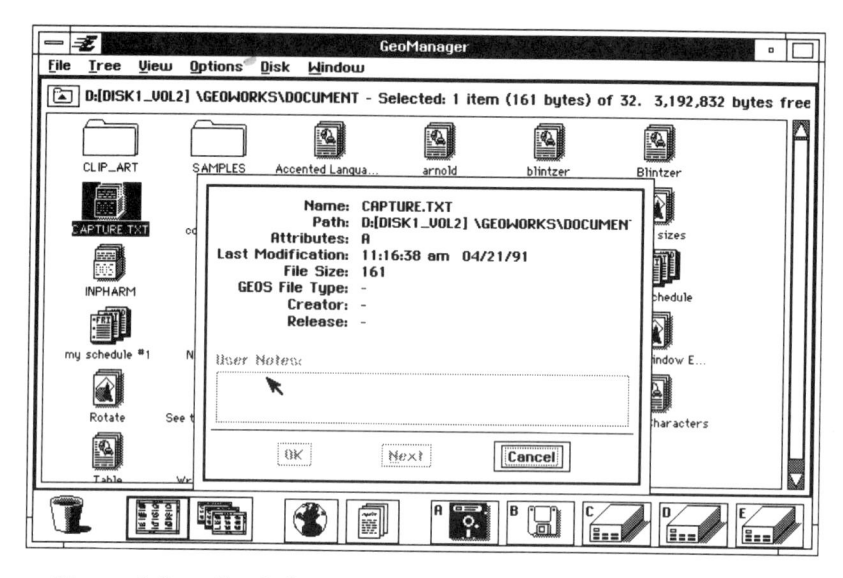

Figure 4-8 — Get Info Dialog Box Display for a DOS Document.

Create directory

Select Create Directory on the file menu to create a new directory. You will usually use this option when the Tree menu is displayed (see below). Figure 4-9 shows the Create Directory dialog box displayed over the Directory Tree for drive A.

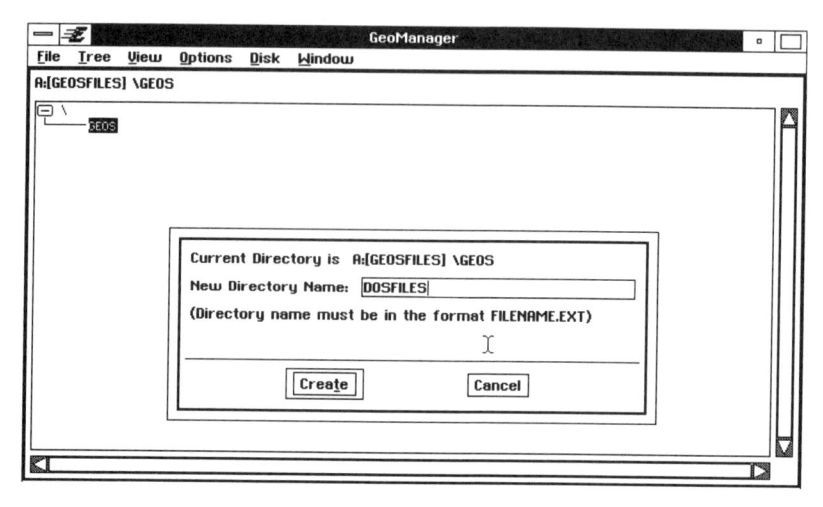

Figure 4-9 — Create Directory Dialog Box.

Suppose you have a subdirectory called MUSIC on your hard drive. You want to create a subdirectory under MUSIC called JAZZ. To create the new directory, first open the MUSIC directory. Select Create Directory from the File menu. Enter the new subdirectory name in the dialog box, then click the Create button. GeoWorks Ensemble creates the new subdirectory. MUSIC is now the parent directory of JAZZ.

Directories must follow the DOS conventions for naming files. This means the directory name must be 1-to-8 characters long, and can have an optional extension of 1-to-3 characters. No spaces or punctuation are permitted.

Move

The move command deletes the item from its current location and relocates it. Highlight the item you want to move by clicking on it, then select Move from the File menu to display the Move dialog box shown in Figure 4-10.

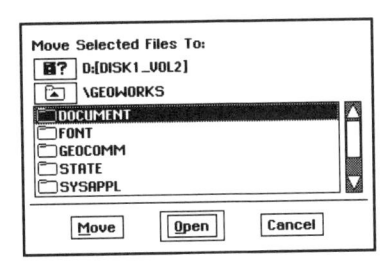

Figure 4-10 — The Move Dialog Box.

In the dialog box, the top icon is the Change Drive icon; the name of the current drive is displayed beside it. Click on the Change Drive icon if you want to move the selected item to another drive. The second icon is the Move Up One Directory Level icon; the name of the destination subdirectory is displayed beside it. The remaining icons are subdirectories under the current directory. (Files are not shown in the dialog box.)

Click on the Move Up One Directory Level icon to select a parent subdirectory. Double-click on a subdirectory icon to move down one level. With every click the destination path and the display change to reflect your choice. Keep clicking until the path displays the destination to which you want to move the item.

4 GeoManager

When you are satisfied with your destination path, click on the Move button in the dialog box. If you highlighted more than one item to move, GeoManager pops up a progress box so you know what is happening. You can stop the Move operation by clicking on the Stop button in the progress box. GeoManager will complete a file move (if one was in process), then stop.

Note: When you highlight a subdirectory and select Move, the program relocates the subdirectory and all its contents in the same operation.

Move by dragging

You can move files and subdirectories — without accessing the File menu — by dragging. Select the items you want to move. Place the mouse cursor on an item then press and hold the right mouse button. The pointer changes to show whether you are dragging one item (pointer shown with a single sheet), or multiple items (pointer shown with three sheets).

You can drag the selected items from one open window to another, as long as a part of the window is visible.

You can also drag directories and files to an icon. Position the mouse pointer on the item you want to move, then press and hold the right mouse button. Drag the pointer onto any of the following (depending on where you want to place the item):

- On a folder icon in a directory window. When the directory represented by a folder icon is on the same disk as the selected item, then the selected item is moved to that directory. If the directory is on a different disk, then the selected item is copied, not moved.

- Anywhere in a directory window except over a folder icon. When the destination directory is on the same disk as the selected item, the item is moved to the destination directory. If the destination directory is on a different disk, then the selected item is copied, not moved.

- On the Up One Directory Level icon in a directory window. The selected item is moved to the parent directory.

- On one of the disk drive icons at the bottom of the GeoManager window. The selected item is moved to the root directory of the disk currently in the selected drive.

GeoManager 4

After you drag the directory or file(s) on the icon you want, release the mouse button.

Copy

The steps to copy an item are almost identical to moving the item. However, when you copy an item it remains in its current location and a copy of it is made at the new location.

Highlight the item you want to copy by clicking on it, then select Copy from the File menu to display the Copy dialog box shown in Figure 4-11.

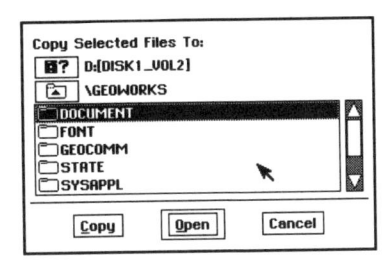

Figure 4-11 — The Copy Dialog Box.

In the dialog box, the top icon is the Change Drive icon; the name of the current drive is displayed beside it. Click on the Change Drive icon if you want to move the selected item to another drive. The second icon is the Move Up One Directory Level icon; the name of the destination subdirectory is displayed beside it. The remaining icons are subdirectories under the current directory. (Files are not shown in the dialog box.)

Click on the Move Up One Directory Level icon to select a parent subdirectory. Double-click on a subdirectory icon to move down one level. With every click the destination path and the display change to reflect your choice. Keep clicking until the path displays the destination to which you want to copy the item.

When you are satisfied with your destination path, click on the Copy button in the dialog box. If you highlighted more than one item to copy, GeoManager pops up a progress box so you know what is happening. You can stop the Copy operation by clicking on the Stop button in the progress box. GeoManager will complete a file copy (if one was in process), then stop.

4 GeoManager

Note: When you highlight a subdirectory and select Copy, the program copies the subdirectory and all its contents in the same operation.

Duplicate

Use the Duplicate command to make a copy of the file under a different name in the same subdirectory. (Remember, copying a file results in two identical, same-named files in different locations.) Highlight the items you want to duplicate, then select Duplicate from the File menu to display the window shown in Figure 4-12.

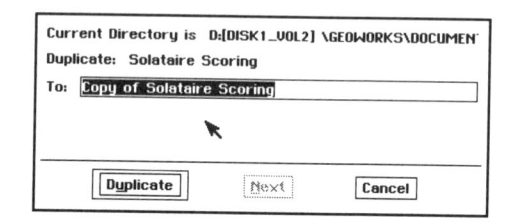

Figure 4-12 — The Duplicate Dialog Box.

GeoManager automatically assigns the new file name "Copy of <filename>." To accept the file name, click on the Duplicate button. To change the file name, tap [←BkSp] to delete the suggested file name, type the name you want (following the DOS or GEOS file naming conventions), then click on the Duplicate button. If you decide not to duplicate the file, click on the Next button to display the next item, or click on the Cancel button to close the dialog box.

Delete

Use the Delete command to delete items. Highlight the files or subdirectories you want to delete, then select Delete from the File menu. If the Confirm Delete option is set in the Options menu (discussed later), then the program displays a dialog box asking you to confirm each deletion: Click Yes to delete, No to save the item.

Caution: If the Confirm Delete option is not set in the Options menu, you will confirm once that you want to proceed, then the program will delete all selected items. Click on Cancel to close the dialog box without deleting any more files.

When you select multiple items to delete, a progress box tells you what is happening. Click on Stop in the progress box to stop the delete operation after the current file.

Delete by dragging

You can delete selected items by dragging them (using the right mouse button) to the Wastebasket icon at the bottom of the GeoManager screen. If the Confirm Delete option is set in the Options menu, the program displays a dialog box asking you to confirm each delete. Click on Cancel to close the dialog box without deleting any more files.

Caution: If Confirm Delete is NOT set on the Options menu, you will not receive a request to confirm the delete. The items are deleted as soon as you release the right mouse button on the Wastebasket icon.

Rename

To change the name of directories or files, highlight the items, then select Rename from the File menu to display a dialog box. Click on the To box and type the new name for the first item. Click on Rename. To skip an item, click on Next. Click on Cancel to close the dialog box without renaming any additional files. If you type in a name that conflicts with an existing file or subdirectory, a dialog box prompts you to select a different name.

Attributes

There are four types of attributes you can assign to DOS files:

- **R**   Read-only
- **H**   Hidden
- **S**   System
- **A**   Archive.

An attribute is either on or off. A file can have any combination of attributes. Perhaps the most useful attribute is Read-only, which protects a file against accidental changes or deletion. These attributes are used only with DOS files

4 GeoManager

(not GEOS files). You can see a file's attributes by selecting Names and Details from the View menu. The far right column displays the file's attributes. For example, Figure 4-13 shows a Names and Details file listing for drive A.

Figure 4-13 — A Names and Details Display.

Highlight the file or files whose attributes you want to change. If you want to change attributes on a group of files, press and hold the left mouse cursor over the first file, then drag the highlight to include all the files you want to affect. Release the button. To select multiple individual files, hold down `Shift` then click on the files you want to select.

Select Attributes from the File menu to display the Change File Attributes dialog box, similar to Figure 4-14.

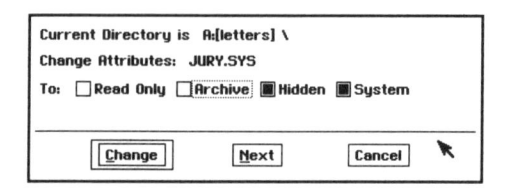

Figure 4-14 — The Change File Attributes Dialog Box.

Click on the attributes you want to select for the file named in the Change File Attributes dialog box. Clicking an attribute toggles it on and off. Click on Change to assign the attributes to the current file. Click on Next to go to the next file without changing the current file's attributes. Click on Cancel to close the dialog box without making any additional file attribute changes. To see the file attribute changes, select Names and Details from the View menu.

Note: If Show Hidden Files is set in the View menu, files with Hidden or System attributes will display. If Show Hidden Files is NOT set in the View menu, you will not see any files with the Hidden or System attributes.

Select all

Use this option to select (highlight) all items (subdirectories and files) in a directory.

Deselect all

Use this option to deselect (remove the highlight) all selected items in a directory.

Exit (F3)

Select Exit from the File menu to remove the application from memory and close the window. You can also exit an application by double-clicking on the Control button.

If GeoManager is the only open application, closing it returns you to the Welcome screen.

Note: Normally you do not exit GeoManager. If you are running several applications and you notice your system is running slowly, you can exit GeoManager to free memory.

Tree Menu

Use the Tree menu to view the subdirectories on a disk. The Tree menu displays the directory structure as an organization tree. The root directory (\ ) is at the top of the tree. Directories and subdirectories are shown with branch lines, indicating their relationship to the root directory and to each other. You can control how much

4 GeoManager

of the tree to display by expanding or collapsing the directories. A plus sign beside a directory name means the directory can be expanded to display subdirectories. A minus sign indicates a subdirectory is fully expanded.

Double-click on a directory to look at its files. Figure 4-15 displays the GeoManager Tree menu.

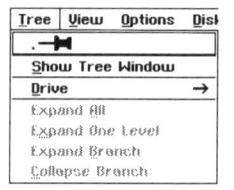

Figure 4-15 — The Tree Menu.

The Tree menu contains the following menu items:

Pin

Select the pin symbol to keep the menu open after you have made your selection from it. Once a menu is pinned, you can relocate it wherever you want.

Show Tree Window

Select this option when you want to display the directory contents of the current drive in tree form. Figure 4-16 shows the structure of a typical directory tree.

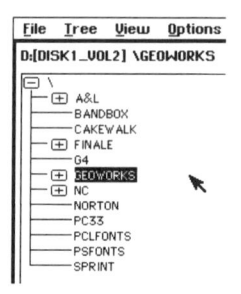

Figure 4-16 — A Directory Tree.

GeoManager 4

Drive

Select this option to change the tree display to a different drive. Select the new drive (for example, drive D:) from the cascade menu as shown in Figure 4-17.

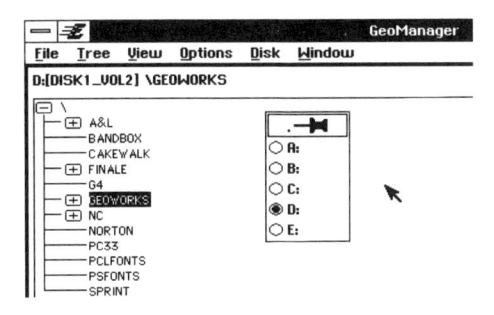

Figure 4-17 — The Drive Cascade Menu.

Expand All

Select this option when you want to Expand All directories shown in the directory tree, displaying the entire subdirectory structure, as shown in Figure 4-18.

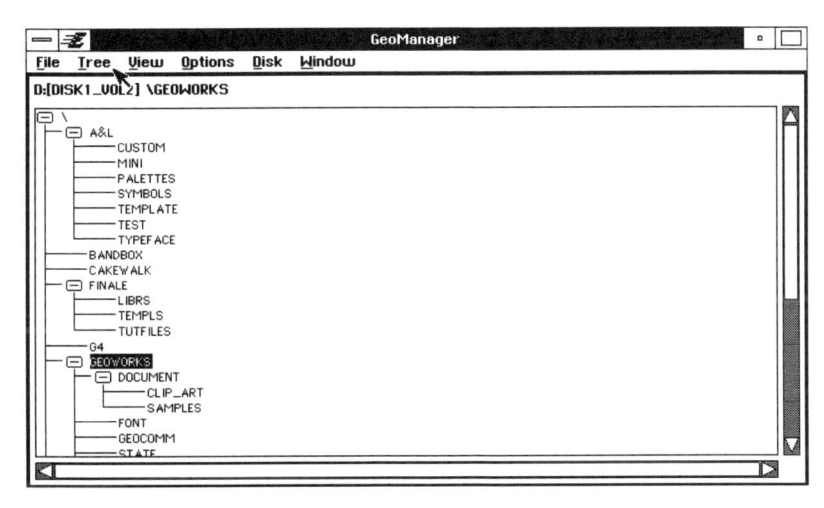

Figure 4-18 — A Directory Tree After Selecting Expand All.

71

Expand One Level

To expand only one level, click the plus sign next to the directory you want to expand. The next subdirectory level displays, if one exists.

You can also click on the name of the directory you want to expand (do not click on the plus or minus sign) to highlight the directory. Then choose Expand One Level from the Tree menu. The selected branch expands one subdirectory level.

Expand Branch

To expand all directories and subdirectories within a branch, click on the name of the directory you want to expand (do not click on the plus or minus sign). Then select Expand Branch from the Tree menu. The selected branch expands to display the complete structure of that directory.

Collapse Branch

To collapse all directories within a branch, click on the name of the directory you want to collapse (do not click on the plus or minus sign). Then select Collapse Branch from the Tree menu. The selected branch collapses. Compare Figure 4-18 and Figure 4-18 to see the difference between the expanded and collapsed displays.

Click on the minus sign beside a subdirectory to collapse that directory branch.

View Menu

The items in the GeoManager directory window are usually represented by small icons arranged alphabetically by name. Use the View menu to change the GeoManager display. Select the subdirectory you want to view, then select one of the View menu options shown in Figure 4-19.

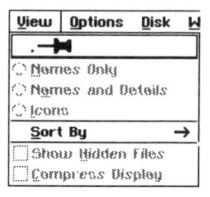

Figure 4-19 — The View Menu.

GeoManager 4

The following describes each of the View menu options.

Pin

Select the pin symbol to keep the menu open after you have made your selection from it. Once a menu is pinned, you can relocate it wherever you want.

Names Only

Select this option to display the contents of the window as a list of small icons with the name to the right of the icon. Use this view if you have a numerous files and you want to see as many of them as possible at one time.

Names and Details

Select this option to display the contents of the window as a list of small icons with the name, size, last modification date, and attributes to the right of each icon. The modification date for a directory is the date it was created.

Icons

Select this option to show the contents of the active directory as icons with the name below the icon.

Sort By

To change the way files are sorted in a subdirectory, first select the subdirectory, then select Sort By in the View menu. Select the sort option you want from the cascade menu. Directories are always displayed before files in any sorting method.

The Sort By cascade menu gives you three choices:

- **Name**   Sorts alphabetically by file name.
- **Date and Time** Sorts files by date and time of the last modification, displaying the most recently modified files first.
- **Size**   Sorts files by size, displaying the largest file first.

4 GeoManager

Show Hidden Files

Toggle this option to display or hide files that have Hidden or System attributes. If the Show Hidden Files menu item is not selected, Hidden or System files are not listed in the active directory display.

Compress Display

When you select this option, the directory display compresses, displaying as much as possible on the screen at one time. Figure 4-20 shows an uncompressed display. Figure 4-21 shows the same directory in compressed format.

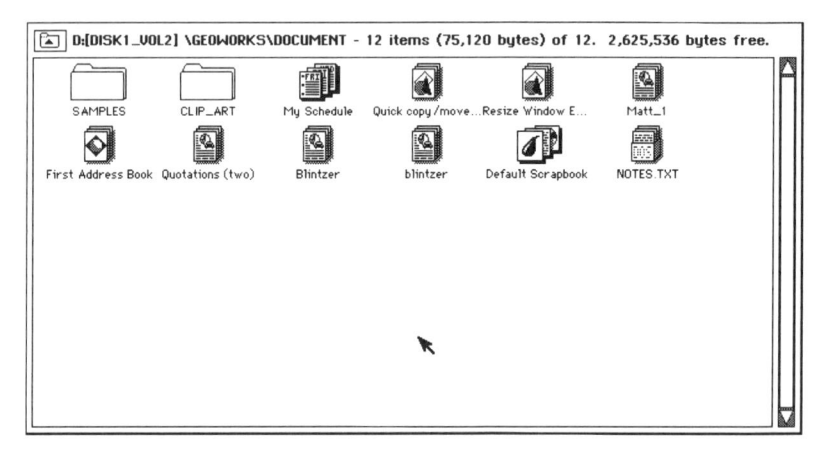

Figure 4-20 — An Uncompressed Directory Display.

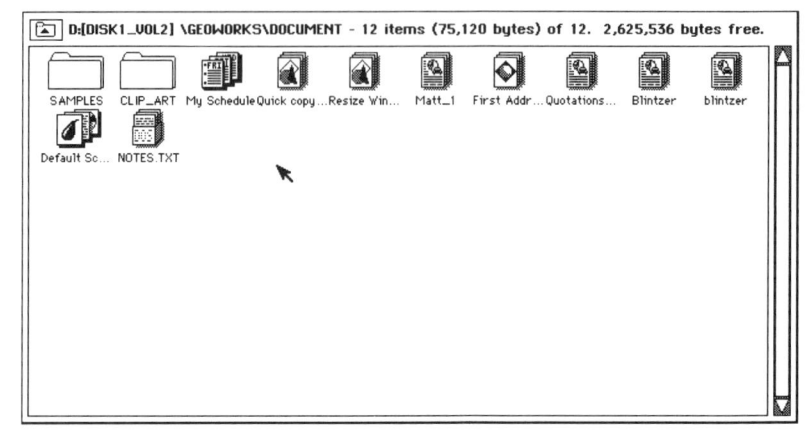

Figure 4-21 — A Compressed Directory Display.

GeoManager 4

Options Menu

Figure 4-22 displays the GeoManager Options menu.

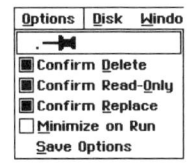

Figure 4-22 — The Options Menu.

Pin

Select the pin symbol to keep the menu open after you have made your selection from it. Once a menu is pinned, you can relocate it wherever you want.

The next three items in the Options menu determine whether a confirmation message will display when you delete or replace a file.

Confirm Delete

Select this option to always display a confirmation box when you delete a file. If the Confirm Read-only option is set, you will get a separate confirmation box when you are about to delete a read-only file.

Confirm Read-Only

Select this option when you always want to display a confirmation box when you are about to delete a read-only file, regardless of whether Confirm Delete is set or not.

Confirm Replace

Select this option to display a confirmation box when you copy or move a file to a directory that contains another file with the same file name. If Confirm Replace is toggled off, the file you are moving or copying will automatically — without confirmation — overwrite (replace) the existing file.

4 GeoManager

Minimize on Run

Select this option if you want GeoManager to shrink to an icon when you run another GEOS application. If Minimize on Run is off, GeoManager remains open when you switch to another application.

Save Options

Select this option to save the current selections in the Options menu. The new menu settings become the default settings and are used whenever you run GeoWorks Ensemble.

Disk Menu

Use the Disk menu to make a copy of a floppy disk, format a disk, rename a disk, or rescan a drive to update a directory display. Figure 4-23 displays the Disk menu. The menu is pinned so it will remain open after you select a menu item.

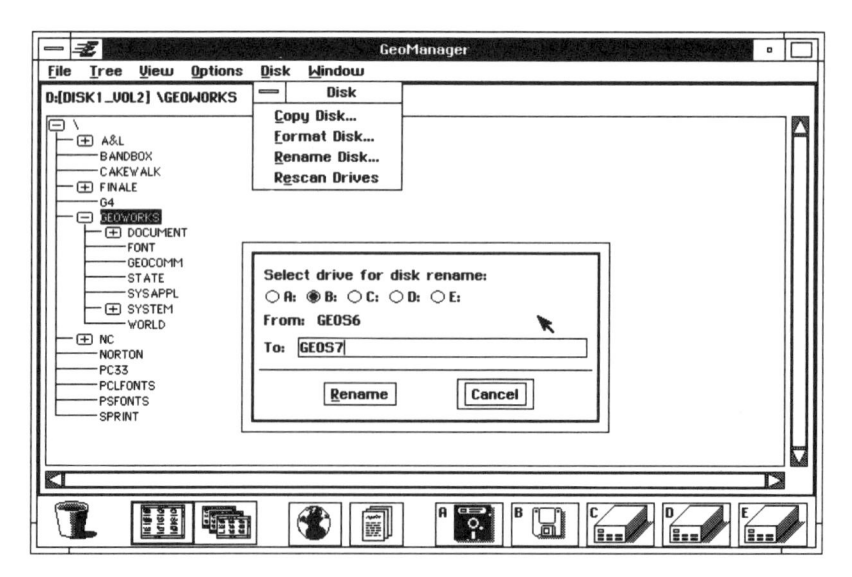

Figure 4-23 — The Disk Menu.

Pin

Select the pin symbol to keep the menu open after you have made your selection from it. Once a menu is pinned, you can relocate it wherever you want.

Copy Disk

This option is similar to using the DOS command DISKCOPY. It duplicates an entire floppy disk onto another floppy disk. The source (original) and target (destination) disks must be the same size; for example, 360K floppy disk to 360K floppy disk. You cannot use Copy Disk to copy files from a 360K floppy disk to a 1.2M floppy disk.

If you have two similar floppy drives, you can copy the disk in one drive to the disk in the other. If you do not have two like drives, you will be instructed to exchange disks as the copy is made.

It is a good idea to label the disks before you start a disk copy so you don't get them mixed up during the exchanges.

Select Copy Disk from the Disk menu to display a dialog box similar to Figure 4-24. In this Figure you can see that when Drive A: is selected as the source, drive B: is not an available target drive. In this case, drive A: is a 5 1/4" drive and drive B: is a 3 1/2" drive. You cannot use Copy Disk with dissimilar drives.

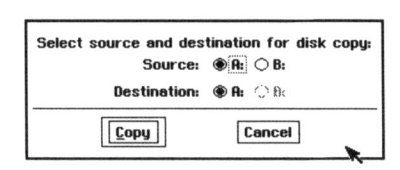

Figure 4-24 — The Copy Disk Dialog Box.

Select the source by clicking on the drive you want to use. Select the destination drive. Select Copy from the Copy Disk dialog box. Screen instructions tell you when and where to exchange disks (if necessary) and when the copy is complete.

4 GeoManager

Format Disk

Disks must be formatted before you can use them. Use the Format Disk command to format (or reformat) a disk.

Note: If you want to know if a disk is formatted, insert it in a drive and click the drive icon in the right corner of the GeoManager window. If the disk is formatted, the program displays a disk directory. If the disk is not formatted — or if the disk drive is empty or the drive door is open — the program displays the message, "Couldn't find a formatted disk in drive."

To format a floppy disk, place it in a disk drive, then select Format Disk from the Disk menu to display the Format Disk dialog box. Click on the drive that contains the disk you want to format. A selection box displays the format options for the selected drive. Figure 4-25 shows the Format Disk dialog box for a 1.2M floppy disk drive.

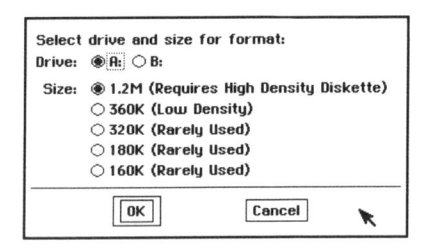

```
Select drive and size for format:
Drive: ●A:  ○B:
Size:  ● 1.2M (Requires High Density Diskette)
       ○ 360K (Low Density)
       ○ 320K (Rarely Used)
       ○ 180K (Rarely Used)
       ○ 160K (Rarely Used)
       [OK]        [Cancel]
```

Figure 4-25 — The Format Disk Dialog Box.

Click on the size (diskette capacity) selection you want. Note that options indicate when they require special high density diskettes, which store more data but are more costly.

It is best to select the highest capacity you can for the diskette and drive you are using. For example, it is possible, but not recommended, to format a 1.2M diskette (which holds 1,200,000 bytes of data) at the lower 360K density (so it holds only 360,000 bytes). It isn't a good idea to format a 1.2M disk as a 360K diskette, unless you have only a 360K disk drive and cannot read a 1.2M diskette.

After you select the size of a disk, another dialog box prompts you for an optional disk volume label (disk name). A volume label can be up to 11 characters long.

Type a volume label if you want one. Click Format. The program formats the disk according to your selections.

A summary screen tells you when formatting is complete and displays the total bytes of disk space, bytes in bad sectors, and bytes available on the disk.

Rename Disk

Use Rename Disk when you want to name an already-formatted disk or change an existing volume label. You can label floppy diskettes and your hard drives. Figure 4-23 shows the Rename Disk dialog box. The volume label in drive B: is GEOS6. A new volume label GEOS7 has been typed in the box. Clicking the Rename button in the dialog box changes the volume label in drive B: from GEOS6 to GEOS7. Clicking the Cancel button closes the dialog box without changing the label.

Rescan Drives

If you change a floppy disk in a drive, select Rescan Drives from the Disk menu to update the directory display. The program rereads all displayed drives (floppy and hard drives) and updates the GeoManager display.

Window Menu

Figure 4-26 shows the GeoManager Window menu.

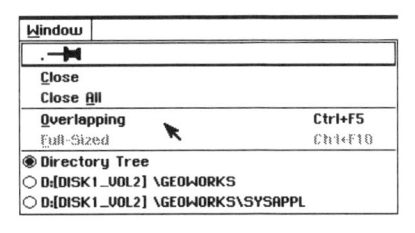

Figure 4-26 — The Window Menu.

The following describes the Window menu options.

4 GeoManager

Pin

Select the pin symbol to keep the menu open after you have made your selection from it. Once a menu is pinned, you can relocate it wherever you want.

Close

Select Close to close the active window.

Close All

Select Close All to close all currently open windows.

Overlapping (Ctrl+F5)

Select overlapping from the Window menu if you want to overlap open windows. You can also use the Overlapping icon at the bottom of the GeoManager window. Figure 4-27 shows three overlapping directory displays.

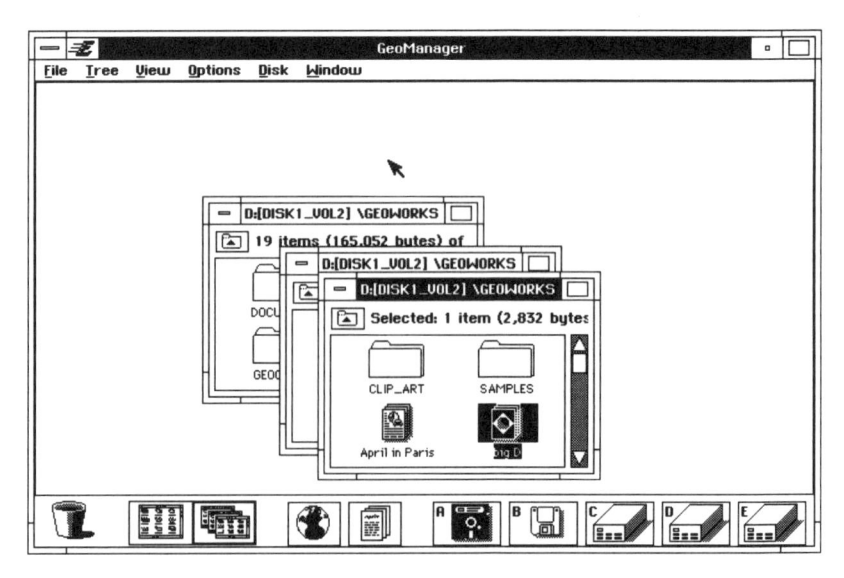

Figure 4-27 — Overlapping Directory Windows Display.

You can maximize the active window, drag the active window to a new location, or resize the active window in an overlapping display.

80

GeoManager 4

Full-Sized (Ctrl+F10)

Select this option to view the active window in an overlapping display as a full-sized window.

Listing and Selection

The bottom portion of the Window menu lists open directory windows. A filled-in circle indicates the active directory window. If you select another directory from this menu, it becomes the active window (and the filled-in circle is displayed next to it).

Information Bar

The third line of the GeoManager window, the Information bar (see Figure 4-1, U), displays the current directory and the path to the current directory. It tells you the total number of files in the subdirectory, how many of those files are visible (not hidden files), how much disk space the visible files use, and how much free space is available on the disk.

At the very left end of the Information Bar line is a small index-card-icon with an upward pointing arrow head. Click on this button to move up one directory level.

Main Display Window

The Main Display Window in the GeoManager window is the primary work and display area (see Figure 4-1, E). When you are viewing the contents of the WORLD directory, you see icons representing the Professional WorkSpace applications. These are representative of the function the application performs.

The selection icons at the bottom of the GeoManager window are divided into four groups (see Figure 4-1). The following is a description of each of these areas and the function of each of the icons.

81

4 GeoManager

Wastebasket

You use the Wastebasket to permanently delete files and directories (see Figure 4-1, G). To do this, place the mouse cursor over the file or directory you want to delete and press and hold the right mouse button. Drag the selected file or directory to the Wastebasket and release the right mouse button. The program asks you to confirm that you want to delete the item. (Once deleted, the item cannot be recovered.)

Full-Sized/Overlapping Buttons

Use these button to toggle between full-sized (see Figure 4-1, H) and overlapping window (see Figure 4-1, I) displays. You can switch between viewing one directory at a time, or simultaneously viewing multiple directories.

World Button

The two main subdirectories in GeoWorks Ensemble are WORLD (see Figure 4-1, J) and DOCUMENT. (The DOCUMENT subdirectory is discussed next.) The WORLD directory contains applications — programs you can run — displayed as icons.

Document Button

The DOCUMENT directory contains your data files (see Figure 4-1, K), the files you create and use while working in a GeoWorks Ensemble application. File icons represent both DOS and GEOS files. (See Chapter 2 for a discussion on the difference between GEOS and DOS files, their icons, and file naming conventions.)

A folder icon represents a subdirectory under the current directory. A subdirectory can contain files and other subdirectories. The folder name (subdirectory name) must adhere to the DOS file naming convention of 1-to-8 characters for the name and an optional 1-to-3 character extension.

Drive Buttons

In the lower right corner of the GeoManager window are the drive buttons (see Figure 4-1, L-P), one for each available drive on your computer (including a RAM disk, ROM disk, or other disk drive type). Click on a drive button to change the GeoManager display to that drive.

Summary

In Chapter 4 you learned how to use the GeoManager application. Each of the GeoManager menu options was explained in detail, including a discussion on subdirectory structure and floppy diskette capacity options.

Chapter 5

The Preferences Application

When you installed GeoWorks Ensemble, you selected monitor, mouse, and printer settings for your computer. You can change these and other settings at any time by using the Preferences application in the Professional Workspace. You can change:

- The look and feel of the program
- The computer's date and time settings
- The background image over which windows are displayed
- The settings for your monitor, mouse, printer, and modem
- Settings for the internal operations of GeoWorks Ensemble.

5 The Preferences Application

Accessing the Preferences Application

You can start the Preferences application two ways:

- Double-click on the Preferences icon in the GeoManager World window.
- Choose Startup from the Express Menu and select Preferences from the cascade menu.

Figure 5-1 shows the Preferences window after accessing it from the GeoManager World window.

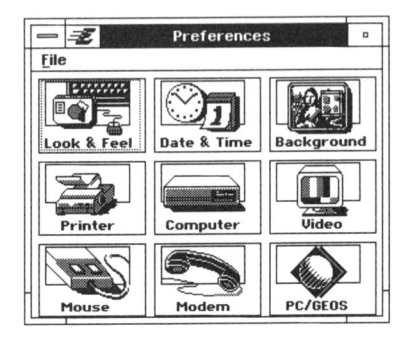

Figure 5-1 — The Preferences Window.

The Preferences window includes the standard application window features: Control button, Title Bar, Minimize button and Menu Bar. File is the only menu option on the Menu Bar. Use the nine Preferences icons to configure GeoWorks Ensemble on your computer to your needs and preferences.

Look and Feel

Use this option to:

- Set the size of text in menus and dialog boxes
- Specify how often an application should safeguard (backup) your open documents
- Turn on or off the computer beep
- Decide which part of the program you want enter automatically when you start GeoWorks Ensemble.

Selecting Look & Feel displays the dialog box shown in Figure 5-2. Filled in circles indicate the active options.

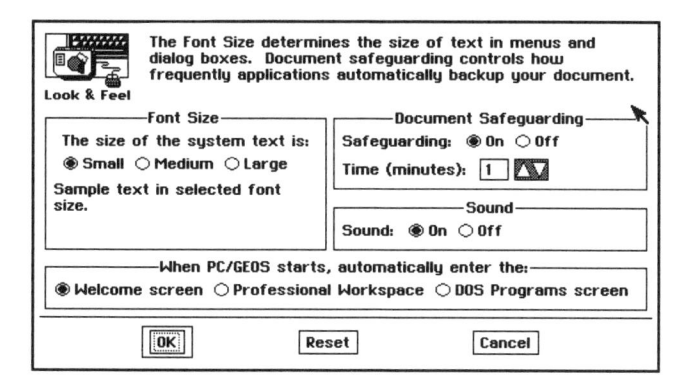

Figure 5-2 — The Look and Feel Dialog Box.

Font Size

You can select one of three options for a display font size: small, medium, or large. When you click on an option, the sample text in the Font Size box changes to demonstrate the active setting. (This setting does not affect your printed documents.)

Document Safeguarding

As you modify a document, your changes are stored in the computer's temporary memory until you save the document. If you turn off your computer before saving your modified document, the changes will be lost. With Safeguarding On, changes stored in temporary memory are periodically and automatically stored to disk, although not as part of your document. When you save a document, safeguarded changes and changes in temporary memory become a permanent part of the document.

Click on the Up and Down triangles to specify the time interval (in minutes from 1 to 18) between saves.

5 The Preferences Application

Note: Under certain circumstances, you can undo changes to a previously-saved document. Select the Revert option in the GeoManager File menu to restore to the screen the last-saved version of your document. All changes in temporary memory and safeguarded changes are erased.

Sound

GeoWorks Ensemble often sounds a beep to alert you to some action or circumstance. Click on your selection to turn on or off the beep.

Opening Screen

In the bottom panel of the Look and Feel dialog box you can select which part of GeoWorks Ensemble you want to enter automatically when you start the program: the Welcome screen, Professional Workspace, of the DOS Programs screen. Click on your selection.

OK, Reset, and Cancel

Click the OK button when you are satisfied with your Preferences selections. The document safeguarding and beep setting changes take affect immediately. The Font Size and Opening Screen settings will not be effective until you exit and re-enter GeoWorks Ensemble.

Click the Reset button to return any settings you may have changed back to the way they were when you opened the dialog box.

Click the Cancel button to close the dialog box and return to the Preferences window without saving any changes.

Date & Time

Use this handy feature to set the current date and time in your computer's internal clock. Selecting Date & Time displays the dialog box shown in Figure 5-3.

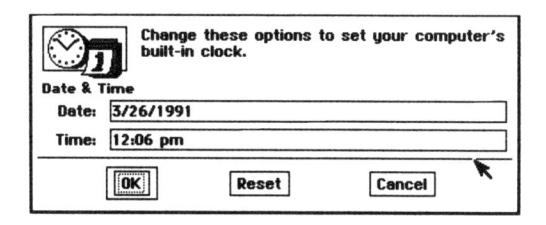

Figure 5-3 — The Date & Time Dialog Box.

Date

Position the mouse cursor in the Date box, then click to activate the text cursor. You can type the date in two ways: 3/26/91 or 3/26/1991.

Time

Position the mouse cursor in the Time box, then click to activate the text cursor. Enter the time using the 12 hour format. Be sure to include am or pm after the time (separated by a space). For example: 12:06 pm or 9:47 am.

OK, Reset, and Cancel

Click the OK button to update the clock.

Click the Reset button to revert to the date and time settings active when you opened the dialog box.

Click the Cancel button to return to the Preferences window without making any changes.

5 The Preferences Application

Background

The background is the area behind all windows in your workspace. This fun item lets you change the background from a solid gray to a pattern or to a picture (graphic). Select Background to display the dialog box shown in Figure 5-4.

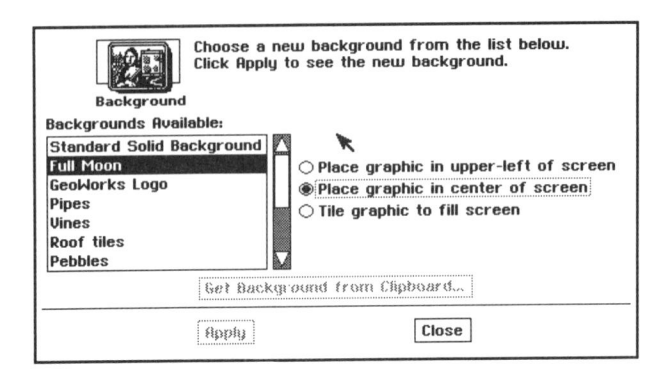

Figure 5-4 — The Background Dialog Box.

Selecting a Background

GeoWorks Ensemble comes with 12 background options, listed in the left panel. You can create your own background and add it to the list (discussed later in this chapter). Use the scroll bar to view the list, then click on your selection.

Display options

Click on one of the three ways to display the background:

- Upper-left of the screen
- Center of the screen
- Tiled (repeated) across the screen to fill it.

Click Apply to view the selected background. (You may have to reduce application windows to icons to adequately view the screen.)

The Preferences Application 5

Inserting New Backgrounds

You can use the Clipboard to save graphics (or text) as a background option. Copy the graphic to the Clipboard. Note that the Get Background From Clipboard button becomes available. Click on it to display a dialog box prompting you for a file name for the Clipboard contents. Type the file name, then click OK to save the file and add it to the list of backgrounds. Select the new entry, then click Apply to see it as a background.

When you are satisfied with the choice of background click Close to return to the Preferences window. The new background is in effect. Figure 5-5 shows the Preferences application displayed over the Full Moon background.

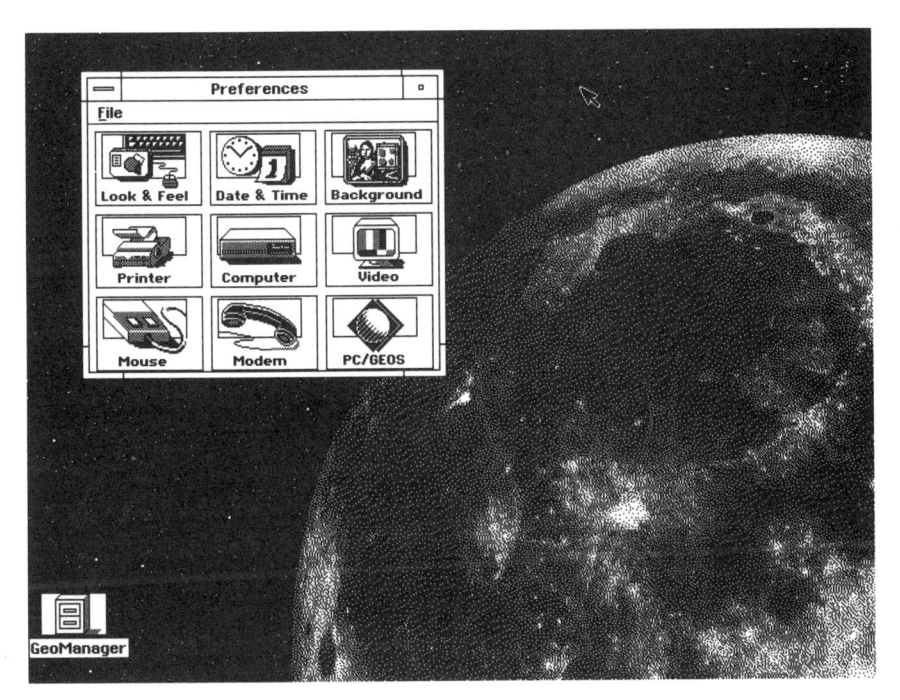

Figure 5-5 — Full Moon Background.

5 The Preferences Application

Printer

Before you can print any documents, you must configure GeoWorks Ensemble so that it works with your printer(s). Selecting this option displays the dialog box shown in Figure 5-6, which lists any printers you selected during the automatic installation program.

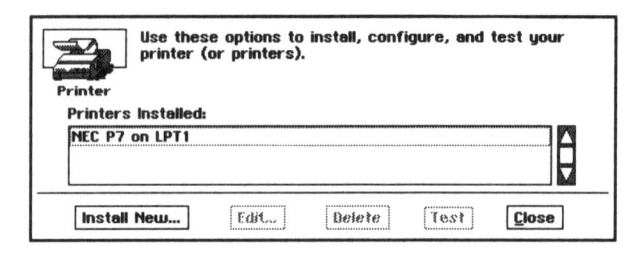

Figure 5-6 — The Printer Dialog Box.

Use the vertical scroll bar to view the list, if necessary. Across the bottom of the dialog box are five buttons: Install New, Edit, Delete, Test, and Close. The options Edit, Delete and Test are not available until you select an installed printer from the list of available printers.

Install New

Selecting this option to install a new printer displays another dialog box listing all printers supported by GeoWorks Ensemble. Scroll through the list to highlight your printer name, then click on it. The printer name displays in the Printer Name box. You can change the printer name to any text you want to identify that printer.

Select the appropriate port from the Port box on the right. Each port on the list corresponds to a possible connection at the back of the computer (not all computers have a connection for every port on the list). Usually, parallel printers plug into LPT1, while most serial printers plug into COM1.

Parallel port

When you select a parallel port, no additional configuration is required.

Serial port

When you select a serial port, the Serial Port Options button becomes activated. Clicking on it displays the Serial Port Options dialog box with the six settings for a serial port. Check your printer manual to determine the correct settings.

See the Protocol section in Chapter 16 for a more through discussion about these settings:

Baud rate indicates the speed at which data will transmit between your computer and the printer, for example: 1200, 2400, 4800, etc.

Word Length signifies the amount of data the computer can process at one time (word). Most personal computers process eight bits (a byte) at one time.

Stop Bits are inserted during the transmission to mark the end of each word. Specify the number of stop bits your printer uses.

Parity specifies the type of error detection used to check the accuracy of data transmission to the printer.

When you are satisfied with the printer settings, click the OK button to add the new printer to the Printers Installed list.

Edit

Click the Edit button to change the settings for an installed printer. Click the OK button to accept the new settings.

Click the Reset button to return the settings to what they were when you opened the dialog box.

Click the Cancel button to return to the Printer dialog box with no changes made.

Delete

Click the Delete button to delete the highlighted printer from the list of installed printers.

5 The Preferences Application

Test

You can test a printer after you install it by selecting Test. The printer should immediately begin printing a test page. If nothing happens, or if you get nonsense as a print out, you can try changing the printer's configuration by selecting Edit.

Close

Click the Close button to return to the Preferences window, saving your printer settings.

Computer

Use this option to take advantage of any computer memory beyond 640K. Selecting Computer displays the Computer dialog box shown in Figure 5-7.

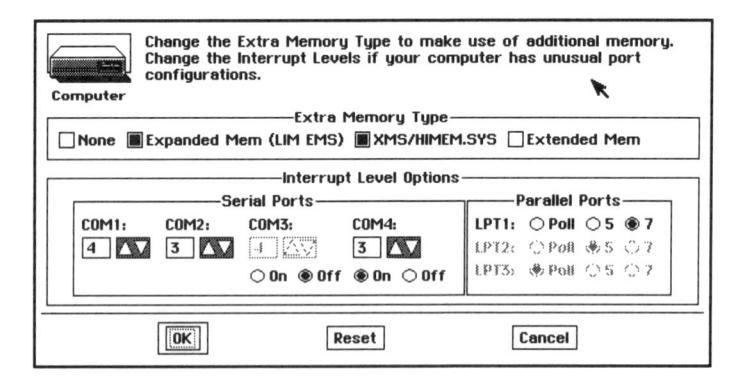

Figure 5-7 — The Computer Dialog Box.

Select the type(s) of memory you have: None, Expanded Memory (LIM EMS), Managed Extended Memory, and Extended Memory.

None

Select this option if your computer does not have extended or expanded memory.

Expanded Memory

This is additional memory accessed through a window in the 640K memory area. If you have an original PC or XT with more than 640K, you have expanded memory. It is also possible to install expanded memory boards for other computers. Expanded memory is defined by the Lotus/Intel/Microsoft Expanded Memory Specification (LIM EMS).

Extended Memory

If you have an IBM 286 or 386 (or compatible) with more than 640K, you probably have extended memory. You may also have expanded memory.

Managed Extended Memory

If you have an extended memory driver such as HIMEM.SYS, you have managed extended memory.

Interrupt Level options

Change the Interrupt Level settings only if your computer has unusual port configurations. You can click the up or down triangles to enter interrupt numbers for up to four Serial Ports. You can choose from three settings for each of three Parallel Ports.

Caution: You should not change the interrupt levels unless you are very familiar with the inner workings of the computer. See the Protocol section in Chapter 16 for a discussion about setting interupt levels.

5 The Preferences Application

Video

Select the Video option if you change your monitor after installing GeoWorks Ensemble or if you want to enable the screen blanking feature. Selecting Video from the Preferences window displays the dialog box shown in Figure 5-8.

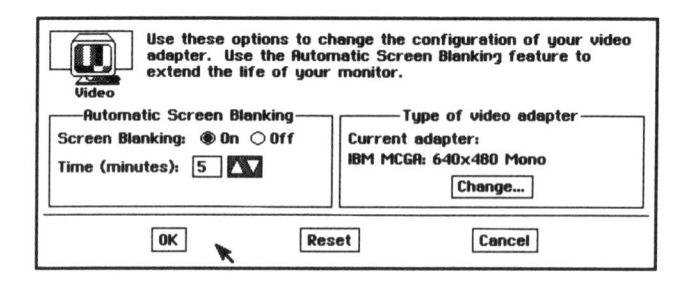

Figure 5-8 — The Video Dialog Box.

Type of Video Adapter

Click the Change button to display a list of video monitors supported by GeoWorks Ensemble. Scroll the list to find the correct monitor, then click on it to select it.

Automatic Screen Blanking

Automatic screen blanking may prevent damage to your monitor. If the same image is left on the screen for a long time, the image may become "burned in" so that a ghost outline of the image is always visible, even when the screen is turned off. With automatic screen blanking active, the picture is automatically turned off after a specified period of inactivity.

After you select On, you can specify the length of time before the screen blanks — from 2 minutes to 30 minutes.

Note: This option does not work with all computers.

The Preferences Application 5

Mouse

Use the Mouse option when you change your mouse type after installation, or you want to modify the mouse sensitivity (how quickly it reacts to your motion and clicks). Selecting Mouse displays the dialog box shown in Figure 5-9.

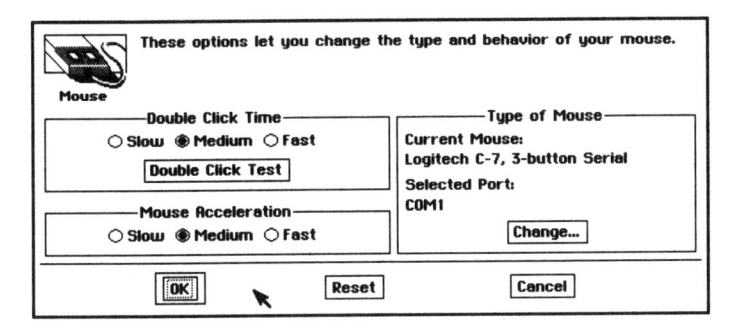

Figure 5-9 — The Mouse Dialog Box.

Double Click Time

You can specify Slow, Medium, or Fast as the double click time. The new speed takes effect immediately. You can test the setting by double-clicking on the Double Click Test button. When you double-click quickly enough for the current setting, the box flashes and beeps.

Mouse Acceleration

Use this option to set how fast the pointer moves across the screen as you move the mouse — Slow, Medium, or Fast.

Type of Mouse

Click the Change button to specify a different mouse type or port than the ones specified during installation. Scroll the list of mouse types supported by GeoWorks Ensemble to select your mouse type. If it is a serial mouse, click the appropriate Serial Port button. An Interrupt setting option may become available, depending on the mouse you select.

5 The Preferences Application

Click the OK button to accept your mouse settings. GeoWorks Ensemble displays a box asking if you want to restart the program in order to activate the new mouse. Click the Yes button to restart GeoWorks Ensemble. You can then test your mouse choice.

Click the Reset button to return the mouse settings to those in effect when you opened the dialog box.

Click the Cancel button to return to the Preferences window with no changes made.

Modem

Use this option to set your modem parameters: the serial port, transmission speed, and format of the transmission. Selecting the Modem option displays the dialog box shown in Figure 5-10.

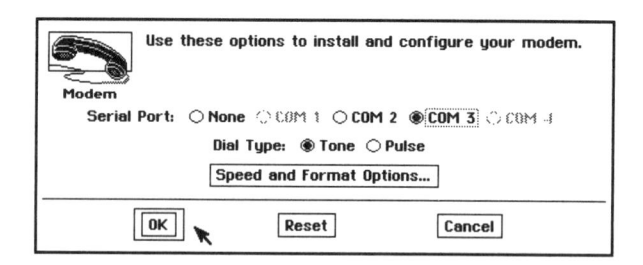

Figure 5-10 — The Modem Dialog Box.

Click on the serial port to which your modem is connected, usually COM1. If you have a serial mouse connected to COM1, you can probably use COM2. Make sure you do not select the same port for your serial mouse and the modem. (See Chapter 16 for additional information.)

Check your modem manual to determine the dial type: tone or pulse.

Click the Speed and Format Options button to display the Modem Options dialog box. Change the options in the dialog box to match the capabilities of your modem. Click the OK button to accept your selections and return to the Modem dialog box.

PC/GEOS

Selecting this option displays the PC/GEOS dialog box shown in Figure 5-11.

Figure 5-11 — The PC/GEOS Dialog Box.

Caution: You should not change any settings in this area unless instructed to do so by an authorized GeoWorks Customer Support Technician. The PC/GEOS settings control internal options; incorrect settings can adversely affect GEOS performance, even prevent GeoWorks Ensemble from working at all. (In this case, you may have to reinstall the program.)

Summary

In Chapter 5 you learned how to use the GeoManager Preferences Application. Each of the Preferences menu options was explained in detail.

Chapter 6

The GeoWrite Application

The GeoWrite application is the GeoWorks Ensemble word processor. In this chapter — which is designed to be first an introduction and then a reference — you will learn about the main elements of the GeoWrite main screen:

- The Ruler bar
- The Selection line
- Justification settings
- Line spacing settings
- Scroll bars
- Main text window
- Typing modes
- Selecting and editing text with the mouse
- Keyboard editing and typing cursor movement.

Chapter 7 discusses the GeoWrite menus. Chapter 8 provides a GeoWrite tutorial in which you can practice using most of the features discussed in Chapters 6 and 7.

6 The GeoWrite Application

Starting GeoWrite

Double click on the GeoWrite application icon in the GeoManager window to display the GeoWrite main screen shown in Figure 6-1.

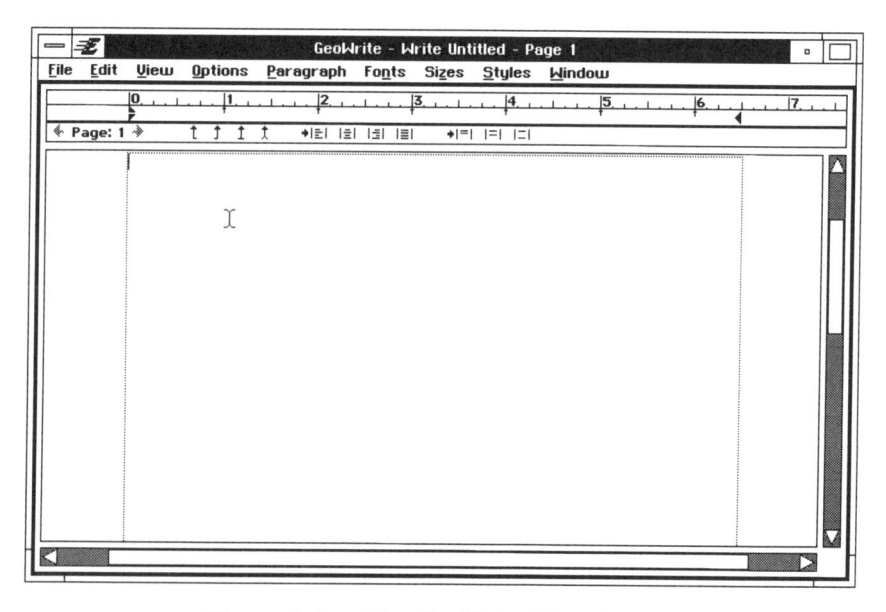

Figure 6-1 — The GeoWrite Main Screen.

GeoWorks starts with a blank, untitled document. Figure 6-2 identifies the important elements of the GeoWrite main screen.

The GeoWrite Application 6

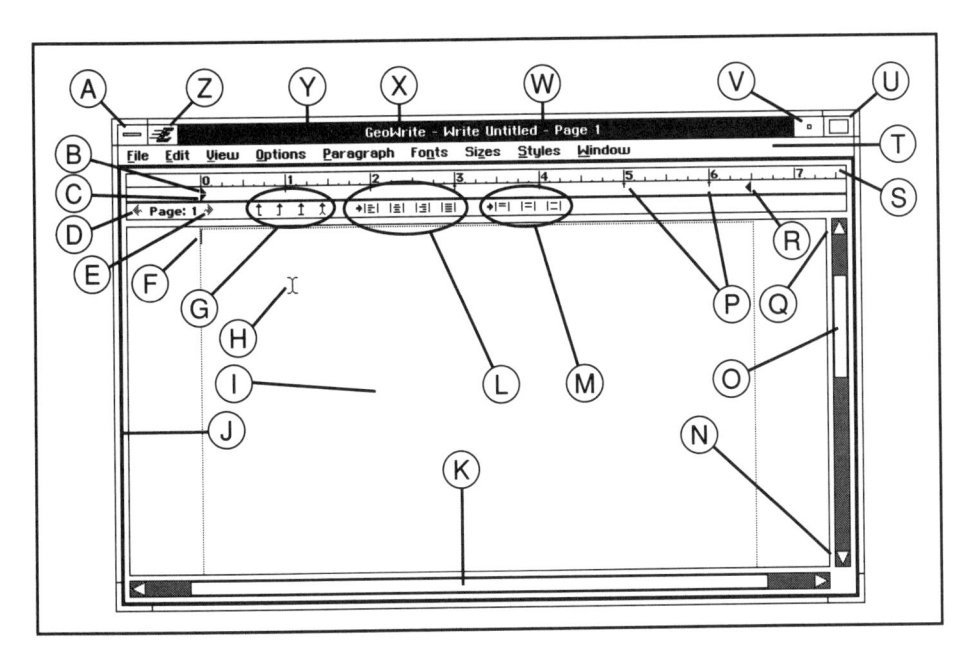

Figure 6-2 — GeoWrite Main Screen Elements Identified.

A. Control menu button.

B. Left indent.

C. Left margin.

D. Previous page.

E. Next page.

F. Text cursor.

G. Tabs.

H. Mouse cursor.

I. Main Text window.

J. Resize border.

K. Horizontal scroll bar.

L. Justification.

M. Line spacing.

N. Scroll arrow.

O. Scroll slider.

103

6 The GeoWrite Application

P. Small tab arrows.

Q. Scroll arrow.

R. Right margin.

S. Ruler.

T. Menu bar.

U. Maximize/Restore button.

V. Minimizer button.

W. Document Name/Page

X. Application name.

Y. Title bar.

Z. Express menu button.

Application Window Elements

At the top of the GeoWrite main screen are five elements common to all application windows: Control menu button, Express menu button, Title Bar, Minimize button, and Maximize/Restore button. These items, along with the horizontal and vertical scroll bars, are discussed in detail in Chapter 3.

The Menu Bar

The second line of the GeoWrite main screen is the menu bar (see Figure 6-2, T) with nine menu options, which are discussed in detail in Chapter 7.

Ruler Bar

The ruler bar consists of two lines (see Figure 6-2, S). The top line is an actual ruler showing the horizontal page measurements. Use the ruler as a guide when changing margins, indenting paragraphs and setting tabs. Below the ruler is a line showing the current margins, indents, and tabs.

Left margin and indent ▸

The left margin marker ʕ and indent marker ▸ are displayed initially as a split arrow head (see Figure 6-2, B and C). Changing these markers affects only the paragraph in which the text cursor is currently located, or any highlighted paragraphs. To set the left margin and indent for the entire document, choose Page Setup from the File menu. (See Chapter 7.)

You can move the indent marker or the left margin marker by placing the mouse cursor on it, then pressing and holding the left mouse button while dragging the marker to the desired location along the rule.

You can move the left margin and indent markers together by pressing ⇧Shift while dragging the markers (as a unit) to the new location.

Right margin ◂

The right margin marker looks like an arrow head pointing left (see Figure 6-2, R). Changing the right margin marker affects only the paragraph in which the text cursor is currently located, or any highlighted paragraphs. To set the right margin for the entire document, choose Page Setup from the File menu. (See Chapter 7.)

To relocate the right margin, drag the marker to the desired location.

Tabs

The tab types (see Figure 6-2, G) and locations are also displayed on the lower portion of the ruler bar. Placing and removing tabs is described below in the Tab section of the Selection Line discussion.

Ruler settings

When you highlight a range of text, the ruler turns gray and shows only those setting that are common to all highlighted paragraphs.

6   The GeoWrite Application

Selection Line

Use the line immediately below the ruler bar to select the displayed page, tabs, justification, and line spacing settings.

Paging arrows

Click on the small arrow before the Page number to display the previous page. Click on the small arrow after the Page number to select the next page.

Tabs

When you open GeoWrite there are small Tab arrows below each of the unit markers on the ruler line (1", 2", 3", etc. see Figure 6-2, P). When you press [tab] the text cursor moves to the nearest tab to the right of its current position. A line tab setting remains in effect for all subsequent lines until you set a new line tab. You could set different tabs for every line of the document.

You can position the text cursor in any line of the document and change the tab setting for that line. The new tab setting will affect only that line. Text which wraps (automatically flows) to the next line falls back to the left margin. A carriage return at the end of a line forces the text cursor to the next line, starting a new line or paragraph at the left margin.

The tabs shown in the lower portion of the ruler bar (see Figure 6-2, G) are relevant to the line in which the text cursor is currently located (or the currently highlighted text).

You can select four tab types. The tab symbols are each represented by an up-pointing arrow, but with a different arrow base. Select a tab type by placing the mouse cursor over it, then pressing and holding the left mouse button. The mouse cursor changes to the selected tab type and jumps to the line below the ruler markings. Drag the tab to the desired location and release the mouse button. The program removes the original small tab arrows at the ruler unit markers.

Left-justified tab ⭡

From the tab, the text you type moves to the right with every character, as if the tab were a left margin. If you press [tab] within a line, all of the text to the right of the cursor position shifts right to start at the next tab location. If the following text needs to wrap and flow to accommodate the relocated text, the document adjusts the text as necessary.

Right-justified tab ⭡

As you type, the text cursor remains at the tab location, but the characters you type move to the left of the tab.

Center-justified tab ⭡

As you type, the text cursor moves to the right with every other character. Alternate characters move the left. The result is centered text at the tab location.

Decimal align tab ⭡

Use this tab on each line of a column of numbers to align the numbers on the decimal point. As you type, the tab operates like a right-justified tab until you type a period (decimal point). Then the tab operates like a left-justified tab.

Selecting a tab type

To select a tab type, place the mouse cursor on the tab type symbol (on the selection line). Then press and hold the left mouse button while dragging the tab to the desired location on the lower portion of the ruler bar.

Copy a tab

You can copy an existing tab on the lower line of the ruler bar by pressing and holding [Ctrl] while dragging the tab to a new location.

Remove a tab

To remove a tab (delete it) from the lower line of the ruler bar, place the mouse cursor over it, then press and hold the left mouse button while dragging the tab off the ruler bar in any direction. Release the mouse button.

6 The GeoWrite Application

Justification Settings

Four symbols — Left, Center, Right, or Full justification — represent text between the left and right page borders. The active symbol for currently-highlighted text, or the text in which the text cursor is located, is identified by a small arrow next to it (see Figure 6-2, L).

Align left |≡|

Use this option to align text along the left margin with a ragged right margin, as indicated in the symbol.

Center align |≡|

Use this option to center text lines, regardless of line length, between the left and right margins.

Align right |≡|

Use this option to align text along the right margin with a ragged left margin.

Fully justified |≡|

Use this option to justify text along both the left and right margins.

Line Spacing Settings

Select a line spacing option to set single spacing |=|, line-and-a-half spacing |=|, or double line spacing |=| (see Figure 6-2, M).

Main Text Window

The Main Text Window (see Figure 6-2, I) displays one page or portion of one page at a time. (You cannot display the bottom of one page and the top of another page at the same time in one window.) This is the area where you create your document.

Headers and Footers

You can create a unique header and/or footer for each page of your document. Or, you can create one header or footer for odd pages and one for even pages. Headers are located at the top of the page, footers at the bottom. The header and footer text can be centered, flush against the left margin, or flush against the right margin. A typical header or footer includes chapter titles, page numbers and names you want repeated on every page. See Chapter 7 for a discussion on creating headers and footers and incorporating graphics in them.

A header or footer, including text and graphics, appears on every page that follows (including the current page) until you set a new header or footer.

Note that when you open a window the slider is not at the top of the scroll bar. Rather, it is positioned so that the panel displays the top of the text area. To see the header area, drag the vertical slider to the top of the scroll bar. You will see the header area boxed off separately, above the main text window. When you want to see the footer area, drag the vertical slider to the bottom of the scroll bar. You will see the footer area boxed off separately, below the main text window.

Typing Mode

There are two typing modes: insertion and overwrite. Press [Ins] to toggle between them. In insertion mode, the text cursor indicates where the next typed character will be inserted. In overwrite mode, the text cursor highlights a character, indicating which character will be overwritten.

Insertion mode

In insertion mode, characters are inserted at the text cursor position, pushing to the right any existing text. The insertion cursor moves one space to the right with each character you type.

Overwrite mode

In overwrite mode, a typed character overwrites an existing character at the text cursor position. The overwrite cursor moves one space to the right with each character you type.

6 The GeoWrite Application

Selecting and Editing Text with the Mouse

To change format settings for a block of text, you must first select the block.

Selecting by dragging

You can use the mouse to select (highlight) a block of text. Position the mouse cursor at the beginning of the text you want to select. Press and hold the left mouse button while dragging the cursor to the end of the text you want to block. Release the mouse button. The program displays the selected text in reverse video — white text on a black background.

Selecting by specifying

Another method of selecting text is to place the text cursor to the left of the first character you want selected. Position the mouse cursor at the end of the block you want to select. Press and hold [Shift] while you click the left mouse button to select the block.

To adjust the selected area, redefining the block of text, press and hold [Shift] while you move the mouse cursor to a new end position for the block. You can redefine a block larger or smaller. Click the left mouse button. The new block is selected.

Selecting words

Double-click the left mouse button to select the word under the mouse cursor. To select a range of words, double click but don't release the left mouse button on the second click. Drag the mouse cursor to highlight the desired words.

You can also use the Selecting by Specifying technique. Place the text cursor at the beginning of the text you want to select. Then move the mouse cursor to the end of the block. Press and hold [Shift] while you click the left mouse button. The specified text is selected.

Selecting lines

To select a line, triple-click the left mouse button with the cursor anywhere over the line you want to select.

You can also use the Selecting by Specifying technique. With the text cursor in the line and the mouse cursor at the end of the line you want to select, press and hold [Shift] while you click the left mouse button.

Selecting larger units

Each time you add a click to a multiple-click sequence, a larger unit of text is specified. For example, double-click specifies words, triple-click selects lines, quadruple-click (four clicks) specifies paragraphs, and six clicks specifies pages.

You can extend a selection by clicking but not releasing the mouse button on the last click, then dragging the highlight to include additional text. For example, you could triple-click to select a line but not release the mouse button on the third click. Then drag the highlight to include several more lines or a paragraph or a page.

You can also use the Selecting by Specifying technique to select larger units of text.

Adjusting range selected

If you want to adjust a still-highlighted block, press and hold [Shift] while you move the mouse cursor to a new location. Click the left mouse button to lock the selected area to the newly specified range.

Deleting selected text

After highlighting an area, press [delete] or [←BkSp] to delete the selected area.

To replace a range of text

After highlighting an area, type the new text you want to appear in the highlighted area. The program deletes the original block of text and inserts the new text in the same location.

6 The GeoWrite Application

Keyboard Editing and Typing Cursor Movement

Proficient typists often prefer to do editing from the keyboard instead of using a mouse. The following list describes keyboard editing commands.

Text cursor movement

One character/line in any direction	Arrow keys
One word backward	`Ctrl`-`←`
One word forward	`Ctrl`-`→`
One paragraph backward	`Ctrl`-`↑`
One paragraph forward	`Ctrl`-`↓`
To beginning of line	`home`
To end of line	`end`
To beginning of text (page)	`Ctrl`-`home`
To end of text (page)	`Ctrl`-`end`

Selecting text

Select left	`Shift`-`←`
Select right	`Shift`-`→`
Select up	`Shift`-`↑`
Select down	`Shift`-`↓`
Select to beginning of word	`Shift`-`Ctrl`-`←`
Select to end of word	`Shift`-`Ctrl`-`→`
Select whole word	`Ctrl`-`space`
Select to beginning of line	`Shift`-`home`
Select to end of line	`Shift`-`end`
Select whole line	`Ctrl`-`home`, followed by `Shift`-`Ctrl`-`end`
Select to beginning of paragraph	`Shift`-`Ctrl`-`↑`
Select to end of paragraph	`Shift`-`Ctrl`-`↓`

Select whole paragraph   [Ctrl]-[↑], followed by [Shift]-[Ctrl]-[↓]
Select to beginning of column/page   [Shift]-[Ctrl]-[home]
Select to end of column/page   [Shift]-[Ctrl]-[end]
Select whole column/page   [Ctrl]-[home], followed by [Shift]-[Ctrl]-[end]

Adjust text selected

Adjust up   [Shift]-[↑]
Adjust down   [Shift]-[↓]
Adjust left   [Shift]-[←]
Adjust right   [Shift]-[→]
Adjust to previous word   [Shift]-[Ctrl]-[←]
Adjust to next word   [Shift]-[Ctrl]-[→]
Adjust to beginning of line   [Shift]-[home]
Adjust to end of line   [Shift]-[end]
Adjust to beginning of paragraph [Shift]-[Ctrl]-[↑]
Adjust to end of paragraph   [Shift]-[Ctrl]-[↓]
Adjust to beginning of column/page [Shift]-[Ctrl]-[home]
Adjust to end of column/page   [Shift]-[Ctrl]-[end]

Deleting text

Delete character to right   [delete]
Delete character to left   [←BkSp]
Delete to end of word   [Ctrl]-[←BkSp]
Delete to beginning of word   [Ctrl]-[delete]
Delete to end of line   [Shift]-[Ctrl]-[delete]
Delete to beginning of line   [Shift]-[Ctrl]-[←BkSp]
Delete selection   [delete] or [←BkSp]

6 The GeoWrite Application

Summary

In Chapter 6 you learned about the elements of the GeoWrite application screen, the basics of formatting text, and how to move the text cursor and select text using keyboard commands.

Chapter 7

GeoWrite Menus

This chapter — which is designed to be first an introduction and then a reference — teaches you how to use the options in the nine GeoWrite menus:

- File
- Edit
- View
- Options
- Paragraph
- Fonts
- Sizes
- Styles
- Window.

Chapter 8 provides a GeoWrite tutorial in which you can practice using most of the features discussed in Chapters 6 and 7. See Chapter 3 for a discussion on the different ways to select menus and menu items in an application window.

7 GeoWrite Menus

To run the GeoWrite application, start GeoWorks Ensemble in the usual way, then select the GeoWrite icon from the Professional Workspace. The program displays the GeoWrite main screen, as shown previously in Figure 6-1. Figure 6-2 identifies the important elements of the GeoWorks main screen.

File Menu

The File menu is the first option on the GeoWrite menu bar, as shown in Figure 7-1.

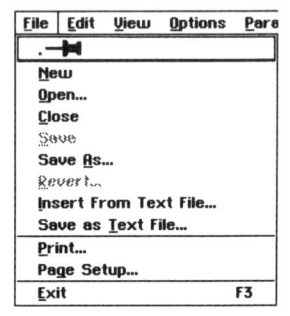

Figure 7-1 — The GeoWrite File Menu.

The Pin Symbol

The first option in each of the GeoWrite menus is the pin symbol. Select this menu option to keep the menu open after you have made your selection from it. Once a menu is pinned, you can relocate it wherever you want by dragging the pinned menu Title bar to a new location. You can then make repeated selections from a pinned menu without reopening it each time.

Figure 7-2 shows a pinned File menu that has been moved to the lower left corner of the window.

GeoWrite Menus 7

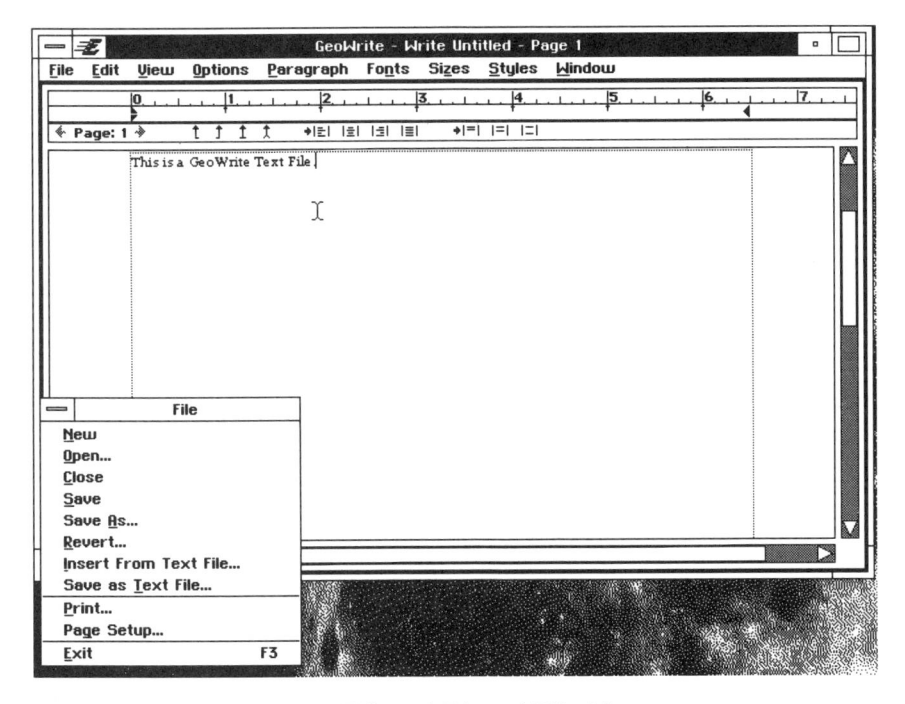

Figure 7-2 — A Pinned File Menu.

Compare the File menu in Figure 7-1 with the pinned File menu in Figure 7-2.

To close (unpin) a pinned menu, double-click on the Control button in the upper left corner of the menu. Or, single click on the Control button, then select Close. (You can also place the mouse cursor on the Control button, then press and hold the left mouse button while dragging to highlight Close. Release the mouse button.)

New

Use this option to create a new, untitled document. When you enter GeoWrite from the GeoManager window, the title of the open document (on the Title Bar) is "Untitled." The document title remains the same until you Save the document and specify a different file name.

117

7 GeoWrite Menus

Suppose you have an open document named "Untitled." You select New to create a second document. The program displays a new blank page (the second document is now active) and the new document Title Bar displays the text: Write Untitled 1 - Page 1. You are now ready to start typing in the second document. You have two documents open (Untitled, and Untitled 1).

If you were to continue opening new documents, each new document would be given a unique name by adding 1 to the assigned number (e.g., Untitled 2, Untitled 3). When you save an Untitled document and give it a new name, the Untitled file name and number become available for assignment to other new documents.

Open

Use the Open command to open (locate and display) a previously-saved file. When you select Open, the Select Document to Open dialog box similar to Figure 7-3 is displayed listing the documents you can open from the default subdirectory.

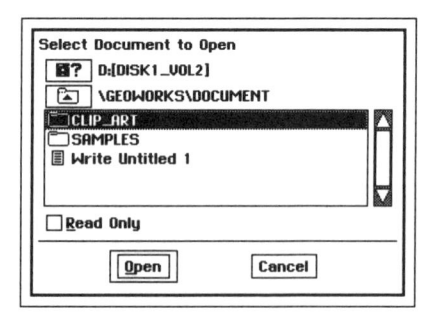

Figure 7-3 — Select Document to Open Dialog Box.

In Figure 7-3 the current directory is DOCUMENT, a subdirectory of GEOWORKS. The DOCUMENT subdirectory contains two other subdirectories (CLIP_ART and SAMPLES) and one file (Write Untitled 1), the only file available to open in this subdirectory. You can move around subdirectories to select a file in a different location.

Note: Double-click on a file name to select it and open it in one operation.

GeoWrite Menus 7

Close

Use the Close command to close the active document. If you have made changes to the document, the program asks whether you want to save the modifications. If you do not elect to save the changes, they will be lost when you close the document.

Save

The Save command saves the active document, storing it to disk to preserve your work. A saved document means you can return to the last-saved version if you subsequently make changes and then decide you don't want to incorporate those changes in the document. To restore the previously saved version, select the Revert option.

The first time you select Save for an active document, the program displays the Select Directory and Enter New Filename dialog box, similar to Figure 7-4.

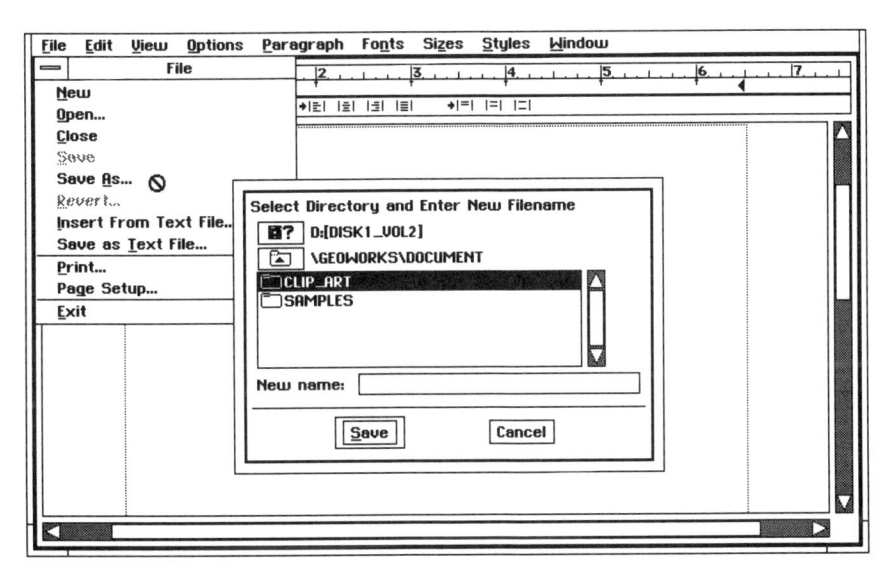

Figure 7-4 — The Select Directory and Enter New Filename Dialog Box.

Note that the File Menu in Figure 7-4 is pinned. You can accept the current drive and subdirectory, or you can select a different drive and/or subdirectory in which to save the document. Then position the text cursor in the New name box and

119

7 GeoWrite Menus

type a document file name. GeoWrite documents are saved in GEOS file format, so you can use up to 32 characters in the file name. A GEOS file name is case sensitive (upper and lowercase letters are considered different characters). You can use spaces between words in a GEOS file name. This allows you to use more descriptive file names for your documents than you can with DOS — one of the seemingly small things that can make a big difference.

After typing the new file name, you can complete the save command in one of three ways:

- Press [Enter]
- Click the Save button, or
- Press [alt]-[S] (the mnemonic method).

The dialog box closes, and you return to the now-saved document which displays the new file name on the Title Bar.

Whenever you select Save for a previously-saved document, the program saves it to disk immediately and automatically in the same location and under the same file name (overwriting the older version).

Save As...

Use this option to save an active, previously-saved document under a different file name. You can accept the current drive and subdirectory, or you can select a different drive and/or subdirectory. Enter a file name in the New name box which is different from the existing document name. The original document remains as last saved. You can use the Save As feature to save several versions of a file as you work.

Revert...

The Revert option retrieves the last saved version of the current document. Any changes made to the current document after the last save are lost. When you choose Revert, the program asks you to confirm that you want to revert to the saved version. Click the Yes button if you are certain you want to revert.

Insert From Text File...

All GeoWrite dialog boxes list only GEOS documents. To use a DOS document in GeoWrite, you must import it using the Insert From Text File option. The Insert From Text File dialog box is shown in Figure 7-5.

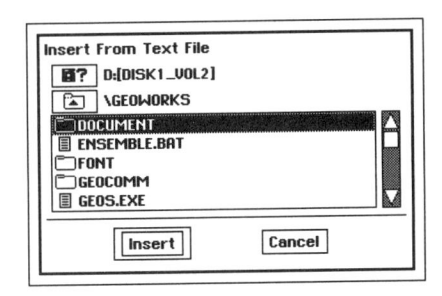

Figure 7-5 — The Insert From Text File Dialog Box.

Select the drive and subdirectory in which the file you want to use is located. The dialog box displays only DOS files. Select the file you want to insert into your GEOS document. The dialog box closes and you return to the document window. The DOS document is inserted at the current text cursor position.

Save as Text File...

To save a GEOS document as a DOS document so you can use it in a DOS application, select the Save as Text File option. The Save to Text File dialog box is shown in Figure 7-6.

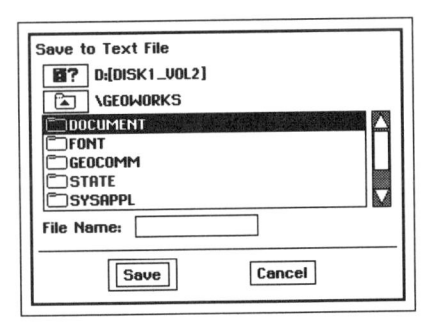

Figure 7-6 — The Save to Text File Dialog Box.

7 GeoWrite Menus

Select the drive and subdirectory in which you want to save the DOS version of your active GEOS document. The dialog box displays only GEOS files. Enter a file name for the DOS document. Click the Save button to save your document and return to the document window.

Print...

Use the Print command to specify the quality of your printed file: draft (for fast printing) or high quality (for the final copy). You can print all or selected pages and specify the number of copies you want to print. The Print dialog box is shown in Figure 7-7.

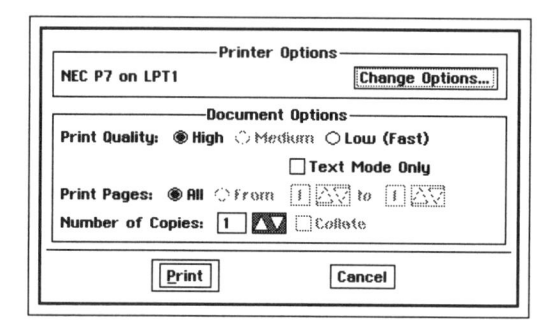

Figure 7-7 — The Print Option Dialog Box.

The upper portion of the dialog box identifies the current printer. Select the print quality and number of copies you want. The following paragraphs discuss the settings in the Print Options dialog box.

Change options

Click the Change Options button to select another printer (if you installed more than one), and to change paper size and paper source. The Change Options dialog box is shown in Figure 7-8.

GeoWrite Menus **7**

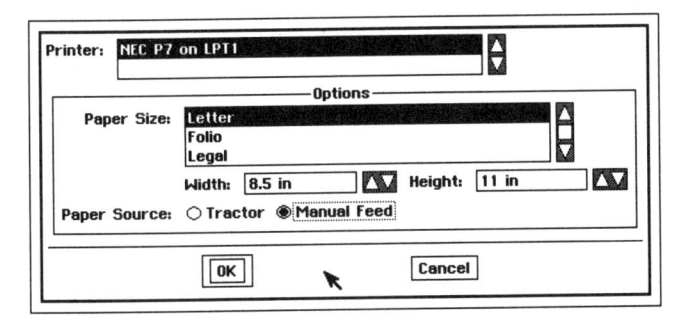

Figure 7-8 — The Change Options Dialog Box.

Note: Use the Print option on the GeoManager Preferences Application menu to install a new printer so you can select it from the GeoWrite Change Options dialog box.

Page Setup...

Before you can print a document, you must specify the paper size and page orientation from the Page Setup option. Selecting Page Setup from the File menu displays the dialog box shown in Figure 7-9.

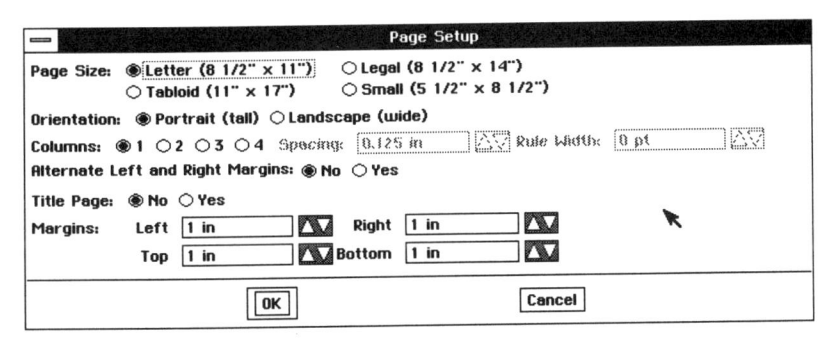

Figure 7-9 — The Page Setup Dialog Box.

123

7 GeoWrite Menus

Printing a Document

Follow these steps to print a document.

1. Select Page Setup from the File menu and verify the paper size and page orientation settings are what you want. Make any changes required.

2. Click the OK button to close the Page Setup dialog box.

Note: The number of columns affects the whole document. You must create different documents if you want a different number of columns on different pages of your final document.

3. Select Print from the File menu. Set the print quality: High, Medium or Low resolution. (Not all options are available for all printers.)

4. (Optional Step) Select Text Mode Only for faster printing at any print quality setting. This option does not print graphics and it uses only the internal printer fonts. Documents printed in Text Mode Only can look considerably different than the screen display.

5. Set the From and To range values to print selected pages. Use Select All if you want to print all pages of the document.

6. Specify the Number of Copies you want to make.

7. Click on Print. The printer starts printing.

Exit (F3)

Use the Exit option to close all open documents and exit GeoWrite. If any documents were modified since the last save, the program asks if you want to save the changes.

Edit Menu

Selecting Edit from the GeoWrite Menu Bar displays the Edit menu shown in Figure 7-10.

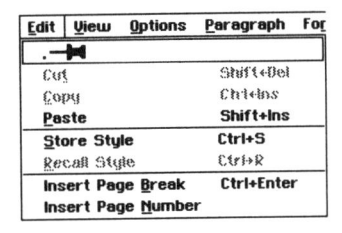

Figure 7-10 — The Edit Menu.

The Pin Symbol

See The Pin Symbol section of the File menu discussion earlier in this chapter.

Cut (Shift+Del)

Use the Cut option to remove selected text from a document, moving it to another location in the same document or to another document. Select (highlight) the text you want to move, then select Cut from the Edit menu.

The Cut option moves the highlighted text to the Clipboard where it is saved until you save something else to the Clipboard. Use the Paste command to copy the Clipboard information to a document.

Copy (Ctrl+Ins)

Use the Copy option to copy text from one location of your document to another, or to another document. Copy is very much like Cut except that the selected material is not removed from its original location in the document.

Select the text you want to copy. Select Copy from the Edit menu. The highlighting disappears. Although it seems as if nothing has happened, Copy places a copy of the highlighted text on the Clipboard. Use the Paste option to copy the Clipboard contents into a document.

7 GeoWrite Menus

Paste (Shift+Ins)

Use the Paste option to copy Clipboard contents to your document. Position the text cursor where you want to insert the Clipboard contents. Select Paste to copy the text.

Paste does not remove the information from the Clipboard. You can paste the Clipboard information into multiple locations in multiple documents, if you wish.

Clipboard contents are saved automatically each time you Cut or Copy text. Even if you turn off your computer, the next time you return to GeoWrite the last Clipboard contents are intact, ready to be pasted into a document.

Store Style

You can save a combination of format settings (margins, indent, tabs, and fonts) as a Style that can be used repeatedly to format new or existing text.

For example, suppose you have set up a special heading in your document that is centered (Paragraph menu), 24 point (Sizes menu), with special Character spacing (Sizes menu), a particular font (Fonts menu), and both bold and italic (Style menu). To save these setting, place the cursor anywhere in the heading and select Store Style from the Edit menu.

Recall Style

Use this option to recall a style to format new text. Position the text cursor at the location where you want to start using the stored style. Select Recall Style from the Edit menu, then type the text you want affected by the style.

You can also recall a style to format existing text. Highlight the text you want to restyle then select Recall Style from the Edit menu. The highlighted text is reformatted to the stored style.

Insert Page Break

Select this option to start a new page at the current cursor position. Any text to the right of the cursor position is carried (with the cursor) to the next page.

Moving between pages

The format bar below the ruler bar displays the current page number. To the left of the page number is a left arrow; to the right of the page number is a right arrow. Click on the left arrow to go to the previous page (if one exists). Click on the right arrow to go to the following page.

You can also use the Window menu to move to another page. Select the page you want from the list of current pages in the document.

Insert Page Number

Select this option to insert the current page number into the text at the text cursor position. When you use this command in a header or footer, the page number is automatically set (updated) for each page of the header or footer.

View Menu

Use the View menu to change the magnification of the page within the window: to view the entire page at once (reduced magnification) or a small portion of it (enlarged magnification). Larger magnifications may help reduce eye strain. Figure 7-11 shows the View menu with seven choices for viewing magnification.

Note: magnification settings do not affect the font size or amount of text on a page when you print the document.

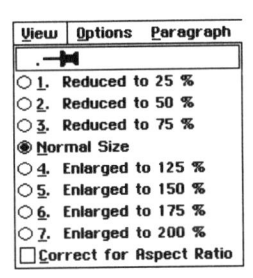

Figure 7-11 — The View Menu.

7 GeoWrite Menus

Correct for Aspect Ratio

You may want to use this option if you have a Hercules or CGA monitor. These monitors use rectangular pixels rather than square ones. (A pixel is the smallest dot your monitor can display.) As a result, images tend to look squashed — too short and too wide. Selecting the Correct for Aspect Ratio option changes the way a document displays so it more closely represents the way it will print. If you select this option and your screen dims, your monitor already has square pixels and no correction is necessary. Selecting this option toggles it on or off.

GOOD IDEA: If your screen writes too slowly with the Correct for Aspect Ratio turned on, try using this option only when previewing your document.

Options Menu

Figure 7-12 shows the Options menu.

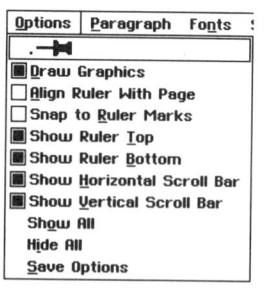

Figure 7-12 — The Options Menu.

Draw Graphics

GeoWrite documents can contain text and graphics. Select Draw Graphics to see the actual graphic images on the screen. Graphics images, however, will slow down scrolling speed as you move through the document. When you turn off Draw Graphics, a graphic image placeholder indicates the image location without slowing down scrolling.

Align Ruler with Page

When you select Align Ruler With Page, the zero on the ruler line aligns with the edge of the page. If you do not set this option, the zero of the ruler line aligns with the text left margin.

Snap to Ruler Marks

When you select this option, the tabs, indents and margin markers snap to the nearest 1/8-inch mark on the ruler. As long as this option is turned on, you cannot set tabs, indents and margins at any increment smaller than 1/8-inch (such as a 1/16-inch mark).

Show Ruler Top

You can choose to show or hide the top line of the Ruler Bar by toggling the Show Ruler Top option. As you learned in Chapter 6, the Ruler Bar contains two lines of information. The top line displays a ruler image with scale gradations.

Show Ruler Bottom

You can choose to show or hide the bottom line of the Ruler Bar by toggling the Show Ruler Bottom option. As you learned in Chapter 6, the Ruler Bar contains two lines of information. The bottom line displays the tab, indent and margin markers.

Show Horizontal Scroll Bar

You can choose to show or hide the horizontal scroll bar by toggling this option.

Show Vertical Scroll Bar

You can choose to show or hide the vertical scroll bar by toggling this option.

Show All

Select this option when you want all screen display options turned on. This option is not a toggle — selecting it activates Show All every time.

Hide All

Select this option when you want all screen display options turned off. This option is not a toggle — selecting it activates Hide All every time.

Save Options

Select this option to save the current Options menu settings and close the menu.

Paragraph Menu

Figure 7-13 shows the Paragraph menu.

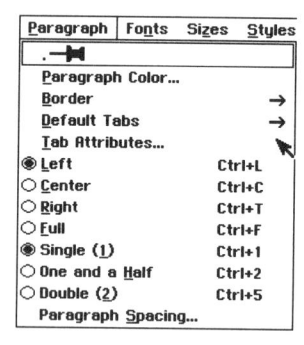

Figure 7-13 — The Paragraph Menu.

Pin

See The Pin Symbol section of the File Menu discussed earlier in the chapter.

Paragraph Color

You can use Paragraph Color settings — which will display as colors or patterns, depending on your monitor — to modify the way your document looks on the screen. Colors always print as black on a black and white printer. A multicolor document created on a monochrome monitor will print multicolor on a color printer.

On a monochrome monitor, patterns of varying intensity represent colors. You cannot apply these patterns to paragraph backgrounds or borders.

GeoWrite Menus 7

In Chapter 8 you will learn how to create a patterned graphic in GeoDraw and then paste it in your GeoWrite document.

Selecting Paragraph Color displays a dialog box similar to Figure 7-14, which shows the dialog box for a monochrome monitor. The patterns representing colors start on the left with black and progress to white on the right.

The dialog box color scale for an EGA or VGA monitor looks slightly different, but functions in the same way as the monochrome dialog box.

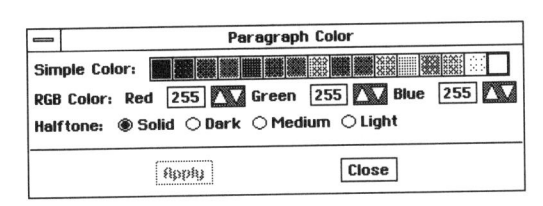

Figure 7-14 — The Paragraph Color Dialog Box.

Halftone

The Halftone setting controls color intensity — the concentration of color — in text, paragraph backgrounds, and borders on color and monochrome monitors. Select Solid for 100%, Dark for 50%, Medium for 25%, or Light for 15% color concentration. Halftones print on color and black-and-white printers. You will learn how to create a halftone in Chapter 8.

RGB color

To change the color mix, select a color box (or pattern box) and vary the amount of red, green or blue for that box. Click on a down arrow to decrease the color amount (down to 0), or click on an up arrow to increase the color amount (up to 255).

Apply

Click the Apply button to see the new color settings.

Close

Click the Close button to close the dialog box and return to the GeoWrite window.

131

7 GeoWrite Menus

Border

Figure 7-15 shows the Border cascade menu.

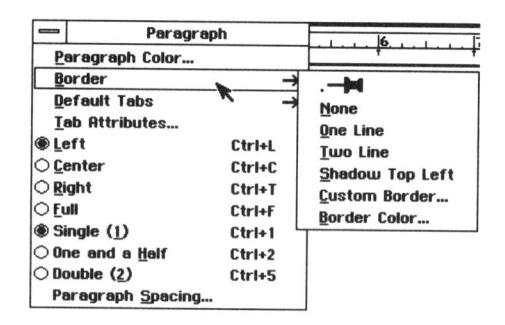

Figure 7-15 — The Border Cascade Menu.

You can use colors and halftones in borders.

None

You must select None when you want to exit a border box and continue typing in your document outside the border. For example, suppose you create a double-line border box for a one-line title. After typing the title text, you must tap [Enter⏎] to insert a blank line in the box, then select None from the Border menu to exit the box.

One Line

Select this option when you want to create text surrounded by a one-line border.

Two Line

Select this option when you want to create text surrounded by a two-line border.

Shadow Top Left

Select this option when you want to create text surrounded by a border box that appears to cast a shadow from an imaginary light source at the top left corner of the screen. The shadow extends from the right and bottom edges of the box.

GeoWrite Menus 7

Custom Border

Select this option to custom design a border. Select a border type — Normal, Shadow, or Double line — as a basis for your custom border. The program displays the Custom Border dialog box similar to the one shown in Figure 7-16.

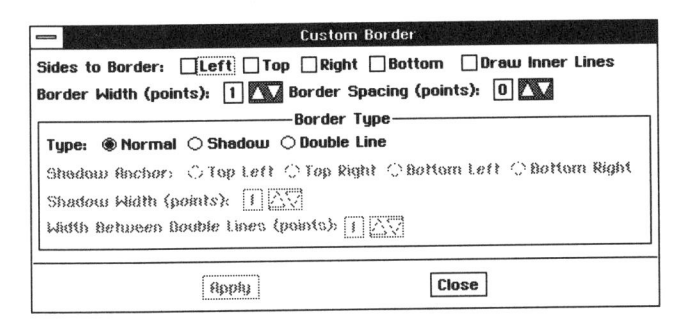

Figure 7-16 — The Custom Border Dialog Box.

Sides to border

You can determine which sides of the box are to have borders by using the Sides to Border option.

Draw inner lines

When the Draw Inner Lines option is active, pressing [Enter] draws a line within the border. When Draw Inner Lines is not active, pressing [Enter] inserts a blank line within the border.

Border width

Select Border Width to adjust the width of the border.

Border spacing

You can adjust the space between the text and border by selecting this option.

133

7 GeoWrite Menus

Shadow anchor

If your custom border includes a shadow, you can change the shadow position by selecting Shadow Anchor. Remember, the shadow appears on the side of the box opposite the light source.

Shadow width

Select this option to adjust the width of the box shadow.

Border Color

Figure 7-17 shows the Border Color dialog box.

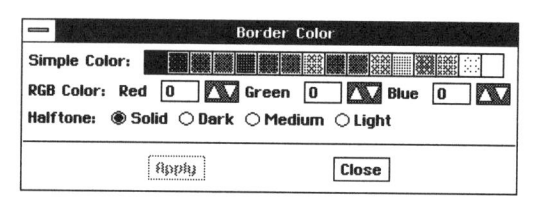

Figure 7-17 — Border Color Dialog Box.

See the Halftone, RGB Color, Apply and Close sections under Paragraph Color above for a discussion of the Border Color dialog box features.

Default Tabs

Figure 7-18 shows the Default Tabs cascade menu.

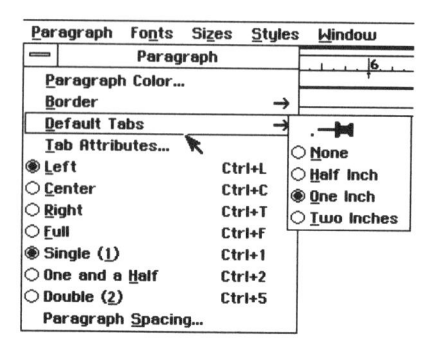

Figure 7-18 — The Default Tabs Cascade Menu.

You can select one of four options as the default tab setting: None, Half inch, One inch, or Two inches. The following paragraphs discuss tab options and settings.

Tab Attributes

Suppose you want to change a left justify tab to a right justify tab with dot leaders. Click on the tab in the Ruler Bar, then select Tab Attributes in the Paragraph menu to display the Tab Attributes dialog box. (Or you can double-click on the tab to select it and display the dialog box in one operation.) Figure 7-19 shows the Tab Attributes dialog box.

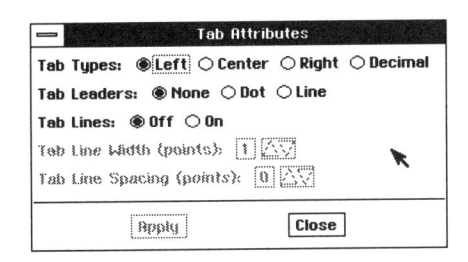

Figure 7-19 — The Tab Attributes Dialog Box.

If you do not first select a tab before displaying the Tab Attributes dialog box, options are dimmed and unavailable.

Tab types

Select the tab type you want: left justified, right justified, centered, or decimal aligned.

Tab leaders

Select the tab leader option you want — line or dots. Use tab leaders to insert a line or a row of dots between text and the leader tab. For example, a Table of Contents often uses dot leaders to fill the space between the content descriptions and the corresponding page numbers.

7 GeoWrite Menus

Tab lines

Toggle on the Tab Lines option to draw vertical lines at the tab location for columns and tables. You can also use it to mark portions of a document that have been changed.

A Tab Line tab is indicated in the Ruler Bar by a vertical line. You can set multiple Tab Line tabs in a document. When you press [Enter] to start a new line in the document, the program draws vertical lines at the Tab Line positions.

Tab line width

Select this option to specify the width of the vertical tab line (from 1 to 3 points).

Tab line spacing

Select this option to specify the spacing between the text and the tab (from 1 to 3 points).

Left (Ctrl+L)

Select this option on the Paragraph menu to left justify the paragraph your text cursor is in or a currently-highlighted paragraph. Left justification aligns the left edge of the text at the left margin and leaves the right margin ragged.

Center (Ctrl+C)

Select this option to center justify the paragraph your text cursor is in or a currently-highlighted paragraph. Center justification centers each line of text between the left and right margins.

Right (Ctrl+T)

Select this option to right justify the paragraph your text cursor is in or a currently-highlighted paragraph. Right justification aligns the right edge of the text at the right margin and leaves the left margin ragged.

Full (Ctrl+F)

Select this option to full justify the paragraph your text cursor is in or a currently-highlighted paragraph. Full justification adds spaces between words so that both the left and right text edges align at the margins.

Note: You can achieve the same justification results by select the left, center, right or full justification icons below the Ruler Bar.

Single (1) (Ctrl+1)

Use this option to single space lines in selected text or the paragraph in which your text cursor is located.

One and a Half (Ctrl+2)

Use this option to space lines one-and-a-half lines apart in selected text or the paragraph in which your text cursor is located.

Double (2) (Ctrl+5)

Use this option to double space lines in selected text or the paragraph in which your text cursor is located.

Note: You can achieve the same spacing results by selecting the Single spacing, One-and-a-half spacing, or Double spacing icons below the Ruler Bar (on the right).

Paragraph Spacing

Select this option to change the spacing above, below and within a selected paragraph or the paragraph in which the typing cursor is located. This is a particularly useful tool. For example, you can add space before or after a heading, stretch columnar text to fill a larger space, or squeeze text to fit a smaller space. Figure 7-20 shows the Paragraph Spacing dialog box.

7 GeoWrite Menus

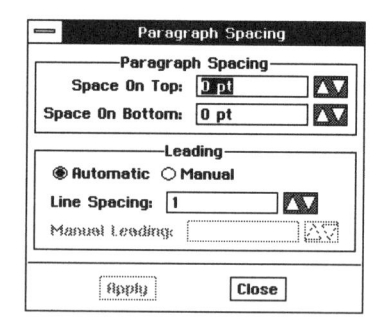

Figure 7-20 — Paragraph Spacing Dialog Box.

Paragraph spacing

Click on the up and down arrows to set the amount of space above or below the affected text (0 to 3 points).

Leading

Use this option to control precisely the distance between lines (leading) in the selected paragraph. Manual leading adds the Line Spacing value as a constant to the space between lines, regardless of the font sizes used in the lines. Manual leading is most appropriate when you use one font size. Automatic leading determines the largest font in a line then multiplies the font size by the Line Spacing value. Use automatic leading when you combine font sizes in a document.

GeoWorks Ensemble dialog boxes display values in inches, but you can enter values in any of the following units: in (inch), pi (pica), pt (point), cm (centimeter), mm (millimeter), ci (Cicero), or ep (European point).

Line spacing

Click on the up or down arrows to select the line spacing value you want to use, or position the text cursor in the Line Spacing box and type a value. (You can use fractions.)

Apply

Select Apply to see how your selection affects the selected paragraph or the paragraph your text cursor is in.

Close

Select Close to accept the paragraph spacing settings, close the dialog box, and return to the GeoWrite window.

Fonts Menu

To set a new font for existing text, highlight the text then select the Fonts menu. Select the font you want to use from the Fonts dialog box. The dialog box closes and you return to the GeoWrite window. The selected text displays in the new font.

To set a font for new text, position the text cursor where you want to begin typing with the new font. Select the Fonts menu. Select the font you want to use from the Fonts dialog box. The dialog box closes and you return to the GeoWrite window, ready to type with the new font.

More Fonts

To see a sample of a font before activating it in the document, select the More Fonts option from the Fonts dialog box. You can pin the More Fonts menu, shown in Figure 7-21, for easy access while creating your document.

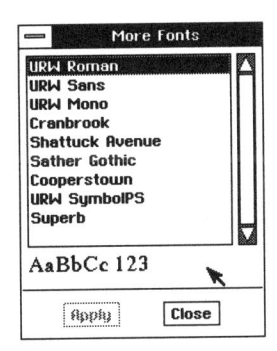

Figure 7-21 — The More Fonts Menu.

7 GeoWrite Menus

Select the font you want to see. Sample text below the font list changes to display the font selection. Click the Apply button to see how the font will look in your document. When you are satisfied with the font selection, click the Close button to return to the GeoWrite window. Figure 7-22 shows a sample of available fonts. The Fonts dialog box is pinned in the upper right corner.

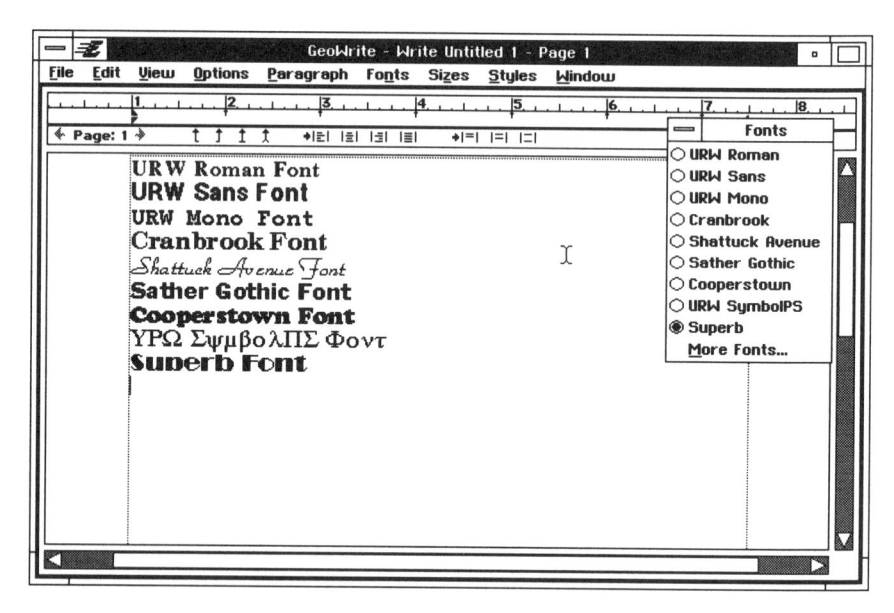

Figure 7-22 — Font Samples.

Sizes Menu

Use the Sizes menu to change the font size of selected text, or to set the font size for new text. Figure 7-23 shows the URW Roman font in eight sizes. The Sizes menu is pinned in the lower right corner of the screen.

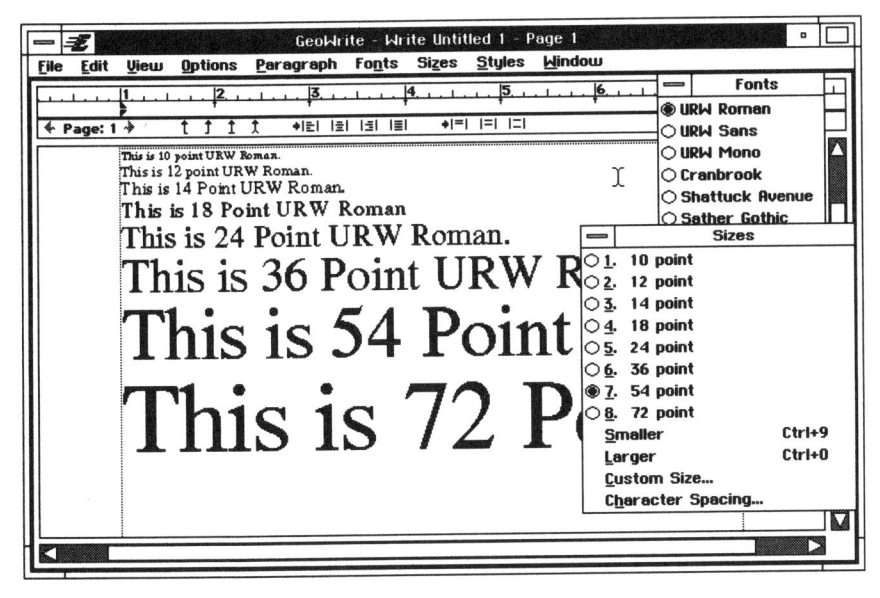

Figure 7-23 — The Sizes Menu and Font Size Examples.

Changing Font Size for Existing Text

Highlight the text you want to change. Select the font size you want from the Sizes menu. The Sizes menu closes and the selected text displays in the new font size.

Changing Font Size for New Text

Position the text cursor where you want to begin typing with the new font. Select the font size you want from the Sizes menu. The Sizes menu closes, and you are ready to begin typing with the new font.

Standard Font Sizes

The Sizes dialog box lists 8 point sizes from 10 to 72. (72 points is equal to one-inch tall.) The menu indicates the active point size by a filled circle next to it.

7 GeoWrite Menus

You can use the Smaller and Larger menu items to either increase or decrease the size of the selected font. The last item on the Sizes menu, Custom Size..., allows you to customize the point size of your text from 4 points to 792 points. (792 points divided by 72 points is 11 inches. This means you can make a character as large as 792 points which can fill an entire 8 1/2-by-11 inch page.)

Changing Existing Text Font Smaller or Larger

Select the text you want to change, then open the Sizes menu. Select Smaller to activate the next smaller standard font size, or choose Larger to activate the next larger font size.

You can also use the Smaller hotkey [Ctrl]-[9] or the Larger hotkey [Ctrl]-[0] to change font sizes from the keyboard.

Changing Font Smaller or Larger for New Text

Position the text cursor where you want to begin typing with the new font. Open the Sizes menu, then select Larger or Smaller.

You can also use the Smaller hotkey [Ctrl]-[9] or the Larger hotkey [Ctrl]-[0] to change the active font size from the keyboard.

Custom Size

To use a size other than a standard font size, select the Custom Size option to display the dialog box shown in Figure 7-24.

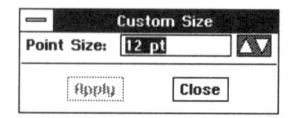

Figure 7-24 — The Custom Size Dialog Box.

Click on the up and down arrows to increase or decrease the displayed font size, or position the text cursor in the font size box and type a font size. You can specify from 4 points to 792 points. (A 792 point font is 11 inches tall — it will fill an 8-1/2 x 11-inch page.)

Click the Apply button to view the font change in your document. When you are satisfied with your selection, click the Close button.

Character Spacing

Select Character Spacing to vary the amount of space between characters in a word (also called kerning). When you select Character Spacing, the program displays the Degree of Spacing dialog box shown in Figure 7-25.

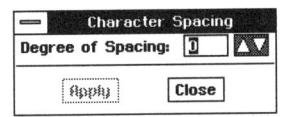

Figure 7-25 — The Character Spacing Dialog Box.

Setting a character spacing amount

Highlight the text you want to affect, or position the text cursor at the point where you want to begin typing with the new character spacing value. Select the Character Spacing option from the Sizes menu.

Click on the up and down arrows to increase or decrease the amount of space, or position the text cursor in the spacing box and type the value you want.

Click the Apply button to see the character spacing in your document. When you are satisfied with the character spacing, click the Close button to return to the document.

7 GeoWrite Menus

Styles Menu

Use the Styles menu shown in Figure 7-26 to display different typefaces: bold, underline, italic, bold and italic, etc.

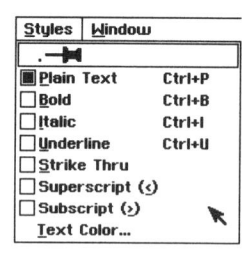

Figure 7-26 — The Styles Menu.

You can select more than one typeface at a time so you can combine bold and italic, for example. The only exception is the Plain Text option which turns off all other typefaces.

Plain Text (Ctrl+P)

Select Plain Text to turn off all other typefaces.

Bold (Ctrl+B)

Use Bold for thicker, darker text than Plain Text. Bold is usually used for headings and word emphasis.

Italic (Ctrl+I)

Use Italic to slant text to the right. Italic is usually used for word emphasis.

Underline (Ctrl+U)

Use Underline to place a line under each character. Underline is usually used for word emphasis.

Strike Thru

Use Strike Thru to place a line through each character. Strike Thru is usually used in editing to indicate text that should be removed from a document.

Superscript (<)

Use Superscript to write characters smaller and above the normal baseline of the text. Superscript is usually used for algebraic exponents and other types of technical notation.

Subscript (>)

Use Subscript to write characters smaller and at or below the normal baseline of the text. It is usually used for mathematical subindex and other types of technical notation.

Text Color

Selecting this option displays the dialog box in Figure 7-27.

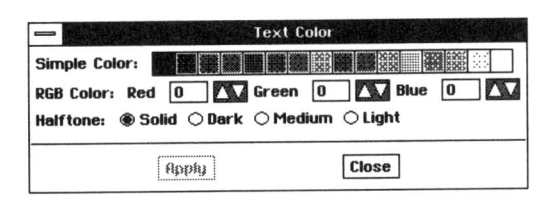

Figure 7-27 — Text Color Dialog Box.

To change the color of text, select the text, or place the typing cursor in the paragraph you want to color. Select Text Color from the Styles menu.

To use the Text Color dialog box, follow the steps covered in the Paragraph/Paragraph Color section earlier in this chapter.

7 GeoWrite Menus

Window

Select the Window menu to display the dialog box in Figure 7-28.

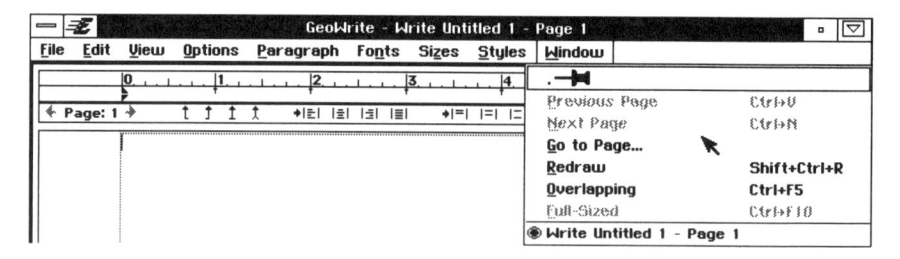

Figure 7-28 — The Window Menu.

Pin

See The Pin Symbol section of the File menu discussed earlier in this chapter.

Previous Page (Ctrl+V)

Select this option to go to the previous page in the document.

Next Page (Ctrl+N)

Select this option to go to the next page in the document.

Go to Page

Select this option to jump to a specific page in the document. Figure 7-29 shows the Go to Page dialog box.

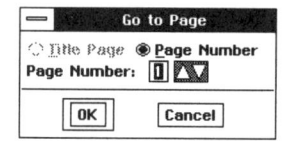

Figure 7-29 — The Go to Page Dialog Box.

GeoWrite Menus 7

You can position the text cursor in the Go to Page box then type the page number. Or you can click on the up and down arrows to specify the page number. Click the OK button to jump to the selected page

Redraw (Shift+Ctrl+R)

Select this option when you want to redraw (refresh) the screen.

Overlapping

Select this option to display multiple pages in overlapping format on the screen. You can also display multiple documents in overlapping format. Figure 7-30 shows three documents in overlapping format.

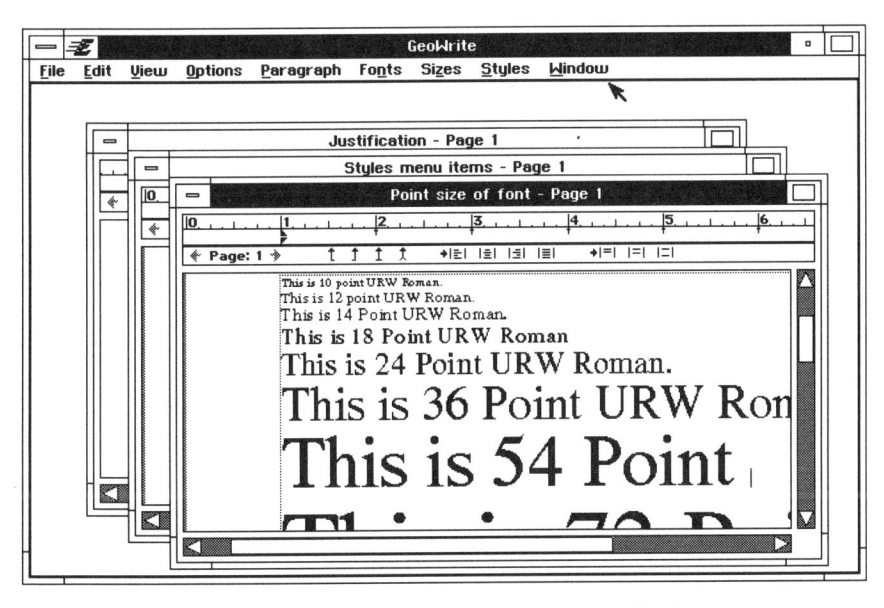

Figure 7-30 — Overlapping Document Windows.

Note that the Title bar of each documents is visible. You can select any Title bar to make it the active document.

147

7 GeoWrite Menus

Full-Sized (Ctrl+F10)

Use this option to change from Overlapping display to a full sized display of the active document.

Page Listing and Select Page

The bottom portion of the Window menu lists the pages in your document. When you select a page from the list, the menu closes and you return to the document on the selected page.

Summary

In Chapter 7 you learned how to use the options on the nine GeoWrite menus. Each menu option was discussed in detail.

Chapter 8

GeoWrite Operations and Tutorial

In this tutorial chapter you will practice using some of the major features of the GeoWrite application. After completing this chapter you will be sufficiently acquainted with GeoWrite to apply the other features to your work on your own.

During the three exercises in this tutorial you will:

- Type a portion of the Declaration of Independence
- Practice formatting techniques
- Insert a graphic image into the document
- Create and format a table
- Enter numbers into the table
- Copy the table
- Respace and format the copied table
- Reset first-line indent and paragraph margin markers.

8 GeoWrite Operations and Tutorial

Accessing GeoWrite

Start the GeoWorks Ensemble program in the usual way. Select the Professional Workspace icon from the GeoWorks Ensemble Welcome screen. If the GeoManager Information Line does not read \GEOMANAGER\WORLD, single-click on the World button at the bottom of the GeoManager window. Then double-click on the GeoWrite icon.

The program displays the GeoWrite window. The document title reads GeoWrite - Write Untitled - Page 1. The typing cursor is in the upper left corner of the typing panel.

Exercise 1

In this exercise you will:

- Create a document
- Enter text
- Format text
- Create a header
- Insert a GeoDraw drawing of a cat into the header
- Save the document.

Create and Save a Document

1. Type the following words:

   ```
   Declaration of Independence
   ```
   Document text.

   `Enter↵` Starts a new line.

The typing cursor moves to the beginning of the second line.

2. Open the File menu and select Save. The program displays the Select Directory and Enter New Filename dialog box.

150

GeoWrite Operations and Tutorial 8

3. Save the new document in the \GEOWORKS\DOCUMENT subdirectory. Change the subdirectory, if necessary, so that the Select Directory information line and the Enter New Filename dialog box both read \GEOWORKS\DOCUMENT.

4. Position the text cursor in the New Name box. Type the name of the new document: Declaration of Independence, and click the Save button. The dialog box will close and you will return to the GeoWrite window. The Title bar should now read: GeoWrite - Declaration of Independence - Page 1.

Setting Options

5. Open the Options menu. Toggle on the following options (a filled square indicates the option is toggled on):

   - Draw Graphics
   - Align Ruler With Page
   - Snap to Ruler Marks
   - Show Ruler Top
   - Show Ruler Bottom
   - Show Horizontal Scroll Bar
   - Show Vertical Scroll Bar.

6. Click on the Save Options button. The Options menu closes and you return to the document with the typing cursor at the beginning of the second line.

Setting a Center Tab ↕

7. Set a center tab at the 4-1/4" position on the ruler. (Move the mouse cursor to the center tab symbol. Drag the center tab symbol to the 4-1/4" position on the ruler.) The program removes the 1" tab symbols to the left of the center tab. The 1" tab symbols to the right of it remain. Your screen should resemble that shown in Figure 8-1.

8 GeoWrite Operations and Tutorial

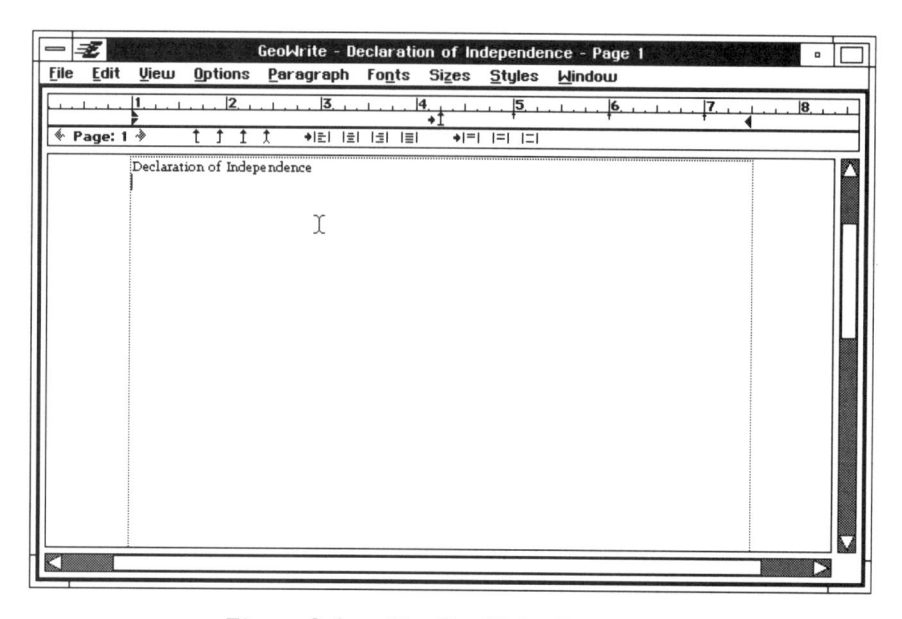

Figure 8-1 — The GeoWrite Document.

Note the horizontal arrow pointing to the center tab you placed on the ruler.

8. Press [tab]. The typing cursor moves to the 4-1/4" position. Type:

   Declaration of Independence   Document text
   [Enter←]   Starts a new line.

   The program centers the second line of text at the 4-1/4" center tab. The typing cursor moves to the third line.

Selecting Text

9. Position the mouse (or text) cursor to the beginning of the first line of text. Select the first line by pressing and holding the left mouse button while dragging to highlight the entire line, then release the left mouse button. The text remains highlighted as show in Figure 8-2.

GeoWrite Operations and Tutorial 8

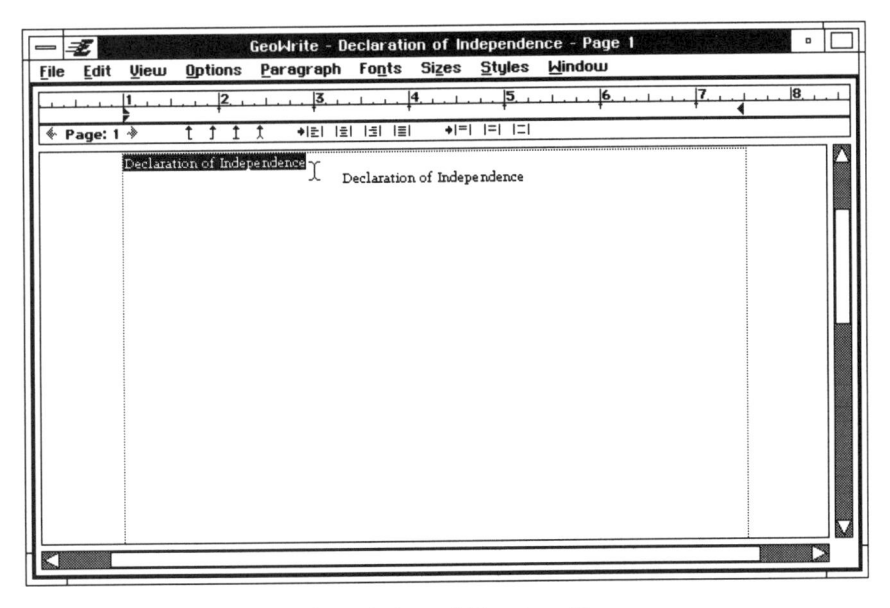

Figure 8-2 — Selected Text in a Document.

Changing Font of Existing Text

10. Open the Fonts menu by pressing [alt]-[N]. Click on the pin symbol to pin open the Fonts menu.

11. Select the Cooperstown font. The program displays the highlighted text in Cooperstown. The text remains highlighted and the Fonts menu remains open.

12. Select the Shattuck Avenue font. The program displays the highlighted text in Shattuck Avenue. The text remains highlighted and the Fonts menu remains open.

Changing Font Size of Existing Text

13. Open the Size menu by pressing [alt]-[Z]. Click on option 4 (or type the number 4) to select 18 point. The program displays the highlighted text in 18 point Shattuck Avenue and closes the Size menu.

153

8 GeoWrite Operations and Tutorial

Changing Text Styles of Existing Text

14. Open the Styles menu by pressing [alt]-[S]. Click on Bold. The program displays the highlighted text in bold 18 point Shattuck Avenue and closes the Styles menu.

15. Pin open the Styles menu. Click on Underline. The program displays the highlighted text in bold and underline style. The pinned Styles menu remains open. Your screen should resemble Figure 8-3.

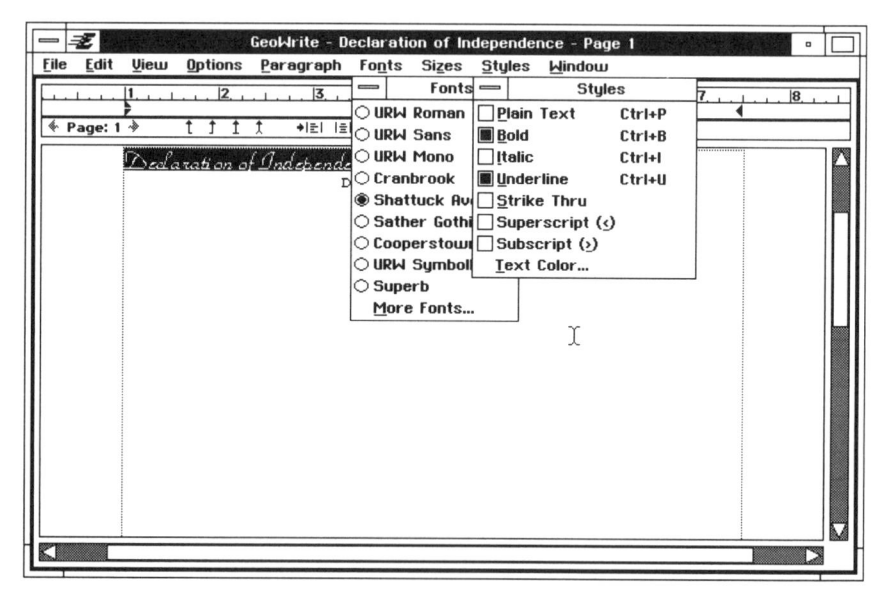

Figure 8-3 — Changing Text Font and Style.

Closing Pinned Menus

16. Close the pinned Styles menu by double-clicking on its Control button. Then close the Font menu.

154

Removing Text Highlighting

17. Click the left mouse button anywhere on the typing area below the third line of the document. The program removes the highlighting and positions the text cursor at the end of the document (the beginning of the third line).

Creating a Blank Line

18. Position the text cursor at the end of the first line. Press [Enter⏎]. The program inserts a blank line between the first and second lines of text, and the cursor moves to the new blank line. Text lines after the new blank line move down one line. Press [Enter⏎] again. The program inserts a second blank line, and the cursor moves to the new blank line.

Changing Font, Size, and Style for New Text

19. Open the Fonts menu and select the URW Sans font. The program closes the Fonts menu.

20. Open the Sizes menu and verify the size is set to 18 point. Close the Size menu by clicking anywhere off the Size menu.

21. Open the Styles menu and select Plain Text to toggle off all text style options. The program closes the Styles menu.

You are ready to type using the URW Sans font in 18 point with plain text (no bold, underline, etc.).

8 GeoWrite Operations and Tutorial

Typing Text

22. Type the following:

> Declaration of Independence
>
> [Enter⏎] [Enter⏎]
>
> The Continental Congress in Philadelphia, on July 4, 1776 adopted the Declaration of Independence. John Hancock was president of the Congress at that time.
>
> [Enter⏎]
>
> [Enter⏎]
>
> IN CONGRESS, July 4, 1776.
>
> [Enter⏎]
>
> [Enter⏎]
>
> A DECLARATION
>
> [Enter⏎]
>
> [Enter⏎]
>
> By the REPRESENTATIVES of the UNITED STATES OF AMERICA,
>
> [Enter⏎]
>
> [Enter⏎]
>
> In GENERAL CONGRESS assembled
>
> When in the Course of human Events, it becomes necessary for one People to dissolve the Political Bands which have connected them with another, and to assume among the Powers of the Earth, the separate and equal Station to which the Laws of Nature and of Nature's God entitle them, a decent Respect to the Opinions of Mankind requires that they should declare the causes which impel them to the Separation.

Your screen should resemble Figure 8-4.

GeoWrite Operations and Tutorial 8

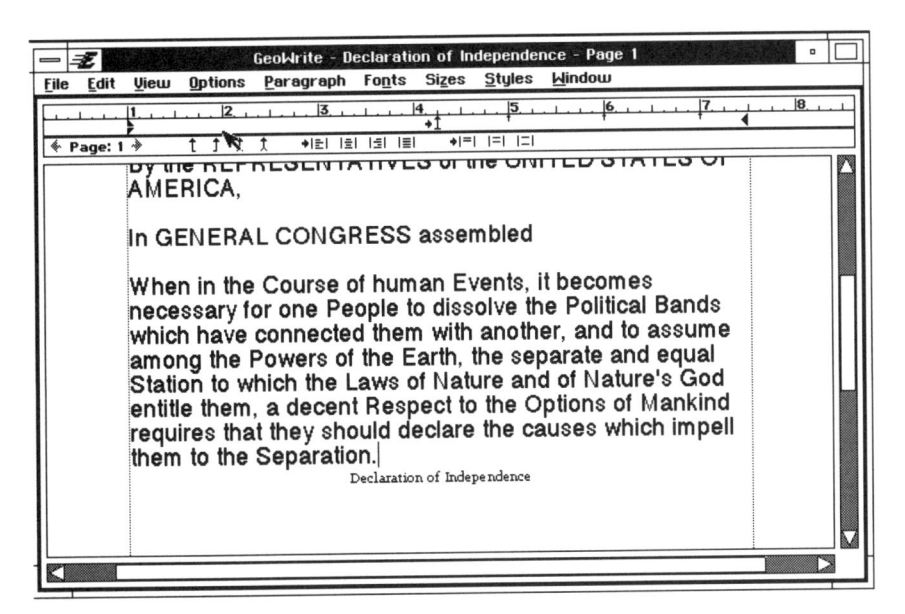

Figure 8-4 — The Document Screen.

Making a Header

23. Scroll to the top of the document until the screen displays the header box. Position the text cursor in the upper left corner of the header box by clicking the mouse cursor anywhere in the box.

24. Type:

> The MARK of the Scribe...
>
> [Enter⏎]
>
> MOTS

157

8 GeoWrite Operations and Tutorial

25. Highlight the letters MOTS and change the size to 72 point. Your screen should resemble Figure 8-5.

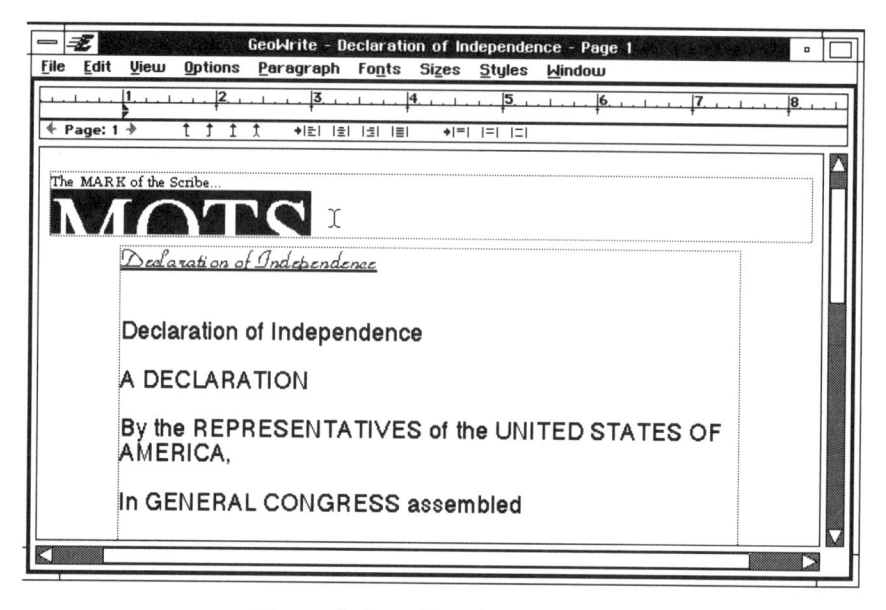

Figure 8-5 — Creating a Header.

Note that the 72 point characters do not fit in the header box.

Changing Header Size

26. Select Page Setup on the File menu. Change the Top Margin setting to 1.5 inches. Click the OK button to close the dialog box. Your screen should resemble Figure 8-6.

GeoWrite Operations and Tutorial 8

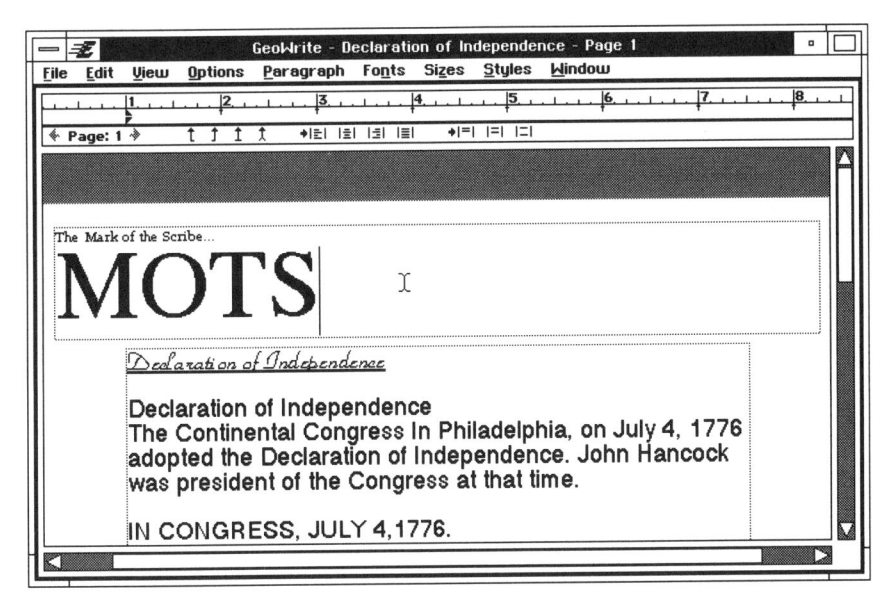

Figure 8-6 — Resized Header.

Inserting a Graphic Image in the Document

To insert a graphic image in a GeoWrite document requires these steps:

- Open the graphics application (in this case, GeoDraw)
- Display the graphic image
- Copy the graphic image to the clipboard
- Resize the graphic
- Switch to the GeoWrite document
- Paste the graphic image into the GeoWrite document.

In this tutorial you will place the graphic image into the header so that it will appear on all pages of your document.

Open a GeoDraw window

27. Open the Express menu and select GeoDraw from the Startup menu. The program opens a GeoDraw window, which is now the active window.

159

8 GeoWrite Operations and Tutorial

Open a graphic image file

28. Select Open from the GeoDraw File menu to display the Select Document to Open dialog box. The current path should read \GEOWORKS\DOCUMENT. Double-click on the CLIP-ART subdirectory icon. The current path changes to \GEOWORKS\DOCUMENT\CLIP_ART. The panel displays the contents of the CLIP_ART directory. Select the Miscellany file in the CLIP_ART subdirectory. Click the Open button to display the Miscellany file — a drawing of a cat.

Copy the graphic to the clipboard

29. Position the mouse cursor anywhere in the drawing and single-click to select it. The program places handles around the drawing. Select Copy from the Edit menu. The program places a copy of the cat drawing on the Clipboard.

Resize the graphic

30. Scroll down the GeoDraw window to display a blank portion of the document. Click the mouse cursor in the blank window.

31. Select Paste from the Edit menu. The program copies the cat drawing back into the document in a new location. The image handles are still visible.

32. Press and hold the left mouse button on one of the image handles. Drag the image smaller. Repeat with other handles as necessary to make the image approximately one-inch square. Use the center handle if you want to relocate the image in the window.

Copy the graphic to the clipboard again

33. Select Copy from the Edit menu. The program copies the small drawing onto the Clipboard.

Exiting GeoDraw

34. Select Exit from the File menu to close GeoDraw. Click the Yes button to save the changes to the Miscellany file. The GeoDraw window closes and you return to the GeoWrite document. The cat drawing remains on the Clipboard.

Pasting the graphic into GeoWrite

35. Position the text cursor after the word MOTS and press [space] seven times. Select Paste from the Edit menu. The program copies the cat drawing into the header box at the cursor location. Your screen should resemble Figure 8-7.

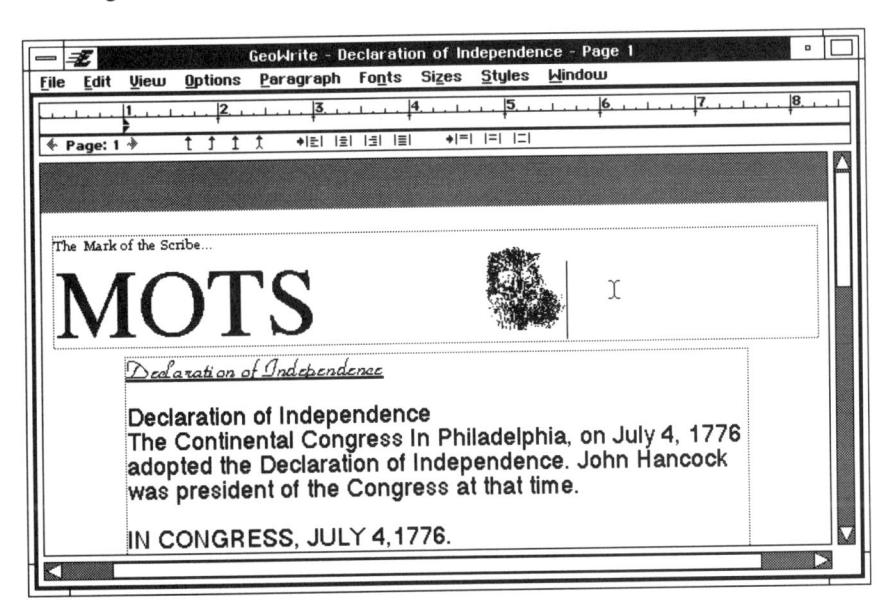

Figure 8-7 — A Graphic Image in a Header Box.

This header with the cat drawing will appear on all pages of your document.

Saving the Document

36. Save the document by selecting Save on the File menu.

8 GeoWrite Operations and Tutorial

Exercise 2

In this exercise you will:

- Create a page break in the document
- Create a table
- Set tabs and margins for the table
- Draw vertical lines in the table
- Enter text in the table
- Format the text
- Format the table
- Copy the table
- Respace the table
- Save the document.

Creating a Table

A table is a collection of data presented in rows and columns. In this exercise you will create a two-column table with a vertical line between the columns. You will place the table in a double-line border box.

You use tabs to create a table. In this exercise you will align numbers using the decimal tab option.

Creating a Page Break

1. Position the text cursor at the bottom of the document. Select Insert Page Break from the Edit menu. The program inserts a page break and positions the cursor at the top of page 2.

2. Press [Enter⏎] four times to create four blank lines.

GeoWrite Operations and Tutorial 8

Setting the Table Margins

3. Drag the left margin symbol (▶) (press and hold [⇧ Shift] while dragging the symbol with the left mouse button) to position 1-3/4 inches on the ruler line. The left margin is set at 1-3/4 inches.

4. Drag the right margin symbol (◀) (press and hold [⇧ Shift] while dragging the symbol with the left mouse button) to 4-1/2" on the ruler line. The right margin is set at 4-1/2".

Drawing Vertical Lines with a Left Tab Marker ↑

5. Drag a Left Tab symbol to 3-1/2" on the ruler line. The program sets a left tab at 3-1/2" and displays a horizontal arrow beside the new tab, indicating it is the currently-selected tab.

6. Double-click on the selected tab (or select Tab Attributes from the Paragraph menu). The program displays the Tab Attributes dialog box similar to Figure 8-8.

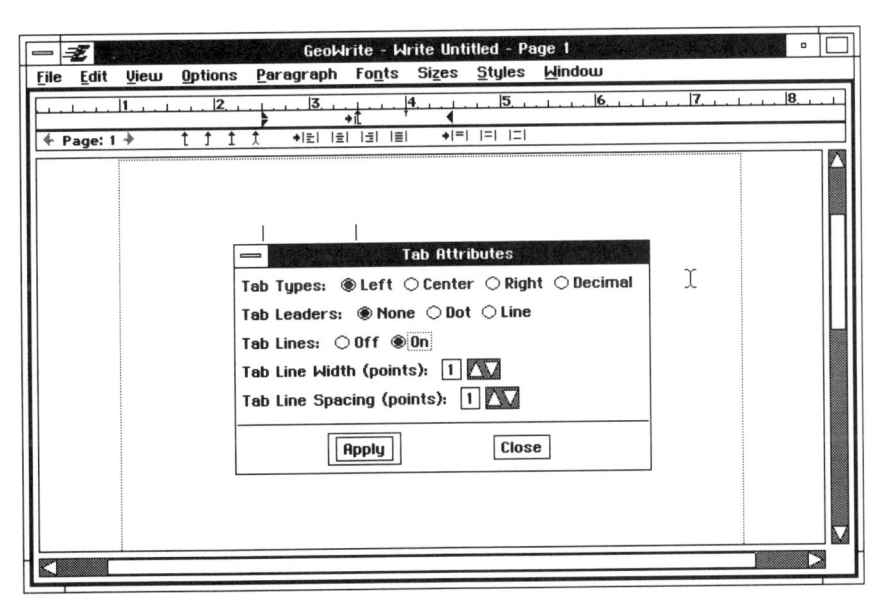

Figure 8-8 — The Tab Attributes Dialog Box.

163

8 GeoWrite Operations and Tutorial

7. Select Tab Lines On, then click the Apply button. The program displays a vertical line next to the selected tab on the ruler line to indicate that it will draw tab lines, and draws a vertical line at the tab position in the typing panel. The left vertical line above the Tab Attributes dialog box in Figure 8-8 is the typing cursor; the right vertical line is the Tab vertical line.

8. Set the Tab Line Width option to 2 points by clicking the up arrow. The allowable range is 1 to 3 points.

9. Set the Tab Line Spacing to 2 points by clicking the up arrow. The allowable range is 1 to 3 points.

10. Click the Close button. The program closes the Tab Attributes dialog box and you return to the document.

Setting Decimal Tabs

11. Drag the decimal tab symbol to position 3" on the ruler line. Copy the new decimal tab (press `Ctrl` while dragging the new decimal tab symbol) to position 4" on the ruler line. The program displays decimal tab symbols at 3" and 4" on the ruler line.

Entering the Table Text

12. Follow these steps to enter the table text:

    `Enter`   Starts a new line

    `tab`   Positions the text cursor on the decimal tab at 3"

    `456.987` Table entry.

    The decimal point aligns on the decimal tab at 3".

    `tab`   Positions the cursor.

    The text cursor moves to a position immediately after the vertical line at position 3-1/2".

    `tab`   Positions the cursor

    `444.88` Table entry.

GeoWrite Operations and Tutorial 8

The decimal point aligns on the decimal tab at 4".

    `Enter`   Starts a new line.

The vertical line at 3-1/2" extends one line.

    `tab`   Positions the cursor

    `3.765`   Table entry.

The decimal point aligns on the decimal tab at 3".

    `tab`   Positions the tab.

The text cursor moves to a position immediately after the vertical line at position 3-1/2".

    `tab`   Positions the cursor.

    `876.087` Table entry.

The decimal point aligns on the decimal tab at 4".

    `Enter`   Starts a new line.

The vertical line at 3-1/2" extends one line.

    `tab`   Positions the cursor.

    `876.909` Table entry.

The decimal point aligns on the decimal tab at 3".

    `tab`   Positions the cursor.

The text cursor moves to a position immediately after the vertical line at position 3-1/2".

    `space` (three times)   Inserts three spaces.

    `76.987`   Table entry.

The decimal point aligns on the decimal tab at 4". The number is preceded by three blank spaces.

8 GeoWrite Operations and Tutorial

Underlining Table Entries

13. Highlight both table entries in the last line. (Position the cursor at the beginning of the line, then press ⇧Shift while clicking the left mouse button to extend the highlight to the end of the line.) Select Underline from the Styles menu. The program underlines both numbers, including the spaces preceding the second number.

14. Click the mouse at the end of the highlighted line to remove the highlighting and position the text cursor at the end of the line.

15. Select Plain Text from the Styles menu.

Continuing Table Text Entry

16. Continue entering table text as follows:

    Enter↵   Starts a new line.
    tab   Positions the cursor.
    1336.661 Table entry.

The decimal point aligns on the decimal tab at 3".

    tab   Positions the cursor.

The text cursor moves to a position immediately after the vertical line at position 3-1/2".

    1397.954 Table entry.

The decimal point aligns on the decimal tab at 4".

    Enter↵   Starts a new line.

Removing Tab Markers

17. Remove the decimal tabs and the vertical line tab from the ruler line by selecting the tab symbols, then pressing delete. The program again displays the small vertical tab arrows at the unit markers of the ruler line and removes the vertical line from the line the cursor is on.

Drawing a Border Around the Table

18. Press [Enter←] to insert a new line. You now have two blank lines following the last line of numbers in your table. When you select the table in a moment, do not include this last blank line or you will not be able to enter text in the document after the table.

19. Press [←] to move up one line.

20. Select the entire table, except for the last blank line.

21. Select Border from the Paragraph menu to display the Border cascade menu. Select the Two Line border option. Click the left mouse button to remove the highlight. The program draws a two-line border around the table as shown in Figure 8-9.

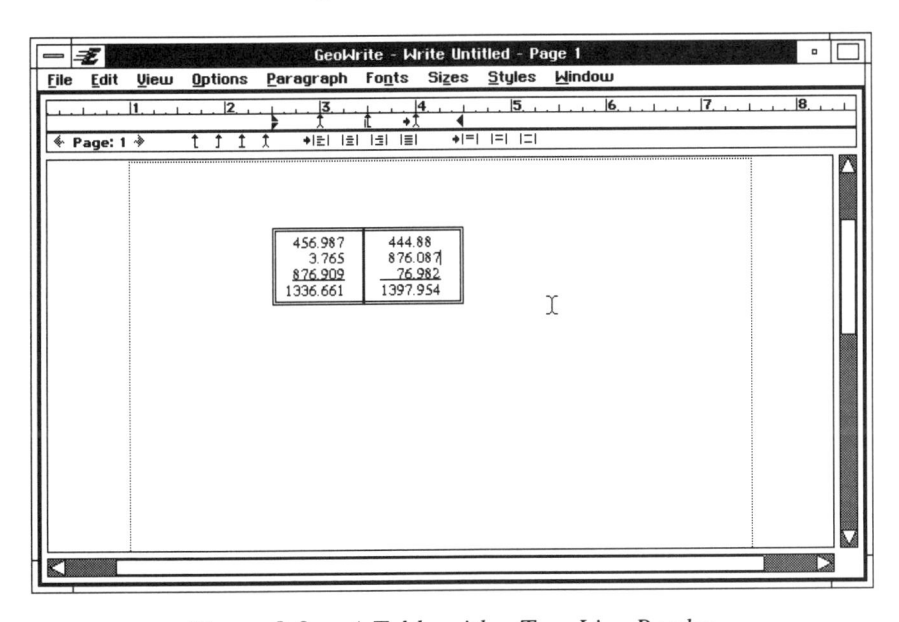

Figure 8-9 — A Table with a Two-Line Border.

Note: You can add or delete lines to the table within the border by pressing [Enter←], [delete], or [←BkSp] as appropriate.

8 GeoWrite Operations and Tutorial

Copying the Table within the Document

22. Highlight the entire table as shown in Figure 8-10.

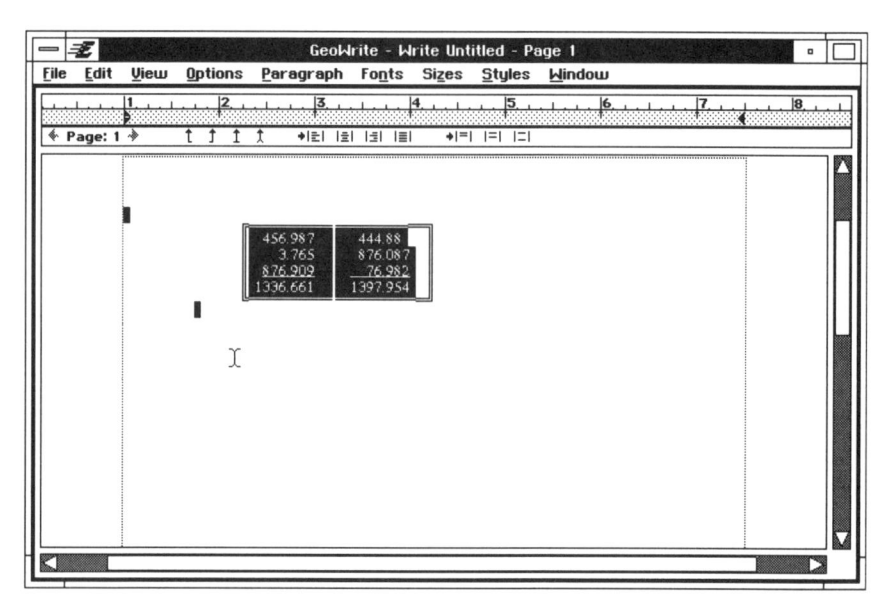

Figure 8-10 — A Highlighted Table.

23. Position the mouse cursor anywhere in the highlighted area, then press and hold the RIGHT mouse button. The cursor changes to the Quick Copy cursor as shown in the highlighted area of Figure 8-11.

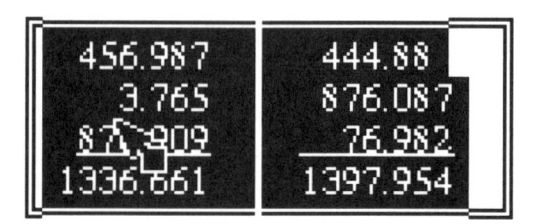

Figure 8-11 — The Quick Copy Pointer.

24. Drag the Quick Copy pointer to the location where you want to place the table copy. Release the mouse button. The program displays the table and the copy of the table. Your screen should be similar to Figure 8-12.

GeoWrite Operations and Tutorial 8

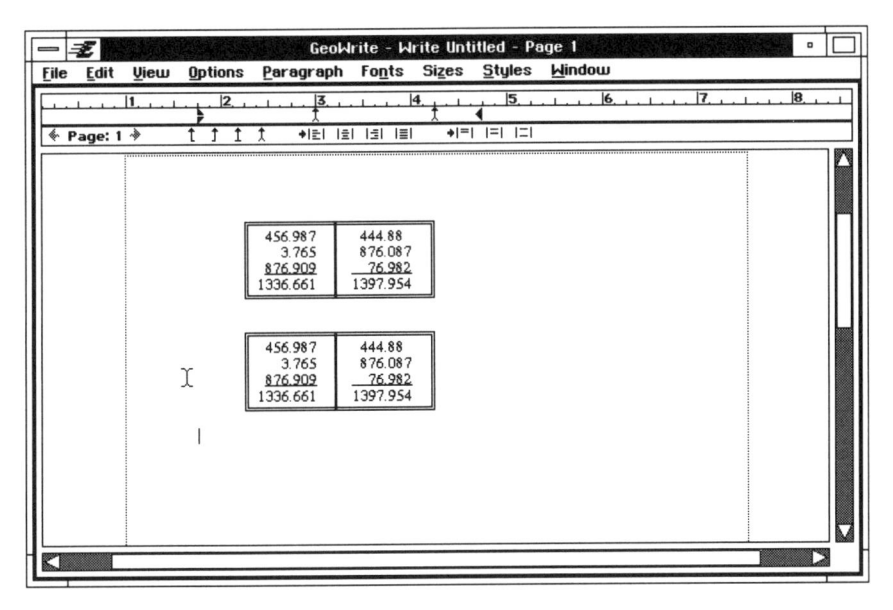

Figure 8-12 — A Copied Table.

Note: You can also use Copy on the Edit menu to copy the table to another document (or to a different location in the same document). Highlight the text, then select Copy from the Edit menu. The program copies the table to the Clipboard. Position the typing cursor in the new document (or in a new location in the same document). Select Paste from the Edit menu. The program places a copy of the table at the cursor location.

Respacing a Table

24. Highlight the entire table. Select the double-spacing icon (above the typing panel). The program changes the table line spacing.

Saving the Document

25. Save the modified document by selecting Save on the File menu.

8 GeoWrite Operations and Tutorial

Exercise 3

In this exercise you will practice changing margins of an existing paragraph to create:

- A first-line indent paragraph
- An indented margin paragraph
- A first-line outdent paragraph (handing paragraph).

You can adjust the left and right margins of any paragraph in the text without affecting any other paragraph. The left margin marker looks like a split arrow head. The top portion controls the indent of the first line only; the bottom portion controls the left margin of the paragraph. Depending on the relative positions of the indent and margin markers, you can create a paragraph with no indents, a first line indent, or a first line outdent (hanging paragraph), as shown in Figure 8-13.

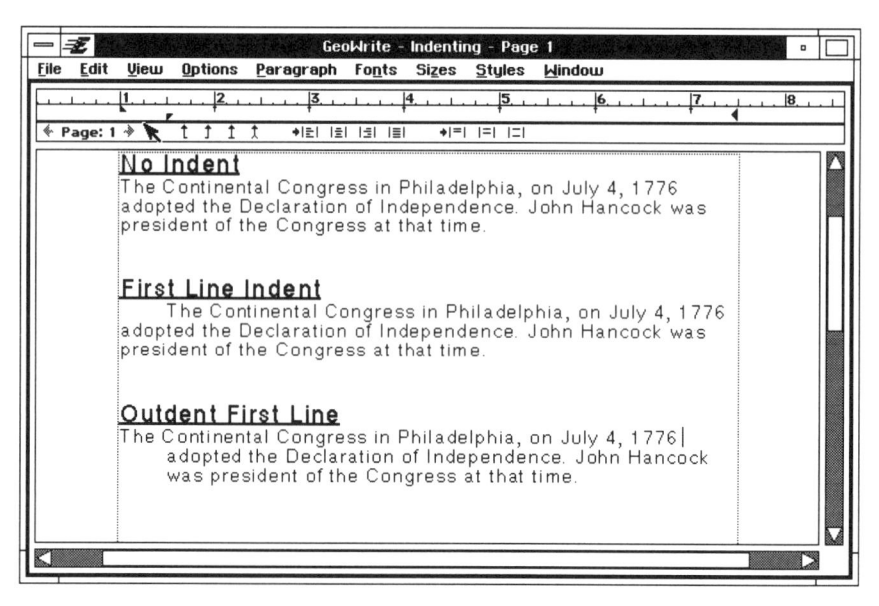

Figure 8-13 — Paragraph Indent and Left Margin Options.

170

GeoWrite Operations and Tutorial 8

1. Scroll to the top of page 1.

2. Position the text cursor anywhere in the paragraph that begins: The Continental Congress in Philadelphia....

The paragraph in which your cursor is located currently has no first-line indent or outdent.

Creating a First-line Indent Paragraph

3. Drag the indent marker (the top portion of the split arrow head) to the right of the margin indent marker along the ruler line. The first line of text moves right to the indent marker position.

Creating an Indented Paragraph

4. Drag the left margin marker (the bottom of the split arrow head) to the right so it aligns with the first line indent marker. The paragraph text displays with a new indented left margin but without a first-line indent.

Creating a First-line Outdent Paragraph

5. Drag the indent marker to the left of the margin marker along the ruler line. The first line of text moves to the left to the new indent marker position.

Saving the Document

6. Save the modified document by selecting Save on the File menu.

Summary

In this tutorial chapter you practiced creating a document with a header, inserting a GeoDraw graphic image in the GeoWrite document, creating and formatting a table, entering table text, drawing a border around the table, copying and respacing the table, and changing the first-line indent and paragraph margin markers.

Chapter 9

The GeoDraw Application

In this chapter you will learn how to use the GeoDraw application, a drawing program that allows you to create graphic images, import graphic images from other graphic programs, and display graphics with text. This chapter discusses most of the options in the eight pull-down menus on the Menu bar:

- File menu
- Edit menu
- View menu
- Options menu
- Modify menu
- Arrange menu
- Text menu
- Window menu.

9 The GeoDraw Application

You will be referred to earlier chapters in the book for discussions about some menu options. You might want to review the Chapter 3 section called, "A Typical Professional Workspace Window" that discusses the elements of the GeoDraw window.

Accessing the GeoDraw Application

Start the GeoWorks Ensemble program in the usual way. Select the Professional Workspace icon from the GeoWorks Ensemble Welcome screen. If the GeoManager Information Line does not read \GEOMANAGER\WORLD, click the World button at the bottom of the GeoManager window. Double-click on the GeoDraw icon. The program displays the GeoDraw main screen, as shown in Figure 3-1 (Chapter 3).

File Menu

The GeoDraw File menu shown in Figure 9-1 is identical to the GeoWrite File menu discussed in Chapter 7 with one exception: GeoDraw has an Import option instead of the GeoWrite Insert as Text option.

Figure 9-1 — The GeoDraw File Menu.

Import...

Use this menu option to import an image saved in two other formats:

- TIFF format files which have a .TIF extension (one of the most universally acceptable bit-mapped file formats)
- PC Paintbrush files which have a .PCX extension.

The GeoDraw Application 9

GeoDraw treats an imported image as an object which you can work with as you would any other object.

Follow these steps to import a file:

1. Select Import from the File menu. The program displays the Select file to import dialog box, as shown in Figure 9-2.

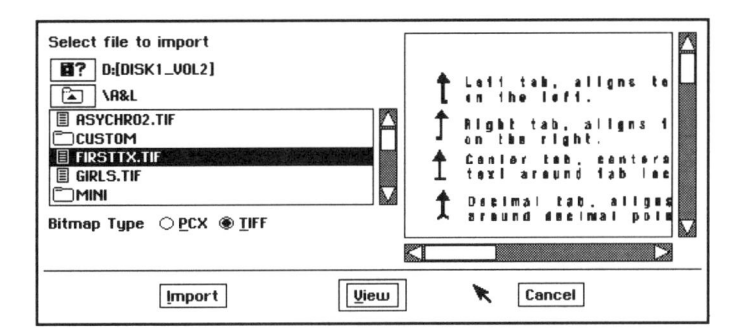

Figure 9-2 — The Select File to Import Dialog Box.

2. If the image you want to import is not in the current subdirectory, double click on the name of the subdirectory that contains the image file. (See Chapter 3, Creating and Saving Documents (Files) section for a discussion about moving around subdirectories and selecting files.)

3. Select the file you want to import from the list in the left panel of the dialog box. In Figure 9-2, the FIRSTTX.TIF file in the A&L subdirectory on the D: drive is the selected file.

4. Click the View button to preview the selected image before importing it. Use the scroll bars to scroll the image in the right panel of the dialog box.

5. Click the Import button when you are satisfied that the correct file is selected. The program closes the dialog box and copies the image into the document window.

Note: Large images may take several minutes to import.

6. Repeat the process for each image you want to import.

175

9 The GeoDraw Application

Click the Cancel button to close the Select file to import dialog box without importing a file.

Edit Menu

You use the Edit menu in all GeoWorks Ensemble applications to copy graphics or text from one document to another, or from one section of a document to another section of the same document. In GeoDraw, the Edit menu also includes options for manipulating graphic images — combining two or more images into a single object (fuse) and separating combined objects (defuse).

Figure 9-3 shows an Edit menu pinned in the lower left of the window with multiple objects selected.

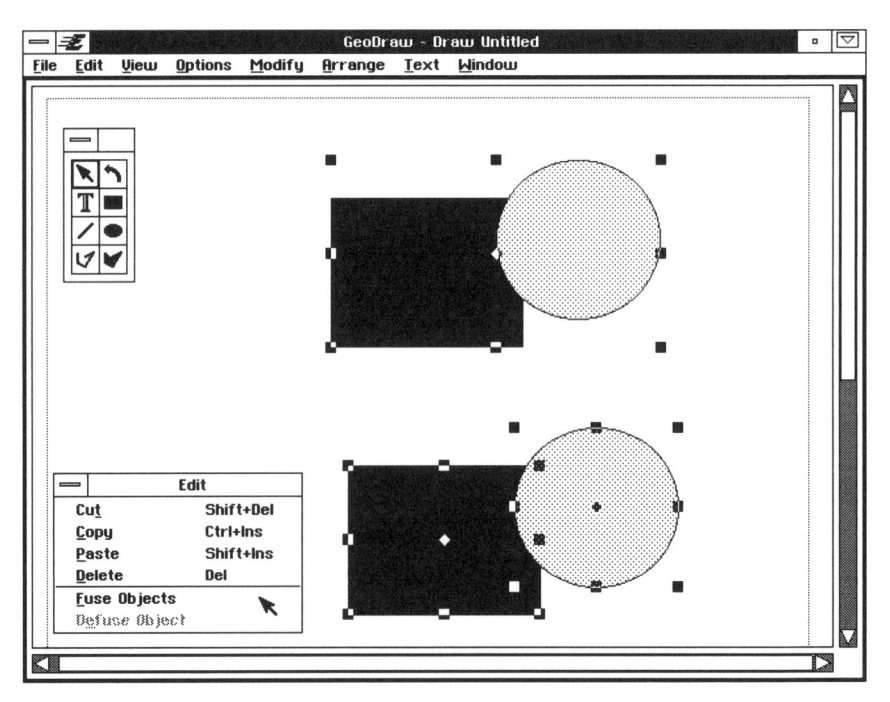

Figure 9-3 — The Edit Menu and Selected Objects.

See the Edit Menu section in Chapter 7 for a discussion about the Pin, Cut, Copy, Paste and Delete Edit menu options.

176

The GeoDraw Application 9

You can manipulate GeoDraw images in a variety of ways: rotate, flip, stretch, shrink, etc. When you select a graphic image by clicking on any portion of it, the program displays handles around the entire object — small squares around the margins and a diamond in the middle. Use the object handles to move the image (middle handle) or manipulate its shape (margin handles) by pressing the mouse arrow on a handle and dragging. You must select an object before you can apply a menu function to the image.

Note: To select an object, be certain that either the Arrow Tool ▣ or the Rotation Tool ▣ is selected from the Tool Box. It is easy to forget to change pointers and find you are drawing in the window instead of selecting an object.

Fuse Objects

To combine two or more separate objects into a group object, select the objects (see below), then select Fuse from the Edit menu. Fused objects lose their individual status and cannot be selected separately. When you position the mouse cursor over any portion of the group object and then click, the entire group is selected as a single object.

Selecting objects by dragging

You can select an object — or multiple objects — by using a selection box. As you look at the GeoDraw window, imagine a rectangle large enough to cover the objects you want to select. Position the arrow pointer or rotation pointer at a corner of the imaginary rectangle.

Click and hold the mouse button while dragging diagonally to the opposite corner of the imaginary rectangle. As you drag, a dotted selection box circumscribes the dimensions you set by the starting drag point and the ending drag point. When the dotted selection box surrounds all the objects you want to select, release the button. The program displays object handles for each of the selected objects. If you miss an object, you can repeat the process, or use the [Ctrl] method described next to add the item.

9 The GeoDraw Application

Selecting objects using [Ctrl]

When you click on an object with the arrow pointer or rotation pointer, the object is selected. If you then position the arrow over another object and click, the second object becomes selected and the first object becomes deselected. To select more than one object at once, hold down [Ctrl] while clicking the mouse button. When you release [Ctrl], the object is added to the selection group. Repeat for each object you want to include. See Figure 9-3 for an example of multiple selected items.

Defuse Object

A group object is comprised of two or more fused objects. Fused objects can be defused — separated and returned to their individual status. To defuse a group, select it, then select Defuse Object from the Edit menu. The defused objects can again be selected and manipulated individually.

View Menu

The View menu allows you to change the size of the displayed image. Use increased magnification to align objects accurately; use reduced magnification to see more of the document and its layout. You can change the display size from 12.5% of actual size to 400% of actual size. Figure 9-4 shows the GeoDraw View menu.

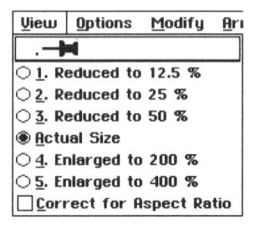

Figure 9-4 — The View Menu.

To select a View menu item, click on the item or press the item number. For example, press [5] to enlarge the display to 400%.

The GeoDraw Application 9

Correct for Aspect Ratio

See the View Menu, Correct for Aspect Ratio section in Chapter 7 for a discussion about this option.

Options Menu

Use the Options menu shown in Figure 9-5 to change the page size, select dragging options (by outline or by rectangle), and displays the Tool Box if you've closed it using the Control button in the Tool Box window.

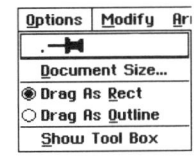

Figure 9-5 — The Options Menu.

Document Size

Select this option to change the size and shape of the drawing area. When you open a new document, the document size is set automatically to 8-1/2" x 11", portrait orientation. To change this setting, choose Document Size from the Options menu. The program displays the Document Size dialog box as shown in Figure 9-6.

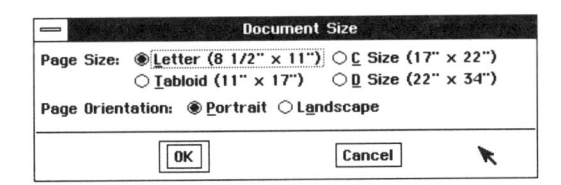

Figure 9-6 — The Document Size Dialog Box.

Click on one of the four page size options. Then select the desired orientation (portrait or landscape). Click the OK button to accept the settings. Click the Cancel button to close the dialog box without making a selection.

Note: Portrait orientation sets the long dimension of the page vertically. Landscape orientation sets the long dimension of the page horizontally.

Drag As Rect

When dragging one or more selected objects with Drag As Rect turned on, a dotted rectangle moves with the pointer showing the new location of the objects. Release the mouse button to anchor the objects in the new location. The Drag as Rect command allows you to drag objects more quickly than the Drag As Outline command.

Dragging with left mouse button

Click and hold the left mouse button on the center handle of one of the selected objects. Release the mouse button to anchor the selected objects in the new location.

Dragging with right mouse button

Click and hold the right mouse button over any portion of one of the selected objects (it does not have to be over a center handle). Release the mouse button to anchor the selected objects in the new location.

Drag As Outline

When dragging one or more selected objects with Drag As Outline turned on, a dotted outline moves with the pointer showing the new location of the objects. Release the mouse button to anchor the objects in the new location. The Drag As Outline command operates more slowly than the Drag As Rect command. Figure 9-10, in the Area Properties section later in this chapter, shows a circle being dragged as an outline to change its shape.

Show Tool Box

You might want to view your drawing without the Tool Box obscuring part of the image. To close the Tool Box, click on the Control button, then select Close. To display the Tool Box again, select Show Tool Box from the Options menu.

The GeoDraw Application **9**

Modify Menu

You can change the way objects are positioned and displayed in the window using the Modify menu. Figure 9-7 shows a pinned Modify menu with the Nudge command cascade menu displayed.

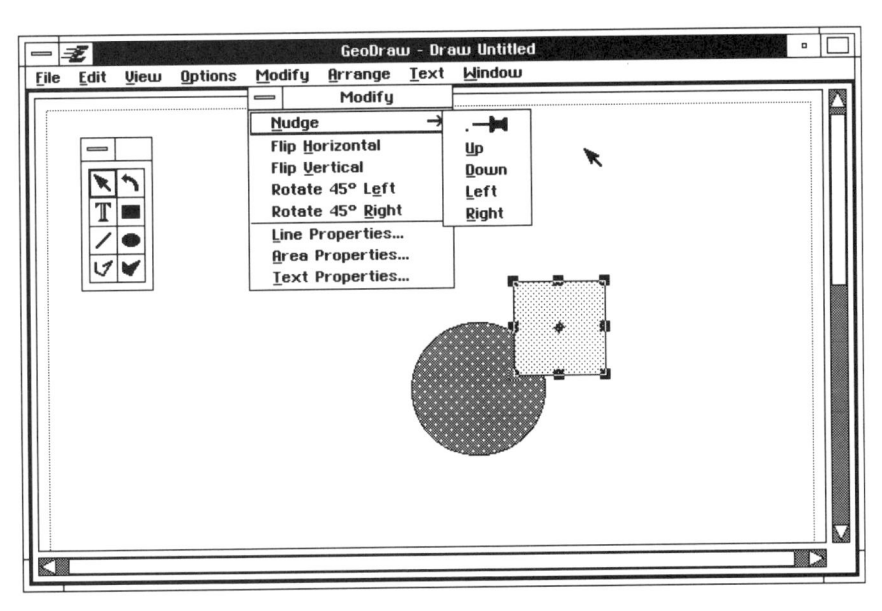

Figure 9-7 — A Pinned Modify Menu with the Nudge Cascade Menu Displayed.

Nudge

Use this option for precise object positioning — moving the object one pixel at a time. (A pixel is the smallest dot that can be displayed on your screen.) The Nudge cascade menu offers four directions in which you can nudge the selected object: Up, Down, Right, and Left.

It is a good idea to pin the Nudge cascade menu because positioning an object frequently requires more than one nudge.

Flip Horizontal

Use this option to flip a selected object horizontally — spin the object 180° around the vertical axis. Figure 9-8 shows two identical objects with the top object flipped horizontally and rotated (see Rotate 45° Left menu item discussed later in this chapter).

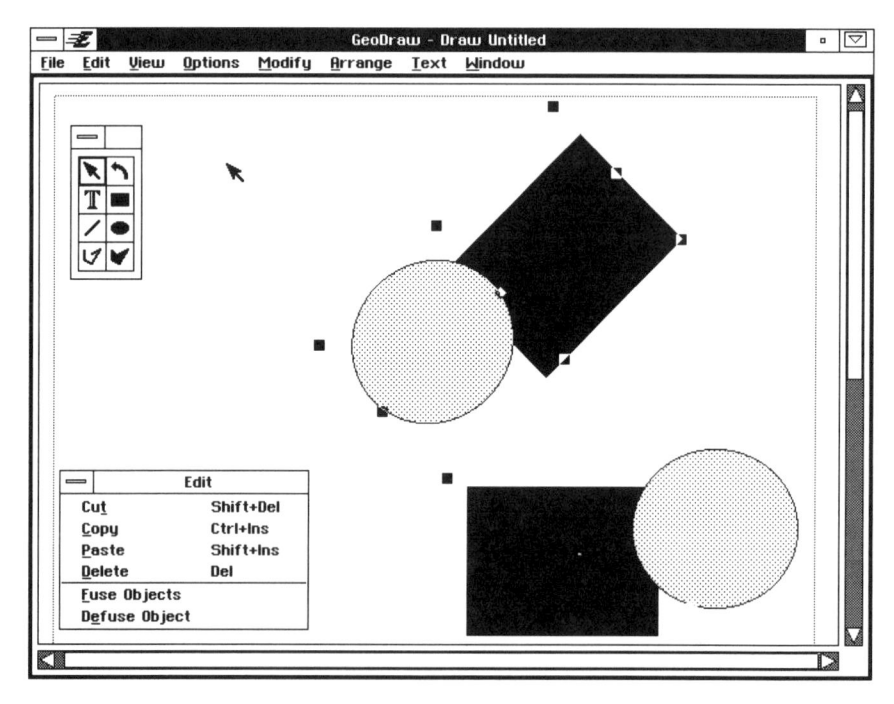

Figure 9-8 — An Object Flipped and Rotated 45°.

To edit text that has been flipped horizontally, you must flip it back to its original position, edit it, then flip it again.

Flip Vertical

Use this option to flip a selected object vertically — spin the object 180° around the horizontal axis.

To edit text that has been flipped vertically, you must flip it back to its original position, edit it, then flip it again.

Rotate 45° Left

Use this option to rotate selected objects 45° counterclockwise. Figure 9-8 shows two identical objects with the top object flipped horizontally and rotated.

Note: Circles, ovals and images imported from another application cannot be rotated.

To edit text that has been rotated, you must rotate it back to its original position, edit it, then rotate it again.

Rotate to any degree

To rotate an object more or less than 45°, select the rotate pointer from the Tool Box. Select the objects you want to rotate. Position the rotation pointer over a corner handle. Click and hold the mouse button while dragging the corner — clockwise or counterclockwise — to rotate the objects to the desired position. Release the button to anchor the objects in the new position.

Rotate 45° Right

Use this option to rotate selected objects 45° clockwise.

Note: Circles, ovals and images imported from another application cannot be rotated.

To edit text that has been rotated, you must rotate it back to its original position, edit it, then rotate it again.

To rotate more or less than 45°, see Rotate to any degree section above.

9 The GeoDraw Application

Line Properties...

Use this option to change the width, style, pattern, and color of the lines that outline selected objects. When you select Line Properties, the program displays the Line Properties dialog box shown in Figure 9-9.

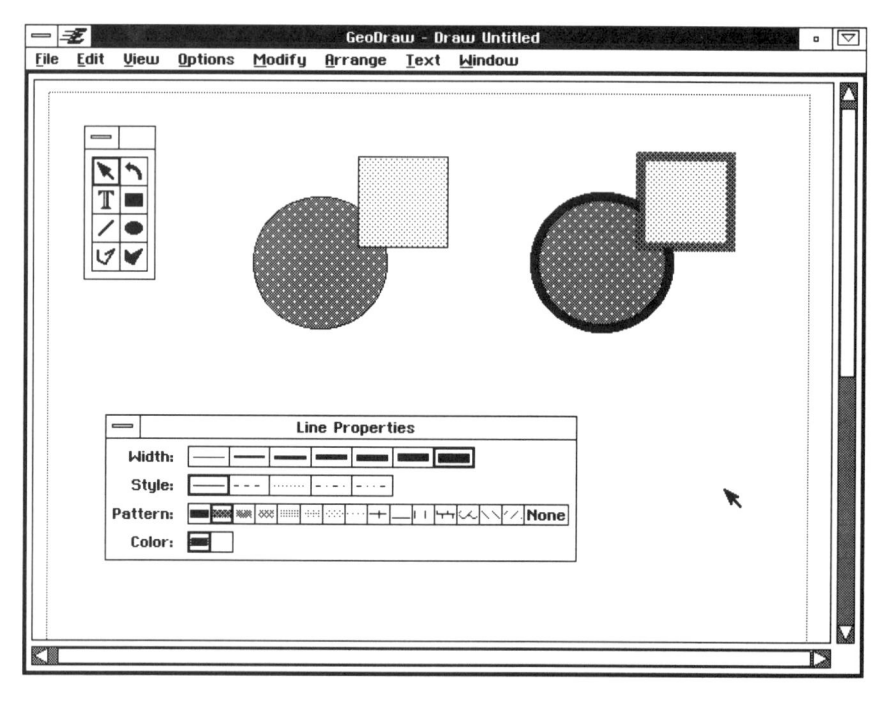

Figure 9-9 — The Line Properties Dialog Box.

Line width

To change a selected object's line width, click on the desired width in the Line Properties cascade menu. In Figure 9-9 the righthand object was originally copied from the lefthand object, so they were identical. Then the righthand object was selected and its line width changed to display thicker lines.

Line style

To change a selected object's line style, click on the desired style in the Line Properties cascade menu. (See Figure 9-9.)

Line pattern

To change a selected object's line pattern, click on the desired pattern in the Line Properties cascade menu. (See Figure 9-9.)

Color

To change a selected object's line color (from black to white or from white to black), click on the desired color in the Line Properties cascade menu. (See Figure 9-9.)

Double-click on the Control button to close the Line Properties dialog box.

Area Properties

Use this option to change the pattern, color, and see-through characteristics of the interior of selected objects. When you select Area Properties, the program displays the Area Properties dialog box shown in Figure 9-10.

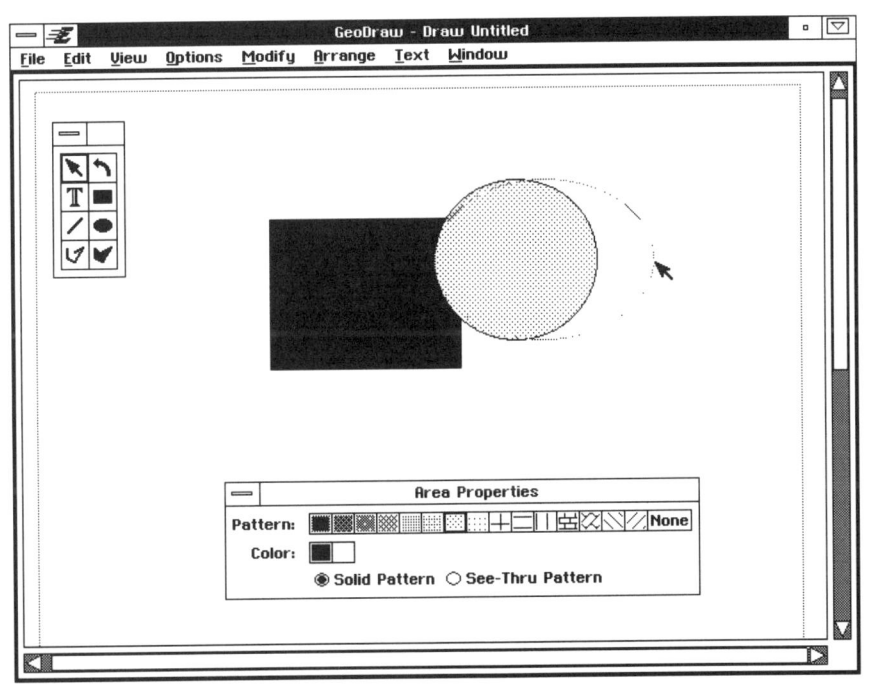

Figure 9-10 — The Area Properties Dialog Box.

9 The GeoDraw Application

Pattern

You can choose one of sixteen patterns to display in an object. First select the object, then click on the pattern you want in the Area Properties dialog box.

Color

You can choose to display an object's area in black or white. First select the object, then click on the color you want in the Area Properties dialog box.

Note: If you do not select an object before you select a pattern or color, the pattern or color will apply to the next object you draw. The object must be a closed object before you can fill it with a pattern. For example, the Square, Circle and Polygon Tools in the Tool Box create objects that can be filled.

Solid/See-Through Pattern

Use this menu option to display a selected object as solid — obscuring any objects behind it, or as transparent — displaying any objects behind it.

Text Properties

Use this option to change the properties of text in a GeoDraw window. You can change the text color and set a solid, dark, medium, or light halftone for the selected text.

- Solid displays all pixels in the text
- Dark displays 75% of the pixels
- Medium displays 25% of the pixels
- Light displays 15% of the pixels.

Figure 9-11 shows text displayed with various halftone settings.

The GeoDraw Application 9

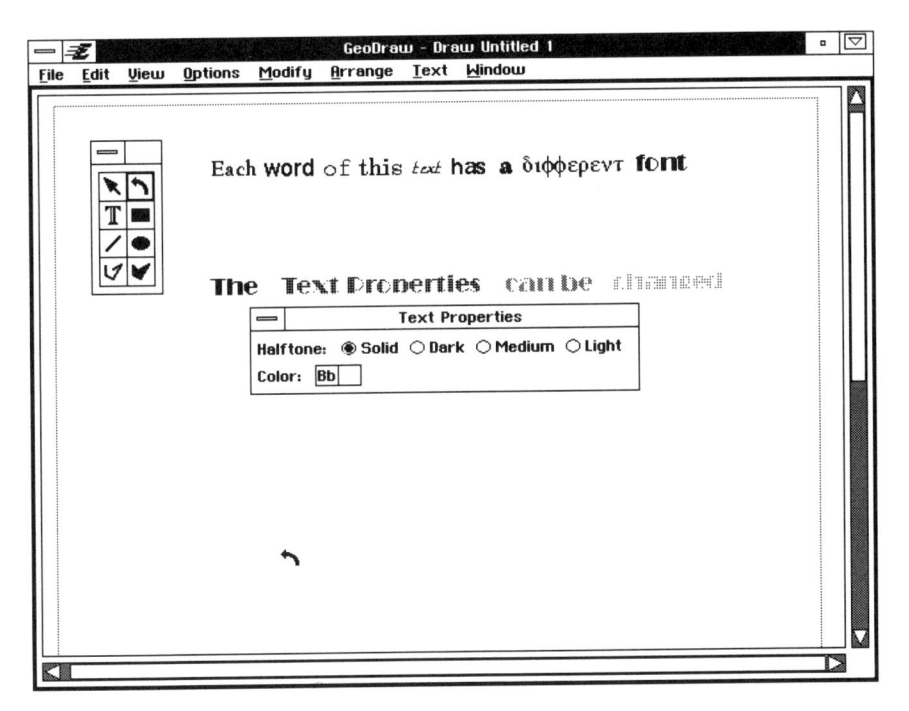

Figure 9-11 — The Text Properties Dialog Box.

To create Figure 9-11, four lines of text with one or two words each were written with different text properties, then the lines were arranged into the single line shown in the Figure.

9 The GeoDraw Application

Arrange Menu

Use this menu to change the display order of overlapping objects, moving them front to back or back to front. You can display multiple levels of overlapping objects. Figure 9-12 shows a pinned Arrange menu.

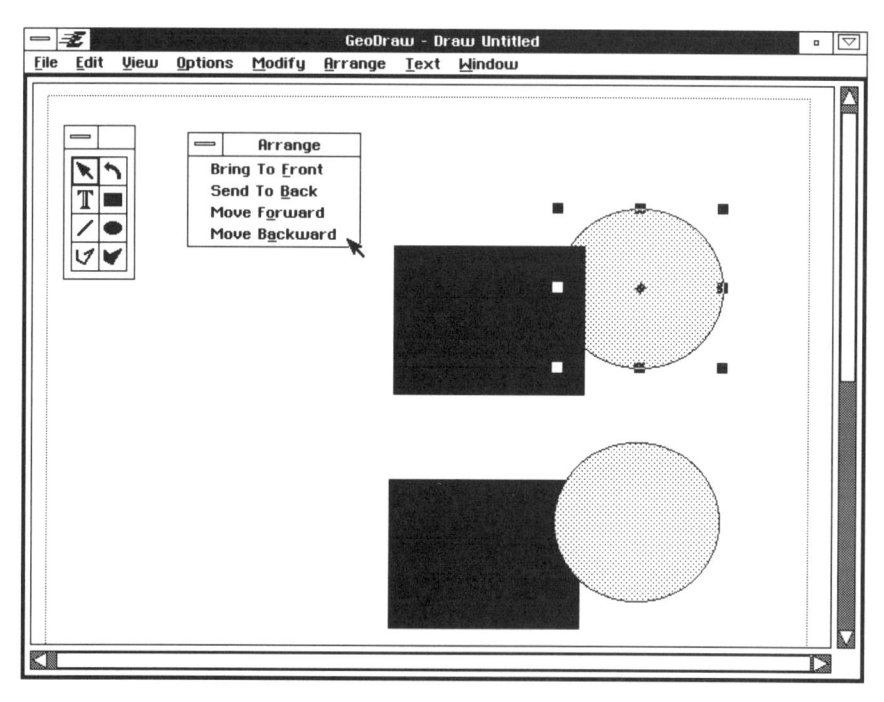

Figure 9-12 — A Pinned Arrange Menu.

Bring To Front

When you select an object at any level in an overlapping display and then select Bring to Front on the Arrange menu, the selected object becomes the top object.

To rearrange overlapping objects in a fused group, defuse the group, then rearrange the individual objects.

Send To Back

When you select an object at any level in an overlapping display and then select Send to Back on the Arrange menu, the selected object becomes the bottom object.

Move Forward

Use this option to move a selected object one level up from its current position. For example, assume you have three overlapping objects. You select the bottom object, then select Move Forward on the Arrange menu. The selected object moves one level higher, becoming the middle object.

Move Backward

Use this option to move a selected object one level down from its current position. For example, assume you have three overlapping objects. You select the top object, then select Move Backward on the Arrange menu. The selected object moves one level lower, becoming the middle object.

Figure 9-12 originally had two identical objects (the top object was a copy of the bottom object). The selected object on the top is shown after the Move Backward command on the Arrange Menu was issued.

Text Menu

You can use the Text menu to change the font, size, style, and justification of GeoDraw text. (Use the Edit menu to copy, cut and paste text.) Figure 9-13 shows the Text menu.

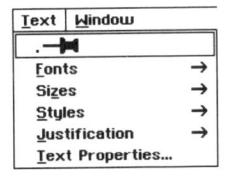

Figure 9-13 — The Text Menu.

See the Edit Menu section in Chapter 7 for a discussion about the Pin, Fonts, Sizes and Styles options on the Text menu.

9 The GeoDraw Application

Justification

Use this option to set Right, Left, Center, or Full justification for selected text. Figure 9-14 illustrates the four justification settings. A pinned Justification menu is shown on the right.

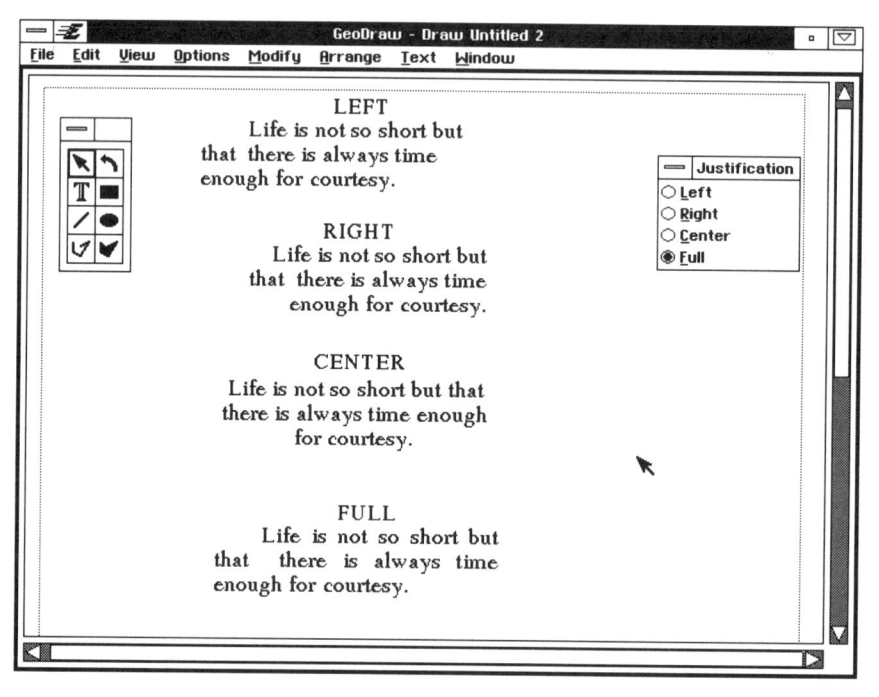

Figure 9-14 — Justified Text.

To change the justification of text, select the text you want affected by the new justification. Then select a justification option from the Justification cascade menu. You can pin the Justification cascade menu for repeated selections.

The following paragraphs describe the four justification options.

Left

Use this option to align text along the left margin with a ragged right margin.

Right

Use this option to align text along the right margin with a ragged left margin.

Center

Use this option to center text lines, regardless of line length, between the left and right margins.

Full

Use this option to add space between words to justify text along both the left and right margins.

Text Properties

See the Modify Menu, Text Properties section earlier in ths chapter for a discussion about this option.

Window Menu

GeoDraw is one of the GeoWorks Ensemble applications that allows you to open more than one document at a time. As you open documents using the Open command on the File menu, the default setting is for the new document to fill the entire GeoDraw window, covering previous documents.

Use the Window menu, as shown in Figure 9-15, to switch between full and overlapping display.

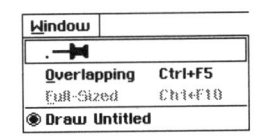

Figure 9-15 — The Window Menu.

9 The GeoDraw Application

Overlapping (Ctrl+F5)

Use this option to display open documents as overlapping windows. When overlapping, all window Title Bars are visible and selectable so you can move, resize, and activate any window.

See the section called A Typical Professional Workspace Window section in Chapter 3 for a review of window functions.

Full-Sized (Ctrl+F10)

Selecting this option achieves the same result as clicking the Maximize/Restore button to maximize a document display.

Page Listing and Page Selection

At the bottom of the Window menu is a list of currently-open documents. When you select an open document from the Window menu, it becomes the active document. In overlapping display, the program places the selected document on top of other open windows. In full-sized display, the selected document fills the document area, covering any other open documents.

Tool Box

To select a Tool Box item, position the cursor over the desired tool icon, then click the left mouse button. The program highlights the selected icon. A selected tool remains selected until you specifically choose another icon, allowing you to use the same tool repeatedly.

Any objects you create using the Tool Box can be manipulated and modified using the GeoDraw menu options described earlier.

The appearance of the GeoDraw cursor changes depending on the tool you select.

- Arrow Pointer Cursor ⬉   The Arrow Pointer is the default cursor when you enter GeoDraw. Use it to select objects.
- Crosshairs Cursor +   When you use a drawing tool, the cursor changes to crosshairs over the drawing area. The intersection of the crosshairs indicates where the shape will begin when you start to draw.
- I-beam Cursor ⌶   When you select the Text Tool, the cursor changes to an I-beam cursor over the drawing area. Click the mouse to position the I-beam where you want to begin typing.
- Rotate Pointer Cursor ↶   When you select the Rotate Tool, the cursor changes to a curved arrow. The Rotate Pointer is similar to the Arrow Pointer, except that it can also rotate objects.

Arrow Pointer Tool ⬉

When you enter GeoDraw, the arrow pointer is selected automatically. Use this tool to select items you want to manipulate.

Text Tool T

Select the Text Tool to enter text into a GeoDraw document. The text you type becomes an object that can be moved, reshaped, rotated, and flipped just as you can any other object. It can also be edited, cut, copied, and pasted.

Creating a text object

Before you begin typing, you can create a text object to define the margins of the text. Position the text cursor where you want to place the first character. Single-click to produce a text object three inches wide (the default width).

9 The GeoDraw Application

To create a wider object for longer text lines, position the I-beam cursor at the desired left margin. Then drag the I-beam cursor to the desired right margin. Release the mouse button.

Note: If the page is wider than the window, continue dragging when you reach the right edge of the window. The page will scroll, allowing you to set the right text margin to the right of the original window display.

As you enter text in the text object, it will wrap automatically at the right margin (just as text wraps in GeoWrite). Press `Enter` only when you want to start a new paragraph or to insert blank lines. As you type, text displays in the currently-selected font, size, style and justification settings.

Text Tool editing

You can select a text object for editing in two ways: dragging and clicking.

To use the dragging method, select the Text Tool from the Tool Box. Position the text cursor to the left of the text you want to edit. Drag the text cursor to highlight the text you want to select.

To use the clicking method, select the Text Tool from the Tool Box. Position the mouse cursor to the left of the first character you want to select. Click the mouse to anchor the text cursor. Position the mouse cursor at the end of the block of text you want to edit. Press and hold `Shift`, then click the mouse button. Release `Shift`. The program highlights the text between the first and second mouse clicks. To change the selected range of text while it is still highlighted, press `Shift` and click the mouse button where you want to reset the end of the selected text. Release `Shift`. The program adjusts the highlighted text to the new range.

Note: To edit more than one text object at a time, press and hold `Ctrl` as you click and drag the cursor over the other items you want to select. To remove an item from the highlighted group, press and hold `Ctrl`, then click again on the item you want to remove from the group. Release `Ctrl`. The program removes the item from the group.

See the following sections in Chapter 6 for more on typing text, selecting text, and editing with keyboard commands:

- Typing Mode
- Selecting and Editing Text With the Mouse
- Keyboard Editing and Typing Cursor Movement.

Line Tool ◰

Select this option to draw a straight line in any direction. When Line Tool is the active option in the Tool Box, the cursor changes to crosshairs. Position the cursor where you want the line to begin, then press and hold the mouse button while dragging the crosshairs to the point at which you want to end the line. When you release the mouse button, the program displays the line with object handles.

Line handles

You can use the three line objects handles (one at each end of the line and one in the center) to move or modify the line.

To move a line, select the Pointer Tool, then position the cursor over the center handle. Press and drag the mouse button to move the line to another location. Release the mouse button to anchor the line in the new location.

To change line length, select the Pointer Tool, then position the cursor over one of the end handles. Click and hold the mouse button while dragging the end point to its new location. Release the mouse button to anchor the line.

To select a line object, double-click the Pointer cursor over the line to select it, displaying the handles. Click the Pointer cursor over the line again to deselect it, removing the handles.

9 The GeoDraw Application

Connect Line Tool ☑

You can use the Connect Line Tool in much the same way as the Line Tool. Select the Connect Line Tool, then position the crosshairs cursor where you want the connected lines to begin. Click the left mouse button to anchor the starting point. Move the crosshairs to the point at which the first line segment will end and the second segment will begin. Click to anchor the junction point. Reposition the crosshairs and click to anchor successive junctions. Double-click on the last point, or press [esc], or press the right mouse button to end the line. When you end the line, the program displays line object handles.

Connected line handles

You can use the handles to move the connected segments as a unit, or to stretch or shrink the object.

To move a connected line, select the Pointer Tool, then position the cursor over the center handle. Press and drag the mouse button to move the connected line object to another location. Release the mouse button to anchor the object in the new location.

To stretch or shrink a connected line object, select the Pointer Tool, then position the cursor over one of the margin handles. Click and hold the mouse button while dragging the handle. Release the mouse button to anchor the object. Dragging a top or bottom handle stretches (or shrinks) the object vertically. Dragging a left or right handle stretches (or shrinks) the object horizontally. Dragging a corner handle stretches (or shrinks) the object both vertically and horizontally.

To select a line object, double-click the Pointer cursor over the line to select it, displaying the handles. Click the Pointer cursor to deselect a line, removing the handles.

Rotate Pointer ↖

You can use the Rotate Pointer to move an object (as you can with the Arrow Pointer). You can also use the Rotate Pointer to rotate an object clockwise or counterclockwise. When you select the Rotate Tool, the cursor becomes a curved arrow.

Rectangle Tool ▪

You can draw a rectangle of any size with the Rectangle Tool. Position the crosshairs where you want one corner of the rectangle. Drag the crosshairs diagonally in any direction. As you drag, the program displays an outline of the rectangle. Release the mouse button to anchor the rectangle and display the object handles.

See the Connect Line Handles section for a discussion about moving and stretching an object.

Circle Tool ●

You can draw a circle of any size with the Circle Tool. Position the crosshairs where you want to begin the circle. Drag the crosshairs in any direction to create the circle. As you drag, the program displays an outline of the circle (or oval). The outline may be a circle or a rectangle, depending on which option is active in the Options menu: Drag as Rectangle or Drag as Outline. Release the mouse button to anchor the circle and display the object handles.

See the Connect Line Handles section for a discussion about moving and stretching an object.

Polygon Tool ✔

You can draw a polygon of any size using the Polygon Tool. Select the Polygon Tool, then position the crosshairs cursor where you want to begin the first line. Click the left mouse button to anchor the starting point. Move the crosshairs to the point at which the first line segment will end and the second segment will begin. Click to anchor the junction point. Reposition the crosshairs and click to anchor successive junctions. When you double-click on the last point to finish the polygon, the program draws a line between the last point and the first point, closing the polygon. The program displays object handles.

See the Connect Line Handles section for a discussion about moving and stretching an object.

9 The GeoDraw Application

Summary

In this chapter you learned how to use the GeoDraw application to create graphic images, import graphic images from other graphic programs, and display and edit text. This chapter discussed most of the options in the eight pull-down menus on the GeoDraw Menu bar.

Chapter 10

The GeoPlanner Application

The GeoPlanner application combines a calendar and an appointment book in one handy program. While it is similar to the Planner in the Appliances section, you will find that it is more powerful and flexible. With GeoPlanner you can:

- Schedule events for any time of day
- Quickly switch to any date (day, month, or year) to view or schedule events
- Set alarms to notify you of upcoming events
- Schedule repeating events
- Search for a string of text (for example, if you don't remember when an event is scheduled, but you do remember what the event)
- Copy or move text within GeoPlanner or to other applications
- Link with GeoDex to access the card file.

10 The GeoPlanner Application

Using GeoPlanner

As with any GeoWorks Ensemble application, you can access GeoPlanner in several ways:

- By double-clicking on its icon in the GeoManager window
- By choosing Startup from the Express menu and then selecting GeoPlanner from the cascade menu
- By clicking the DOCUMENT directory on the GeoManager screen, then clicking a GeoPlanner document icon.

When you open GeoPlanner, the program displays a window similar to the one in Figure 10-1.

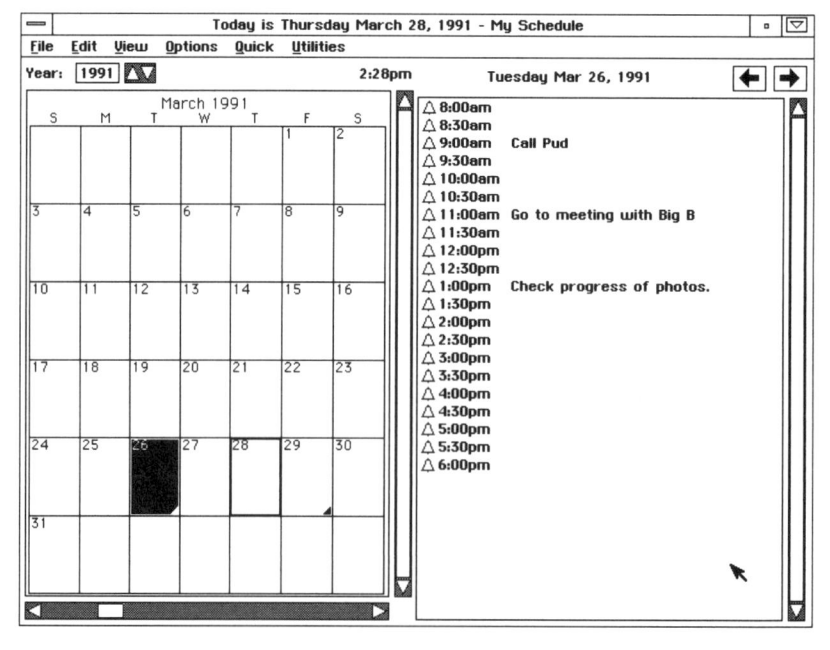

Figure 10-1 — The GeoPlanner Window.

The program displays the current day, current date, and the document name in the top line of the window. In Figure 10-1, the day is Thursday, March 28, 1991. The open GeoPlanner document is titled My Schedule. The displayed title of an open, unnamed document is Unnamed Schedule.

The standard GeoWorks menu bar is displayed on the second line of the window.

The third line of the GeoPlanner window displays the selected year on the left, the current time in the middle, and the selected day and date on the right.

Selected Year

The year box displays the currently-selected year. Every click on the small up arrow advances one year; every click on the small down arrow moves back one year. In Figure 10-1, the calendar displays March for 1991. If you click on the year box up arrow, the calendar display will change to March for 1992.

Current Time

The program displays the current time as set in your computer. If the displayed time is incorrect, you can reset the computer clock using the Preferences application. (See Chapter 5, Date & Time section.)

Selected Day and Date

The program displays the day of the week and the date of the highlighted calendar day. In Figure 10-1, March 26 is highlighted (shown in black). You can select a different day in two ways:

- Click on a day in the calendar. The highlight moves to the new day and the selected day and date display changes.
- Scroll through dates by clicking on the Previous Day arrow and the Next Day)arrow at the far right of the third line.

Calendar

The large panel on the left displays a one-month calendar. When you first start GeoPlanner, the calendar displays the current month for the current year. The current day is heavily outlined on the calendar. In Figure 10-1, the current date is March 28; the corresponding day in the calendar is outlined. To select another day on the calendar, click on the day box. The highlight moves to the selected day.

A small triangle in the lower right corner of a day box indicates one or more scheduled events for that day.

At the bottom and to the right of the calendar are scroll bars. Use the scroll bars to scroll through the months.

Schedule of Events

The large panel on the right displays a list of times and any scheduled events. The default list of times is from 8:00am to 6:00pm, incremented every half hour. When you enter an event into the list, you can accept a default time setting, or specify your own (for example, 10:50am or 8:45pm). Use the vertical scroll bar on the right to scroll through the events list.

Scheduling an Event

Follow these steps to schedule an event:

1. Click on the day in the calendar panel that you want to schedule. The program displays in the right panel the schedule list for that day.

2. Click on — or scroll to — the time (or the nearest time) you want to schedule in the list of events.

3. Select New Event from the Edit menu. The program displays a blank event in the Event window. Type the time you want to schedule for the event (for example, 11:15am or 11:15pm). If you do not want the event to start at any particular time, leave the time area blank.

4. Press [tab]. The cursor moves to the event description area. Type the event description — you can enter more than one line.

Note: If you enter an event out of time sequence, GeoPlanner reorders the display the next time you open the schedule.

Viewing Scheduled Events

To view the events schedule for the previous day, click on the Previous Day arrow above the events window. To view the events schedule for the next day, click on the Next Day arrow.

Viewing Scheduled Events for Several Days

You can view the events for several days at a time. Press and hold the mouse button as you drag the mouse cursor over the days you want to select. The program highlights the selected days and displays the range of dates above the events window. View the events schedules for the range of days by scrolling through the list.

Click on the Next Day arrow or Previous Day arrow above the events window to display additional blocks of days. For example, if you highlight five days in the calendar, clicking the Next Day arrow changes the list of events to the five days following the highlighted days.

The Menu Bar

The Menu Bar, the second line in the window, contains six menus. You can access the menu option by holding down [alt] while pressing the underlined letter in the menu name, or by clicking on the menu name with the left mouse button. You can access the options on the menus by typing the underlined letter in the option name or by clicking the mouse button.

10 The GeoPlanner Application

File Menu

When you select File, the menu provides you with nine options for handling your GeoPlanner documents (see Figure 10-2).

Figure 10-2 — The GeoPlanner File Menu.

See the File Menu section in Chapter 7 for a discussion about the New, Open, Close, Save, Save As, Revert and Exit File menu options.

Page Setup

Use this option to specify how you want to print a schedule or calendar. When you select this option, the program displays the Document Options dialog box shown in Figure 10-3.

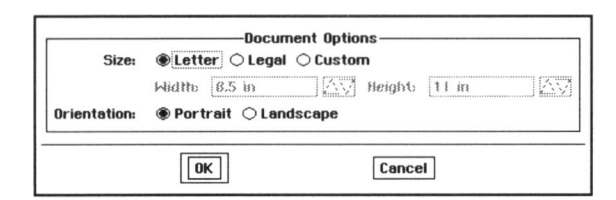

Figure 10-3 — The Document Options Dialog Box.

You can choose the size paper you want: Letter, Legal, or Custom. If you choose custom, the program displays two boxes in which you enter the Width (from 2" to 4-1/4") and Height (from 2" to 3-1/4") of your paper. You can then select whether you want the calendar or events schedule to print Landscape (the long edge of the paper at the top and bottom) or Portrait (the long edge of the paper at the left and right).

The GeoPlanner Application 10

Print

When you are ready to print, select this option to display the dialog box shown in Figure 10-4.

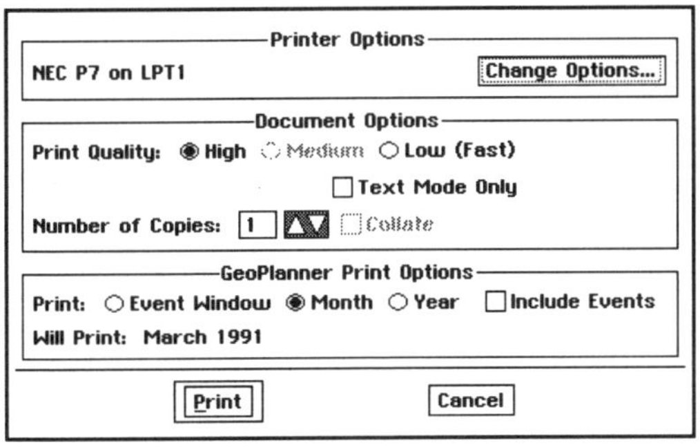

Figure 10-4 — The Printer Options Dialog Box.

The currently-selected printer is listed at the top left of the dialog box.

Click on the Change Options button beside the printer name to:

- Select a different printer, if you have installed more than one printer for GeoWorks Ensemble
- Select a different paper size
- Specify the paper source: tractor feed or manual.

The second panel in the Printer Options dialog box allows you to specify Document Options: which print quality — high, medium, or low (fastest option), whether to print text only, and the number of copies to print. See the File Menu section in Chapter 7 for a discussion about print quality settings.

The third panel in the Printer Options dialog box, the GeoPlanner Print Options panel, allows you specify what to print. You can choose to print:

- The Events window
- A calendar for the selected month(s)
- A calendar for the selected year.

10 The GeoPlanner Application

To include scheduled events when printing a calendar, select the Include Events option. The month to print is selected by clicking on any day box in that month.

When you are satisfied with your selections, click on the Print button to begin printing.

Edit Menu

The Edit menu contains seven options, as shown in Figure 10-5, that allow you to move or copy text, enter new events, delete events, and set alarms.

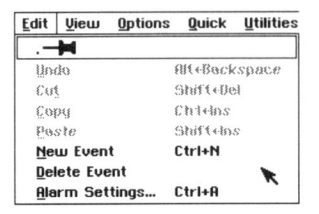

Figure 10-5 — The Edit Menu.

See the Edit Menu section in Chapter 7 for a discussion about the Undo, Cut, Copy and Paste options.

Quick Copy and Quick Move

In addition to the cut and paste or copy and paste operations on the Edit menu, you can use Quick Copy or Quick Move to place text in another application. To use Quick Copy or Quick Move, open another application window (for example, GeoWrite). Select the text you want to copy or move. Position the mouse cursor over the highlighted text. For Quick Copy, press and hold the RIGHT mouse button (the pointer changes to the Quick Copy pointer). For Quick Move, press and hold [alt] then press and hold the RIGHT mouse button (the pointer changes to the Quick Move pointer). Move the pointer to the target location. Release the button. The program copies or moves the selected text.

The program bypasses the Clipboard in a Quick Copy or Quick Move operation. Any text already saved on the Clipboard remains intact.

New Event

You can use this option to insert incremental times into the events list. When you click on New Event, a box containing the new time is inserted with a blinking cursor positioned in the box.

If you did not previously click on a specific time, the inserted time begins with 8:00am (duplicating the 8:00am entry). If you click New Event again, the program inserts a new time halfway between the currently-chosen time and the next time on the list. In this case, the program would insert 8:15am. If you click New Event seven more times, the program inserts these time increments: 8:27, 8:29, 8:30, 8:45, 8:53, 8:57, 8:59 and 9:00am. The 8:30am and 9:00am times duplicate existing times on the list.

You can enter events for any of the new times by pressing [tab] after the time entry to type the event description.

If you click on a time before clicking New Event, the new time is inserted just after the selected time. For example, if you select 1:00pm, the inserted time is 1:15pm (half way between 1:00pm and the next entry 1:30pm).

The shortcut for inserting new times is [Ctrl]-[N].

Delete Event

This option allows you to remove an event from the schedule. When you click on the event to select it, the program draws a box around it. Select Delete Event from the Edit menu. The program deletes the event from the list.

GeoPlanner does not have a shortcut for this operation.

Alarm Settings

Use this option to set an alarm as an event reminder. Click on an event in the events list to select it. The program draws a box around the event. Select Alarm Settings from the Edit menu to display the Event Information dialog box. The dialog box displays the date, time and description of the selected event.

10   The GeoPlanner Application

Setting an alarm

Enter the date and/or time that you want the alarm to go off. Click the Alarm On button to activate the alarm. Click the OK button to close the dialog box. The program fills in the bell next to the event to indicate the alarm is set.

When the alarm goes off, the program displays a dialog box telling you the event and time for which you set the alarm. You can turn off the alarm or set the Snooze option. If you turn off the alarm, the program closes the dialog box. If you select Snooze, the program closes the dialog box temporarily, then sounds the alarm and displays the dialog box again after five minutes.

View Menu

Use the View menu to modify the way GeoPlanner displays the events window and/or the calendar. When you select View, the program displays the menu shown in Figure 10-6.

Figure 10-6 — The View Menu.

The first three options, Calendar Only, Events Only, and Both, are mutually exclusive — you can select only one at a time.

Calendar Only

When you select this option, the program displays only the calendar window, using a full window display. You cannot view or enter events, although the alarm feature still works if you have set the alarm for any events. You can use the scroll bars at the bottom or at the right to view other months. Depending on your setting, you can scroll through one month at a time, or a block of four months at a time.

Events Only

This option displays the events window only. You can add, change or delete events. To change the displayed day, click the Next Day and Previous Day button at the top right of the window.

Both

When you select this option (the program default setting), the calendar and events windows display side by side. You can scroll through the months using the bottom and right scroll bars on the calendar. You can also scroll through the list of events using the scroll bar at the right of the events window.

The next two options in the View menu allow you to choose whether to view the calendar one month at a time or a full year at a time.

Single Month

When you select this option (the program default setting), the calendar displays only one month.

Full Year

This option displays 2 months at a time, or, if Calendar Only is selected, 4 months at a time. Scroll through the months using the scroll bars at the bottom and right of the calendar.

Options Menu

Select this option to change the way GeoPlanner displays, vary the start and end times in the events list, and set how far in advance the alarm should go off before an event's scheduled time.

10 The GeoPlanner Application

Change Preferences

When you select this option, the program displays the Change Preferences dialog box shown in Figure 10-7.

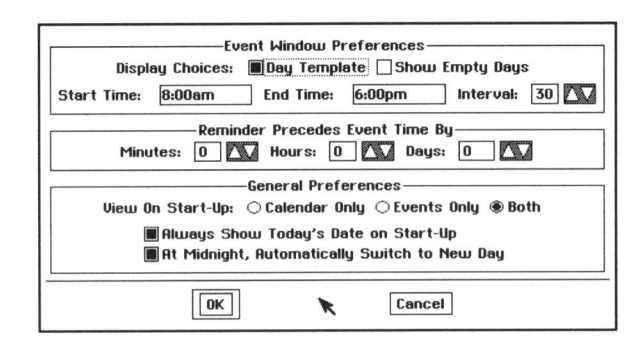

Figure 10-7 — The Change Preferences Dialog Box.

Day Template

When you activate this option, the events window shows the entire day in small (usually half-hour) time increments (the default setting), whether or not an event is scheduled for that day. If Day Template is Off, the program displays only scheduled events.

Show Empty Days

When Show Empty Days is active (the default setting) and you select a range of days on the calendar to display in the Events window, the program displays all days, whether or not events are scheduled. When Show Empty Days is off, the Events window displays only days with scheduled events when you select a range of days on the calendar.

Start Time

Enter in the Start Time box the time of day to begin the events list. The default is 8:00am.

End Time

Enter in the End Time box the time of day to end the events list. The default is 6:00pm.

Interval

You can click on the up and down arrows to change the interval between times in the events list. The default is 30 minutes.

Reminder Precedes Event Time By

You can use this option to set a buffer time between when the alarm goes off and the event's scheduled time. Click on the up or down triangles to set the minutes, hours and days options for the buffer. The default settings are 0, which means that the alarm goes off at the time the event is scheduled. The new settings become the program default.

Note: You can use the Alarm Settings option on the Edit menu to set the alarm buffer for a specific event, overriding the program default for that event.

Set options in the General Preferences section to determine how the GeoPlanner displays when you start the program.

View On Startup

You can select one of three options for the initial display: Calendar Only, Events Only, or Both. See the View Menu section in this chapter for a discussion about these display options.

Always Show Today's Date on Startup

When you turn on this option, the current day's date is always shown. When you turn it off, the date is not shown.

At Midnight, Automatically Switch to New Day

When you turn on this option, the program switches the next day's date at midnight. When you turn off this option, the program will not switch automatically to the next day's date.

When you are satisfied with your selections in the Change Preferences dialog box, click on OK to activate the settings and return to the Options menu. Any changes become effective immediately for the current session.

10　The GeoPlanner Application

Save Preferences

To save permanently any changes in the Change Preferences dialog box — setting them as the new program defaults — select Save Preferences from the Options menu.

Quick Menu

Select this option when you want to quickly display event schedules. When you select Quick, the program displays the menu shown in Figure 10-8.

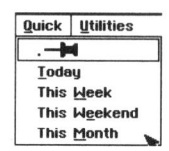

Figure 10-8 — The Quick Menu.

Today

Select this option to display the events scheduled for the current day.

This Week

Select this option to display events scheduled for the entire week. The program does not display days for which no events are scheduled.

This Weekend

Select this option to display events scheduled for the weekend.

This Month

Select this option to display events scheduled for the entire month. The program will not display days for which no events are scheduled.

The GeoPlanner Application 10

Utilities Menu

The Utilities menu options allow you to schedule repeating events, to search for a text string, and to link with the GeoDex application. When you select this option, the program displays the dialog box shown in Figure 10-9.

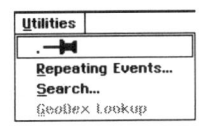

Figure 10-9 — The Utilities Menu.

Repeating Events

Selecting this option displays the Repeating Events dialog box which lists all scheduled repeating events. If there are none, the box displays the words "no events." At the bottom of the dialog box are four buttons: New, Change, Delete, and Close.

New

Clicking on the New button displays the Type of Event dialog box. Select the frequency of the event (Weekly, Monthly, or Yearly). Then select how the event is identified (by Date, or by Day of Week). Depending on your selection, some of the following options will be dimmed (unavailable).

Use the Select Day(s) option to specify the day(s) of the week on which the repeating event occurs. This option is active when you choose Weekly in the previous section.

Use the Day of Month option to specify the day on which the repeating event occurs (if you selected Monthly or Yearly and Specify by Date earlier). If you selected Yearly, you can also enter a month in the box labeled Month.

Use the Day of Week option to specify which week in the month (first to fifth) the repeating event occurs, and which day in the week. This option is available when you select Monthly or Yearly and also select Specify by Day of Week. For example, if an event always happens on the third Tuesday of the month, enter third and Tuesday in the respective boxes.

10 The GeoPlanner Application

Click on the Time box to enter a time for the event.

Enter a description (which is required) of the repeating event in the Event box.

Use the Repeat option to select the frequency of reoccurrence. For example, select Forever if the event always occurs. If there is a specific time limit for the event, choose From. The first box now displays the current date. The To box displays the last day of the current year. You can change the dates in these boxes to whatever dates you want.

When you are satisfied with your selections, click the OK button to save your choice and return to the GeoPlanner window. Click the Cancel button to return to the GeoPlanner window without making changes.

Change

When you select this option, the program displays the dialog box previously described in the New section. Make whatever changes you want, then click the OK button to save the changes.

Delete

Select this option to delete a repeating event. Highlight the event and select Delete. The program removes the event from the list.

Close

Select this option to close the Repeating Events dialog box and return to the GeoPlanner window.

Search

You can use this option on the Utilities menu to search for a string of text. When you select this option, the program displays the Search dialog box. The text string you enter can be a word, part of a word or a group of words.

Note: GeoPlanner is case-sensitive. You must enter the string exactly as it occurs in the event listing.

When you are satisfied with the text string, click the Start Search button. The search begins at the current day and continues through the list of future events. If the program cannot match the string, a message asks if you want to search past events, also. If the program finds the text string, it displays the text in the event window.

To find the next occurrence of the string, click the Find Next button to continue the search. When no further matches can be found, the program displays a message saying the search is complete.

GeoDex Lookup

Suppose you want to telephone a person mentioned in an event description for whom you have a card in the GeoDex address book. From within GeoPlanner you can search GeoDex for the name, then have GeoDex dial the number for you.

Follow these steps to look up a GeoDex card from within GeoPlanner:

1. Start GeoDex from the Express menu if it is not already running.

2. Switch back to the GeoPlanner window by clicking anywhere in the GeoPlanner window or by selecting it from the Express menu.

3. Select (highlight) the text (name, address, or any other identifying text string) you want to locate in GeoDex.

4. Select GeoDex Lookup on the Utilities menu. The program searches the GeoDex cards for a matching text string and displays in the GeoDex window the first card containing a match.

5. Switch to the GeoDex window by clicking anywhere in the GeoDex window or by selecting it from the Express menu.

6. Scroll to the appropriate phone number and have GeoDex dial it for you.

10 The GeoPlanner Application

If the displayed card is not the one you want, or if you want to look at more cards that match the text string, follow these steps to continue the search:

1. Select the GeoDex View menu.

2. Select the Both View option. The left side of the window displays the first card containing the text (shown highlighted). The right side of the window displays all the entries in your card file listed alphabetically. At the bottom of the window is the text you selected in GeoPlanner. You can enter a different text string, if you wish.

3. Click the Find Next button to continue the search. Continue clicking until you find what you want.

You can confine the search to only Index entries by clicking the Confine Search To Index button. Otherwise, the search includes all the text. You can click the Clear button to remove the text string and stop the search.

Note: From the GeoDex application you can search for a text string in GeoPlanner. After selecting the search text in GeoDex, use the GeoPlanner button in the bottom right of the GeoDex window to perform the search.

Summary

The GeoPlanner application is a combination calendar and date book. You can enter events in the date book and easily switch to any day, month and year you want to view on the calendar. It is also easy to view events for a day, week, or the entire month. You can change some GeoPlanner settings to your preference, and set an alarm to remind you of events. The Utilities menu allows you to schedule repeating events, and conduct a search for text within GeoPlanner or within GeoDex.

Chapter 11

The Calculator Application

This application works much like a hand-held calculator. You can perform addition, subtraction, multiplication and division, calculate percentages, and store numbers in memory. In this chapter you will learn:

- How to perform calculations
- How to switch between Standard and Hewlett-Packard Reverse Polish Notation (RPN) configurations
- How to set order of precedence for formula calculations in the Standard configuration
- How to calculate using RPN notation
- How to use the menu options.

11 The Calculator Application

Using the Calculator

You can access the Calculator application by:

- Double-clicking on the Calculator icon in the GeoManager window
- Selecting Calculator from the Express menu/Startup option.

When you start the Calculator application, the program displays a window similar to Figure 11-1.

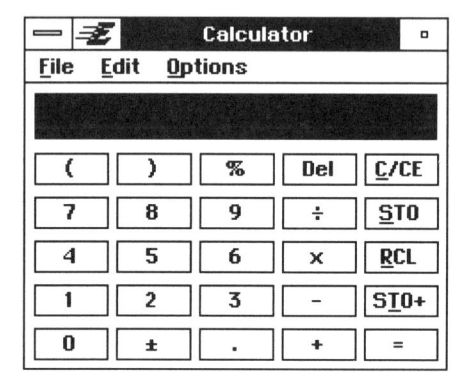

Figure 11-1 — The Calculator Window.

The Calculator application is similar to the Calculator appliance in the Appliances section. You will find, however, that the Calculator application is more flexible and powerful. You can operate the calculator by clicking the mouse cursor on the calculator buttons or by pressing keys on the keyboard. Table 11-1 sets out the calculator functions and indicates which calculator buttons to click or which keyboard keys to press.

218

The Calculator Application 11

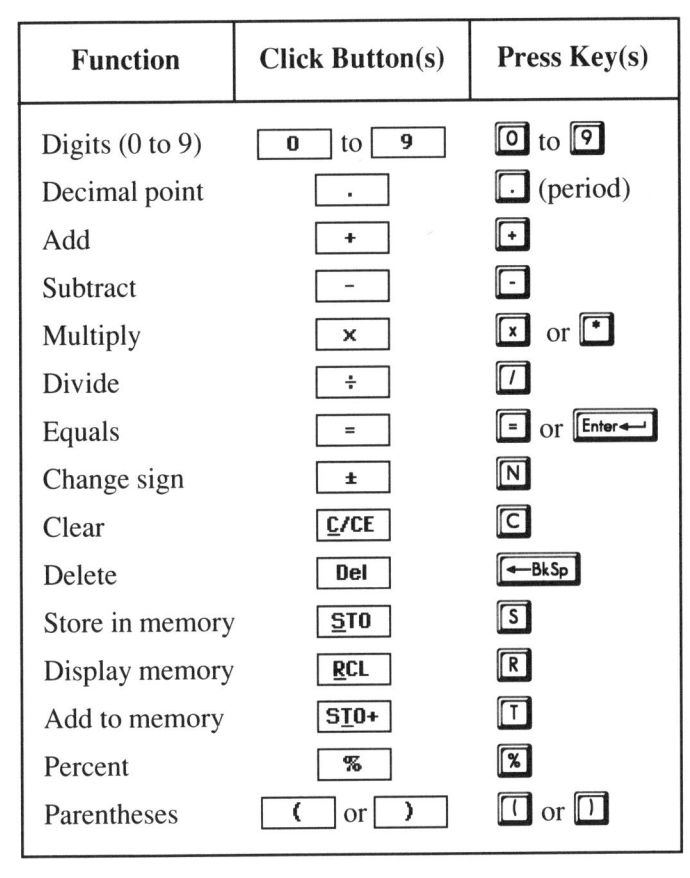

Table 11-1 — Calculator Functions

Function	Click Button(s)	Press Key(s)
Digits (0 to 9)	`0` to `9`	`0` to `9`
Decimal point	`.`	`.` (period)
Add	`+`	`+`
Subtract	`-`	`-`
Multiply	`x`	`x` or `*`
Divide	`÷`	`/`
Equals	`=`	`=` or `Enter`
Change sign	`±`	`N`
Clear	`C/CE`	`C`
Delete	`Del`	`←BkSp`
Store in memory	`STO`	`S`
Display memory	`RCL`	`R`
Add to memory	`STO+`	`T`
Percent	`%`	`%`
Parentheses	`(` or `)`	`(` or `)`

You can use the regular typing keys, or you can use the numeric keypad if `num lock` is ON.

Delete

This function erases the last (leftmost) digit in a number.

Parentheses (Standard Configuration)

You can use parentheses to group numbers together so that they are operated on as a unit. Parentheses change the order of operations — the value inside the parentheses is calculated before any other operation.

11   The Calculator Application

Clear

You can click the [C/CE] button once to clear the displayed number. When you double click the [C/CE] button, the program clears everything, including any calculations in progress. To clear the memory from the keyboard, press [0], then press [S] to store the value of zero.

Error

If you try to divide by zero, or if your result is a value greater than the calculator can handle, the program displays an error message. A result cannot be greater than 2,147,483,647 or less than -2,147,483,647. Click on [C/CE] or press [C] to clear the error message.

Order of Operations (Standard Configuration)

The Calculator application in Standard configuration follows this order of precedence when performing calculations:

First: quantities in parentheses

Second: multiplication and division

Last: addition and subtraction.

Arithmetic operations with the same order of precedence (multiplication and division, or addition and subtraction) are performed in the order they occur from left to right. The following example illustrates the order of operation.

Suppose you enter the formula:

4 + 5 x 6 =

You may expect 54 as the answer (4 + 5 = 9; 9 x 6 = 54). However, the answer you get is 34. The reason is that the multiplication operation has precedence over addition. Therefore, the first calculation is 6 x 5 (= 30), then 4 is added to 30, with a result of 34.

The Calculator Application 11

To ensure that the sum of 4 + 5 is the value multiplied by 6, you must enter the formula like this:

(4 + 5) x 6 =

or like this:

6 x (4 + 5) =

The calculator first evaluates the sum in the parentheses, then multiplies the sum by 6 for a result of 54.

Memory Use

You can store a frequently-used number in the calculator memory so you can call it up with a single click. You can also use the memory function to keep a running total when performing a series of calculations.

STO [STO]

This button stores the currently-displayed number in memory, replacing any previously stored value.

STO+ [STO+]

This button adds the currently-displayed number to the value stored in memory.

RCL [RCL]

This button displays the value stored in memory. You can then use this number in a calculation.

11 The Calculator Application

The Calculator Menu Bar

At the top of the calculator display is a menu bar with three menu options: File, Edit, and Options.

File Menu

The only option on the Calculator File menu is Exit.

Exit (F3)

Select this option to close the Calculator application and return to the GeoManager window.

Edit Menu

You can cut and paste, or copy and paste, numbers from the calculator into other applications using the Edit menu. Before you can cut or copy a number, you must first select it: press and hold the mouse button on the first digit, then drag the mouse cursor to the last digit. Release the button to highlight the number.

Cut

You can use this option to remove the selected number from the calculator and place it on the Clipboard. Open a window for the application into which you want to paste the number. Select Paste from the Edit menu in the target application. The program inserts the number at the cursor position.

Copy

This option is identical to Cut, except that the number remains in the calculator and a copy is moved to the Clipboard.

Paste

You can reverse the procedure previously described in Cut and Copy by copying or moving a number from another application into the calculator. Select Paste from the calculator Edit menu to paste the number on the Clipboard into the calculator.

The Calculator Application **11**

Quick Copy ▪ *and Quick Move* ▫

In addition to the cut and paste or copy and paste operations on the Edit menu, you can use Quick Copy or Quick Move to place text in another application. To use Quick Copy or Quick Move, open another application window (for example, GeoWrite). Select the text you want to copy or move. Position the mouse cursor over the highlighted text. For Quick Copy, press and hold the RIGHT mouse button (the pointer changes to the Quick Copy pointer). For Quick Move, press and hold [alt] then press and hold the RIGHT mouse button (the pointer changes to the Quick Move pointer). Move the pointer to the target location. Release the button. The program copies or moves the selected text.

The program bypasses the Clipboard in a Quick Copy or Quick Move operation. Any text already saved on the Clipboard remains intact.

Options Menu

You can use this menu to specify the number of decimal places for the calculator to display. You can also switch the calculator between Standard operation (the default) and Reverse Polish Notation (RPN), which is used by Hewlett-Packard calculators.

Decimal Places

Select this option to display the Decimal Places dialog box. Click on the small triangles to increase or decrease the number of decimal places shown. The range is 0 to 8 decimal places.

Note: When a value includes more decimal places than the number specified for display, the calculator will round off the number for display purposes only. The actual value used in calculations retains its full number of decimal places. For example, if you have the number 223.413 and have set the decimal places to 1, the number will display as 223.4, but the calculator will use 223.413 in its calculations.

Standard

Select this option to configure the calculator as a standard hand-held model. The operations of the Standard configuration are described earlier in this chapter.

11 The Calculator Application

RPN

When you select this option, the calculator is reconfigured, as shown in Figure 11-2, and operates as a Hewlett-Packard calculator.

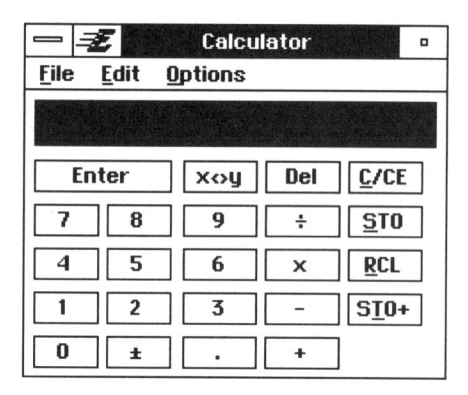

Figure 11-2 — The RPN Calculator.

In general, the buttons on Standard and RPN calculators are the same, with the following exceptions:

Enter button `Enter`

Use this button to separate the first and second numbers, storing the first number in a register so it can be recalled automatically for the calculation. RPN notation can use up to four registers and the displayed number in its calculations.

Note that there are no parentheses and no equal sign buttons on the RPN calculator.

Exchange button `x<>y`

Use the exchange button to reverse the order of two numbers entered in the calculator.

For example, suppose you want to divide 8 by 4, but you inadvertently entered the 4 first, then the 8. Click the exchange button — or `E` on the keyboard — to reverse the numbers.

The Calculator Application 11

Performing RPN Calculations

Click these buttons to perform the calculation 768 ÷ 16:

`7`	Displays 7
`6`	Displays 76
`8`	Displays 768
`Enter`	Stores displayed number in first register
`1`	Displays 1
`6`	Displays 16
`÷`	Divides value in register by displayed number

The calculator displays the result: 48.

To erase the last displayed digit, click the `Del` button.

To switch the displayed number from negative to positive (or positive to negative), click the `±` button.

What happens if you click the Enter button after entering the second value in this calculation: 8 x 4?

`8`	Displays 8
`Enter`	Stores displayed number in first register
`4`	Displays 4
`Enter`	Moves value in first register to second register, then stores displayed number in first register
`x`	Multiplies value in first register by displayed number: 4 x 4

The calculator displays the result: 16. The value 4 in the first register (which has been used) is deleted. The value 8 in the second register moves down to the first register.

225

11   The Calculator Application

To add 9 to the displayed result 16:

> **9** Moves value in first register (8) up to second register. Stores displayed number (16) in first register. Displays 9.
>
> **+** Adds value in first register and displayed number: 16 + 9.

The calculator displays the result: 25. The value 16 in the first register (which has been used) is deleted. The value 8 in the second register moves down to the first register.

To divide the displayed value by the value in the first register:

> **x◇y** Switches displayed value and value in first register
>
> **÷** Divides value in first register (25) by displayed number (8).

The calculator displays the result: 3.125. The value in the first register (which has been used) is deleted.

Unlike standard calculators, RPN calculators perform operations in the order they are entered, not according to an order of preference. In other words, the same numbers entered in the same order do not necessarily give the same answers on the two calculators. The following example illustrates this.

Standard calculator: 6 + 2 x 4 = 14

> Performed as 2 x 4 = 8, 8 + 6 = 14 because multiplication takes precedence over addition.

RPN calculator: 6 + 2 x 4 = 32

> Performed as 6 + 2 = 8, 8 x 4 = 32 because the calculation is done as entered.

There is no need to use parentheses in RPN calculations. For example, to perform the calculation 50 x (6-4), first calculate 6 – 4 = 2, then calculate 2 x 50 to get the answer 100.

Memory Functions

The memory register is separate from the calculation registers, so calculations will not affect the number stored in memory unless you click a memory function button.

The Calculator Application 11

To store the displayed number in memory, click the `STO` button.

To add the displayed number to the value in the memory register, click the `STO+` button.

To display the value in the memory register, click the `RCL` button. You can then use that value in a calculation.

For example, suppose you want to divide the number 3 by the value in the memory register (5):

`3`	Displays 3
`Enter`	Stores displayed number in first register
`RCL`	Displays value in memory register (5)
`÷`	Divides value in first register (3) by displayed value (5).

The calculator displays the result: 0.67.

Now suppose you want to divide the value in the memory register (5) by the number 3:

`RCL`	Displays value in memory register (5)
`3`	Stores displayed value in first register. Displays 3
`÷`	Divides value in first register (5) by displayed value 3.

The calculator displays the result: 1.67.

Summary

This chapter explained how to access and use the Calculator application in the Professional Workspace. You can perform calculations the same way you would with a hand-held calculator. In addition, you can cut, copy, and paste numbers to other application documents. You can switch the calculator from a Standard configuration to the Hewlett-Packard Reverse Polish Notation configuration.

Chapter 12

The Notepad Application

In this chapter you will learn how to use the Notepad application in two ways: as a pad for jotting down notes to yourself, and as a DOS (ASCII) text editor. Unlike GeoWrite, which creates GEOS-type documents, Notepad documents are saved as DOS-type documents.

12 The Notepad Application

Accessing the Notepad Application

You can access the Notepad application by:

- Double-clicking on the Notepad icon in the GeoManager window
- Selecting Notepad from the Express Menu/Startup option.

Note: You cannot open Notepad by opening one of its documents from the GEOMANAGER/DOCUMENT directory.

When you select the Notepad application, the program displays the window shown in Figure 12-1.

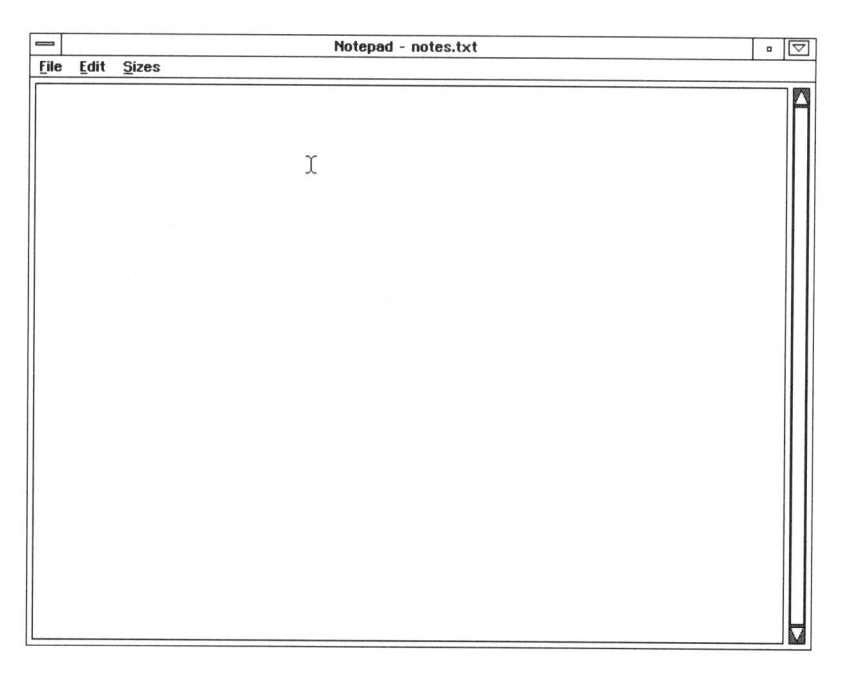

Figure 12-1 — The Notepad Window.

When you enter Notepad the first time, the program creates a blank NOTES.TXT file in the DOCUMENT subdirectory and displays it.

When you return to Notepad after exiting, the window displays the way it was when you last left the program. In other words, if a Notepad document was open when you last exited, the same document is open when you return to the application. If a NOTES.TXT file exists but was not displayed when you last exited, the program displays "Notepad - No File" in the Title Bar.

Using Notepad for Notes

You can use the Notepad application as a free-form pad for jotting and saving notes that do not require the special formatting features available in GeoWrite. When you save a Notepad document, you can choose to follow GEOS filenaming conventions or DOS filenaming conventions. (See the DOS and GEOS Files section in Chapter 3 for details.)

To help you decide which application is more appropriate for a task, the following table summarizes the differences between The Notepad and GeoWrite:

Table 12-1 — Comparison of The Notepad and GeoWrite

The Notepad	GeoWrite
Only one document can be open at a time.	Multiple documents can be open at once.
Creates and uses DOS-type documents.	Creates and uses GEOS-type documents.
Does not safeguard documents.	Safeguards documents.
No choice of fonts.	A selection of fonts.
No rulers, no formatting or justification options.	A variety of formatting and justification options.

12 The Notepad Application

Using Notebook as a DOS Text Editor

You can use the Notepad to create and edit DOS text files such as your computer's AUTOEXEC.BAT file or other batch files for running routines at the DOS prompt. Although editing DOS files in the Notepad is quite similar to working with GEOS files in GeoWrite, it is important to realize that all Notepad files are DOS files and are not interchangeable with GEOS documents.

When saving a DOS batch file, you must use the DOS filenaming conventions or DOS will not recognize the file as one it can use.

The Notepad Menus

As you can see in Figure 12-1 displayed earlier, the menu bar at the top of the Notepad screen contains three menus: File, Edit, and Sizes.

File Menu

When you select this option, the program displays the File menu shown in Figure 12-2.

Figure 12-2 — The File Menu.

The File menu contains eight options, not all of which are available all the time. Unavailable items are shown dimmed on the menu. For example, if you do not have a file open, you will notice that the only choices you can make are: New, Open, and Exit.

The Notepad Application **12**

New

When you select New, the heading at the top of the Notepad screen changes to Notepad - Notes. You can enter any text you want in the notepad window. Text can be edited using the same techniques you use to edit any documents.

Open

Use this option to open an existing Notepad file. Selecting Open displays the dialog box shown in Figure 12-3.

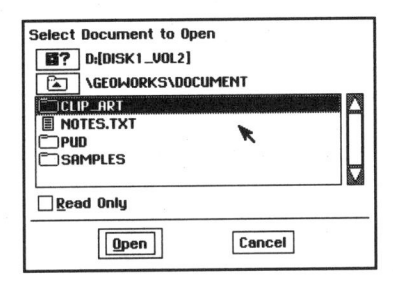

Figure 12-3 — Select Document To Open Dialog Box.

Selecting a file

You can scroll through a long list of filenames by clicking on the scroll bar arrows. Double-click on a filename to select it and open it in one operation, or click on a filename, then click the Open button.

Read Only file

In the lower left of the Select Document to Open dialog box is a Read Only button. To set a file as read only, highlight the filename, then click the Read Only button. A read only file cannot be edited or deleted. This can be useful if you want to make sure you (or someone else) does not accidentally alter your note. To turn off Read Only, highlight the file, then click the Read Only button again.

Close

Select this option to remove a file from the Notepad window. If you modified the file since the last save — or if it has never been saved — the program displays this message: "Note has been changed. Do you wish to save it?" You can choose Yes, No or Cancel.

If you select No, the program closes the file without saving your changes. If the file had never been saved, it is deleted entirely.

If you select Cancel, the program takes you back to the file window.

If you select Yes, one of two things will happen. If the document had been saved before, the program saves the file immediately and closes the file. If the file was never saved, then the program displays the Select Directory and Enter New Filename dialog box shown in Figure 12-4.

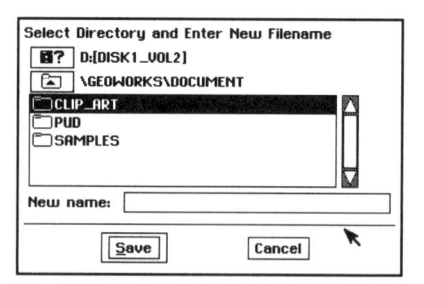

Figure 12-4 — Select Directory and Enter New Filename Dialog Box.

Select the directory in which you want to store the file, or accept the current directory, and enter a filename in the filename box. Click the Save button to save the file. Click the Cancel button to return to the Notepad window without saving the document.

Save

When you select this option to save a note the first time, the program displays the dialog box shown previously in Figure 12-4. Select the directory and enter a filename. Click on Save to save the document. The new name displays in the Title Bar.

The Notepad Application **12**

When you select this option to save a previously-saved note, the program saves the document immediately.

Note: Unlike most other GeoWorks Ensemble applications, the Notepad does not safeguard your changes as you work. Every time you make important changes to a file, select Save to preserve the changes.

Save As

You can use this option to save a previously-named file under a different name. The program saves a copy of the file under the new name, preserving the original file. You can select the subdirectory and filename for the new document.

Revert

If you are working in a previously-saved document and you decide you don't want to keep the changes made since the last save, select Revert from the File menu. The program displays a dialog box asking you to confirm that you want to revert to the last saved version of your document. If you select Yes, the program deletes the changes.

Print

You can print your note using this menu. When you select Print, the program displays the Printer Options dialog box shown in Figure 12-5.

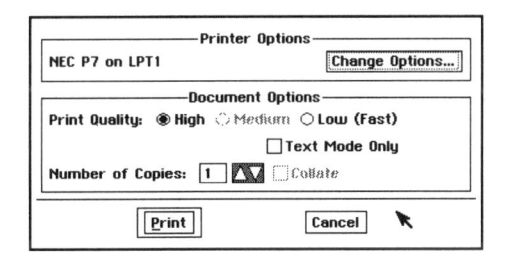

Figure 12-5 — The Printer Options Dialog Box.

See the File Menu/Print section in Chapter 7 for a discussion about this option.

235

12 The Notepad Application

Exit

Select this option to exit Notepad and go to the Welcome screen. The shortcut keystroke for Exit is [F3].

Edit Menu

When you select this option, the program displays the Edit menu shown in Figure 12-6.

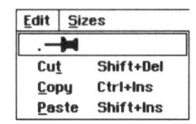

Figure 12-6 — The Edit Menu.

See the Edit Menu section in Chapter 7 for a discussion about these Notepad Edit menu options: Cut, Copy and Paste.

See the Edit Menu section in Chapter 10 for a discussion about using the Quick Copy and Quick Move commands.

Sizes Menu

When you select this option to change the size of displayed text in the Notepad window, the program displays the dialog box shown in Figure 12-7.

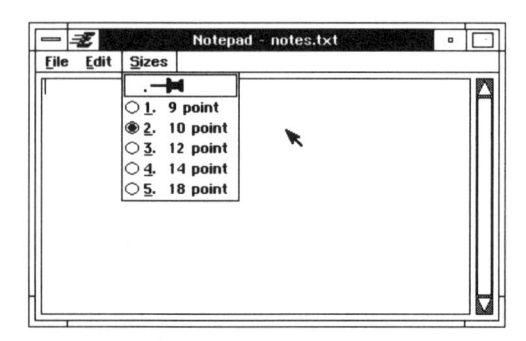

Figure 12-7 — Sizes Menu.

The Notepad Application 12

You can click on a size to select it, displaying all text in the Notepad in the selected point size. You can choose only one size at a time: 9 point, 10 point, 12 point, 14 point, and 18 point. Select a smaller size to display more text in the window at a time; select a larger size for readability.

Note: The size of text on the screen does not affect the way the document will print.

Summary

In this chapter you learned how to use the Notepad to jot down quick notes which don't require the formatting capabilities of GeoWrite. You can print these notes, save them, or copy them to other documents. The Notepad is also ideal for creating DOS files or for editing DOS files from other sources, for example, your computer's AUTOEXEC.BAT file.

Chapter **13**

The Scrapbook Application

In this chapter you will learn how to use the Scrapbook application to collect your favorite graphics and text items. While the GeoWorks Ensemble Clipboard is a handy way to transfer text and pictures from one document to another, it can hold only one item at a time. Use the scrapbook for permanent storage of the items you use frequently, such a company logo or a favorite drawing.

One scrapbook file can contain as many "scraps" of text or graphics as you wish, each on its own page. You can also create multiple scrapbooks, perhaps organizing your text and graphics by topic.

13 The Scrapbook Application

Accessing the Scrapbook

You can access the scrapbook in several ways:

- Double-clicking on the Scrapbook icon in the GeoManager window
- Selecting Scrapbook from the Express menu/Startup option.
- Clicking on a Scrapbook document icon in the GeoManager DOCUMENT directory.

The Scrapbook Window

When you open the Scrapbook application, the program displays the scrapbook window shown in Figure 13-1.

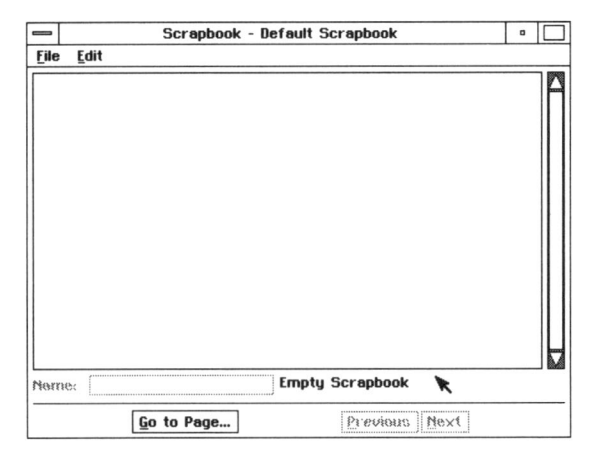

Figure 13-1 — The Scrapbook Window.

The Title Bar displays the document name: Default Scrapbook. The first time you open Scrapbook, the program creates the Default Scrapbook and displays it for you. Even if you have more than one scrapbook, the Default Scrapbook always appears when you open the program.

If you have not yet saved anything in the Default Scrapbook, the window area is empty and an "Empty Scrapbook" notation displays at the bottom of the window.

Two menu options display on the Menu Bar: File and Edit.

The Scrapbook Application 13

Below the Menu Bar is the scrapbook window where you can view the contents of the scrapbook. If the contents of a page are larger than the window area, scroll the page using the scroll bar at the right of the window.

Below the window is a box labeled Name. You can name each page in the scrapbook by entering a name in this box. The program displays the page name in this box if the page is already named.

Next to the Name box the program displays the notation "Empty Scrapbook," or, if you have saved images, the program displays the current page number and the total number of pages. (For example, Page 1 of 2.)

Below the Name box is the Go to Page button. You can select any page in the scrapbook by clicking this button to display the Go to Page dialog box shown in Figure 13-2. The dialog box displays a list of pages and page numbers in the scrapbook, with the current page highlighted. You can view any page you want by highlighting it and clicking the View Page button. Click the Close button to close the dialog box. The program displays the selected page in the scrapbook window.

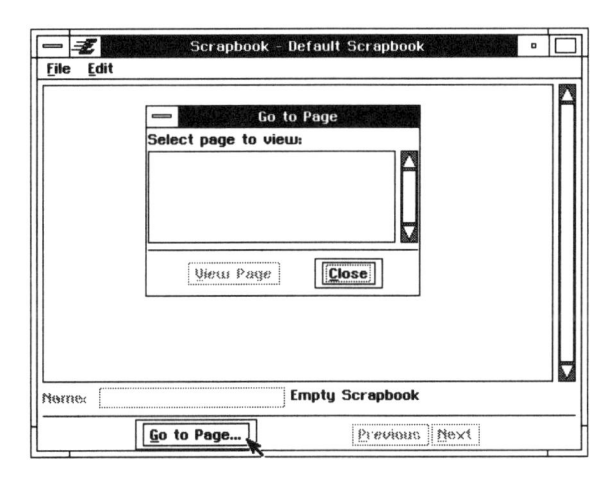

Figure 13-2 — The Go to Page Dialog Box.

To the right of the Go to Page button in the scrapbook window are the Previous and Next buttons. Clicking the Previous button takes you to the previous page in the scrapbook. If you are viewing the first page, the Previous button takes you to the last page. Clicking the Next button takes you to the next page. If you are viewing the last page, the Next button takes you to the first page.

241

13 The Scrapbook Application

The Menu Bar

The two menus on this bar, File and Edit, work in much the same way as they do in other GeoWorks Ensemble documents.

File Menu

When you select File from the Menu Bar, the program displays the File menu shown in Figure 13-3.

Figure 13-3 — The File Menu.

See the File Menu section in Chapter 7 for a discussion about the options on the scrapbook File menu.

Edit Menu

When you select this option, the program displays the Edit menu shown in Figure 13-4.

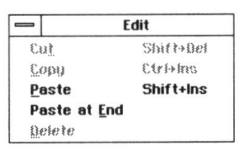

Figure 13-4 — The Edit Menu.

This menu contains five options which allow you to add text or graphics to your scrapbook, either on a new page or on the page you select. You can move or copy from a scrapbook to another application, or delete a page from the scrapbook.

Cut

You can use this option to move (cut) text or graphics from another application to the scrapbook, or from the scrapbook to another application. In either case, the transfer goes by way of the Clipboard. The shortcut for this option is `Shift`-`delete`.

Select (highlight) the text or graphics you want to move from an application to the Clipboard. Select Cut from the Edit menu in the application. The program removes the selected item from the application and places it on the Clipboard. Paste the item from the Clipboard to the scrapbook.

When moving an item from the scrapbook to the Clipboard, it is not necessary to highlight it first. Selecting Cut from the scrapbook Edit menu automatically selects the contents of the displayed page and moves it to the Clipboard. The program renumbers any pages that follow the cut page.

Copy

This option works the same as Cut, except that the original material remains intact and a copy is placed on the Clipboard. The shortcut for this is `Ctrl`-`Ins`.

Paste

Select Paste from the Edit menu to copy the Clipboard contents into the scrapbook. The program inserts a page in the scrapbook at the current location and places the item on the page. For example, if page 2 is displayed when you select Paste, the program inserts a new page 2, renumbers the original page 2 as page 3, and renumbers subsequent pages. The shortcut for this is `Shift`-`Ins`.

Paste at End

This option places Clipboard material on a new page at the end of the scrapbook. If you had 5 pages in the book, it paste the material on a new page 6. No shortcut exists for this option.

13 The Scrapbook Application

Delete

This option deletes the contents of the displayed page. The contents are not copied to the Clipboard, so they cannot be retrieved. There is no shortcut for this command.

Caution: The program does not prompt for confirmation before deleting the material — as soon as you select Delete, the program removes the contents.

Changing the Default Scrapbook

Since the program opens the Default Scrapbook every time you run the application, you might want to change the Default Scrapbook to the one you use most often.

Follow these steps to change the Default Scrapbook:

1. Exit the Scrapbook application. If you return to the Welcome screen, select the Professional icon to go to the GeoManager window.

2. Activate the DOCUMENT directory by clicking on the Document icon at the bottom of the window.

3. Highlight the document called Default Scrapbook.

4. Rename the document to some other unique name.

5. Highlight the scrapbook document you want as the default.

6. Rename the highlighted scrapbook file Default Scrapbook.

Note: You must name the file exactly as shown, otherwise the Scrapbook application will not recognize the name.

The next time you start the Scrapbook application, the new Default Scrapbook will open automatically.

Opening More Than One Scrapbook at a Time

You can open more than one scrapbook in two ways:

- From the GeoManager window by clicking the Scrapbook icon each time you want to open another document
- From the Express menu/Startup option by clicking the Scrapbook each time you want to open another document.

In either case, if the program displays a message that the Default Scrapbook is already in use, click the OK button. Then you can select Open from the File menu to open another scrapbook.

The open scrapbooks display in overlapping format on the screen as shown in Figure 13-5.

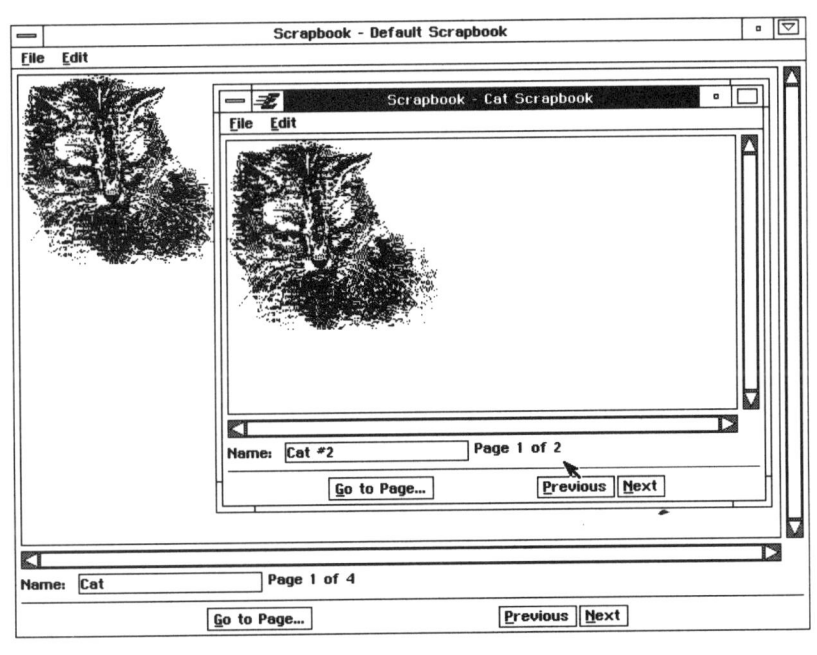

Figure 13-5 — Overlapping Scrapbook Windows.

13 The Scrapbook Application

You can resize the windows (see Resizing a Window in Chapter 4) so they display side by side, as shown in Figure 13-6.

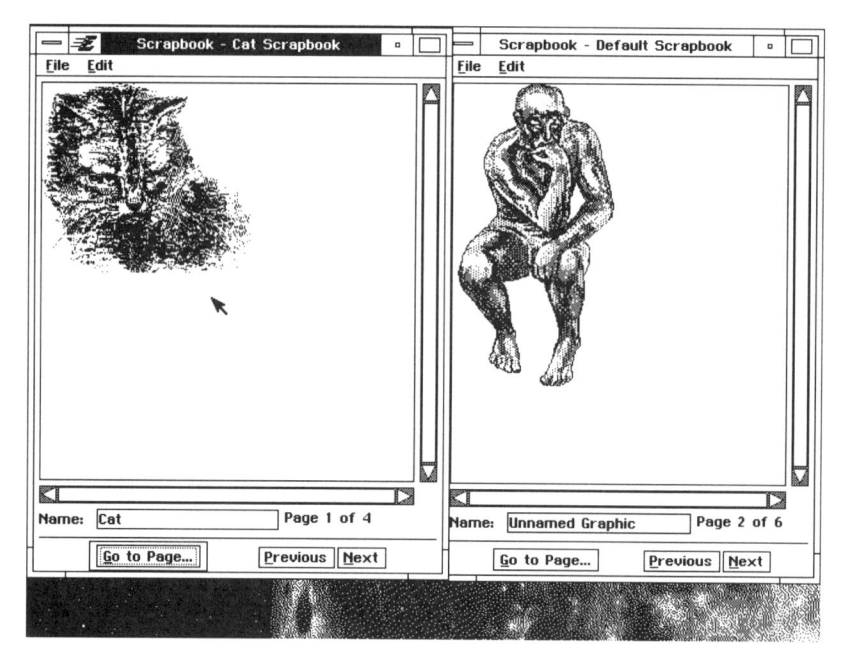

Figure 13-6 — Resized Scrapbook Windows.

Cutting or Copying Between Scrapbooks

Follow these steps to cut or copy between open scrapbooks:

1. Click the Maximize button (the rectangle in the upper right corner of the window) of the scrapbook that contains the item you want to cut or copy. The program displays the scrapbook as a full window.

2. Display the scrapbook page that contains the item.

3. Select Cut (or Copy) from the Edit menu. The program cuts (or copies) the item, placing it on the Clipboard.

The Scrapbook Application 13

4. Click the Minimize button (same as the Maximize button). The program displays the scrapbook as an overlapping window again.

5. Click the Maximize button on the scrapbook into which you want to paste the item. The program displays the scrapbook as a full window.

6. Select Paste (or Paste at End) from the Edit menu. The program copies the item from the Clipboard into the scrapbook.

Note: You can also reduce the scrapbooks to icons, selecting and reducing them as necessary to move between them to cut (or copy) and paste.

Summary

The Scrapbook application is a handy way to store frequently used text or graphics. You can create multiple scrapbooks, each with as many pages as you want. You can cut (or copy) items from one scrapbook to another, from a scrapbook to another application, or from another application to the scrapbook.

Chapter 14

The GeoDex Application

In this chapter you will learn how to use the GeoDex application, a combination card file and automatic phone dialer. GeoDex is convenient for keeping track of names, addresses, and other notations. You can print lists of names and phone numbers. If you have a modem, you can use the GeoDex phone dialing feature.

14 The GeoDex Application

Accessing the GeoDex Application

The GeoDex program can be accessed in several ways:

- Double-clicking on the GeoDex icon in the GeoManager window
- Selecting GeoDex from the Express menu/Startup option
- Clicking a GeoDex document icon in the GeoManager DOCUMENT directory.

The GeoDex Window

When you open the GeoDex application, the program displays the window shown in Figure 14-1.

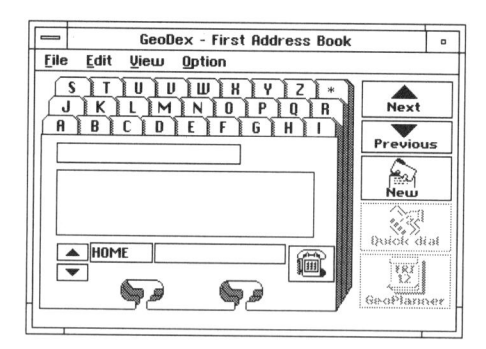

Figure 14-1 — The GeoDex Window.

The GeoDex Title Bar displays the default file name, Address Book, or the name you have given the displayed card file. In Figure 14-1 the card file is named First Address Book.

The Menu Bar contains four options: File, Edit, View, and Option. The GeoDex menus are described later in this chapter. The program displays the card files on the left in the GeoDex window. Above the top card are letter tabs from A to Z and an * (asterisk) tab. You can click on a letter tab to flip to the cards listed under that letter. When you click the * tab, the program flips to cards that are not grouped under a letter. The program highlights the selected tab.

The GeoDex Application 14

The top card is the GeoDex work area. Enter into the index field (the small box at the top of the work area) the word or words by which you want to identify the card. Remember that GeoDex alphabetizes according to the first word, so when entering a name, type the last name first.

You can enter the name, address and other information in the large box. Use the scroll bar at the right of the large box to scroll the contents.

Below the large box is the phone number box. Each card can store up to seven phone numbers. The default phone number display is HOME. You can click the up and down triangles to switch to OFFICE, CAR, FAX, and three blank areas in which you can enter custom phone number designations. Enter the phone number in the box beside the designation.

The program displays five buttons to the right of the card window: Next, Previous, New, Quick dial, and GeoPlanner.

Next

You can click this button to display the next card in alphabetical sequence. If you are viewing the last card in the file, the program flips to the first card in the file.

Previous

You can click this button to display the previous card in the alphabetical sequence. If you are viewing the first card in the file, the program flips to the last card in the file.

New

You can click this button to create a new card. The program files the card alphabetically for you.

14 The GeoDex Application

Creating a card

Follow these steps to create a new card:

1. Enter in the index field the word or words which identify the card. If you are entering a person's name, type the last name followed by a comma, then type the first name.

2. Press [Enter⏎]. The program copies the index field contents into the address area below. If the identifying text is the way you want it, press [Enter⏎] again to move down a line. Type in the address information, pressing [Enter⏎] each time you want to begin a new line. Press [←BkSp] to correct mistakes.

3. Press [tab] to move to the phone number area. Click the buttons to select the appropriate number designation (home, office, car, or fax), or create your own designation.

4. If you will be using the Dial or Quick dial features, enter the phone number following the guidelines outlined in the Entering Phone Numbers section that follows.

5. Click any of these buttons to insert the new card in the index: New, Next, Previous, or a Tab button.

Entering phone numbers

Follow these guidelines when entering phone numbers:

- You can insert a dash (-) or a space within the number to make it easier to read.

- Omit the area code for local numbers.

The GeoDex Application 14

- Include any number you must dial to place a call manually. For example, if you must always dial 9 to access an outside line, include the 9 like this: 9-555-1212.

- Include any necessary access number for your long distance service.

- For a long distance number, include the 1 and the area code. For example: 1-508-555-1212.

- If your modem software supports it, you can place a comma anywhere in the number to pause briefly the dialing procedure, which is sometimes necessary to make a modem connection. For example, you could enter 1-505,-555-1212. Check your modem manual for information about this feature.

You can configure GeoDex to insert preliminary numbers automatically for every number dialed. It is then not necessary to include these numbers in every phone listing. See the Option Menu section later in this chapter.

Note: To use the Quick Dial and Dial features, you must have a Hayes-compatible modem which shares the same line as your telephone. You should refer to your modem manual for instructions on installing and setting up the modem.

Use the Preferences application to configure GeoWorks Ensemble for your modem.

See the Dialing a Phone Number section later in this chapter for information about dialing a number.

14 The GeoDex Application

Quick Dial

Select this option to display two lists: the most frequently and the most recently called names and phone numbers, as shown in Figure 14-2.

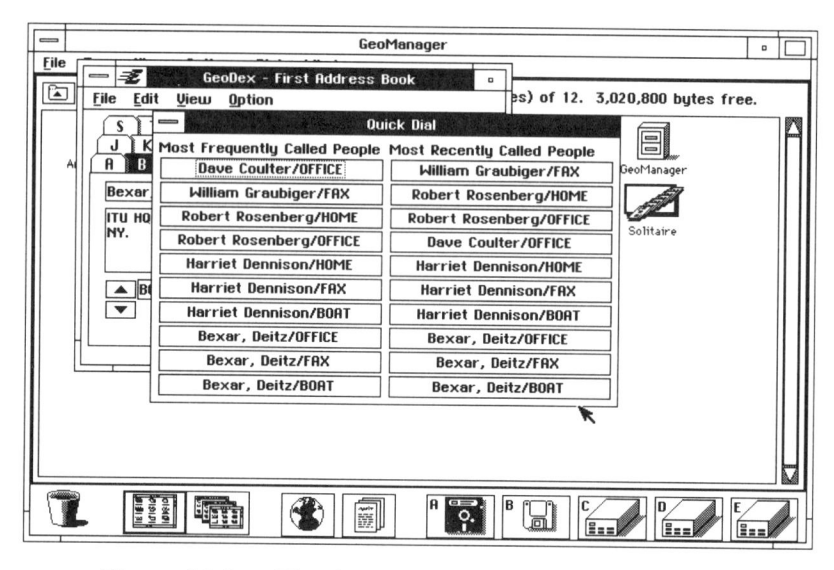

Figure 14-2 — The Quick Dial Phone Number Listings.

The program updates the lists every time you make a phone call from GeoDex, modifying the lists to reflect your calling pattern.

See the Dialing a Phone Number section later in this chapter for information about dialing a number.

GeoPlanner

This item is shown dimmed unless you have selected Both View from the View menu (or double-clicked on a tab) and are conducting a search for a text string. You can then click this button to search GeoPlanner for the text string. See Chapter 12 for a discussion about searching for text strings in GeoPlanner and GeoDex.

The Menu Bar

Two of the four menus on this bar, File and Edit, work in much the same way as they do in other GeoWorks Ensemble documents.

File Menu

When you select File from the Menu Bar, the program displays a File menu with 8 options. See the File Menu section in Chapter 7 for a discussion about the options on the GeoDex File menu.

Edit Menu

This menu contains six options which allow you to delete cards, move or copy text from a file card to another card or to another applications. Some of the options are shown dimmed (unavailable) until you select text.

Undo

You can select this option when you change your mind about an alteration to a card — whether you added, deleted, or edited text. When you select Undo, the program returns the card to its contents before you made the change. The shortcut for this is [alt]-[←BkSp].

Cut, Copy, and Paste

See the Edit Menu section in Chapter 7 for a discussion about using the Cut, Copy and Paste options.

See the Edit Menu section in Chapter 10 for a discussion about using the Quick Copy and Quick Move commands.

Clear

If you have created an address card but have not inserted it in the card file, you can remove the card by clicking Clear on the Edit menu. The program removes the card immediately, without confirmation.

Delete

You can select this option to get rid of a previously-saved file card. The program removes the card immediately, without confirmation.

View Menu

The View menu allows you to select three options for viewing the information in the GeoDex file: Card View, Browse View, and Both View.

Card View

This option displays the default card file view. You can flip through cards by clicking the Next or Previous buttons, and you can display the cards for a specific letter of the alphabet by clicking on a letter tab.

When Card View is active, you can create new cards or edit existing cards.

Browse View

When you select this option, the display changes to a list of names sorted alphabetically. You can scroll through the list to find the name you want. At the bottom of the list is a box for a phone number. When you click on a name to highlight it, the program displays that person's phone number in the box. You can click the up and down triangles to scroll through the list of phone numbers for the selected card.

You can dial the displayed phone number following the dialing instructions in the Dialing a Phone Number section later in this chapter.

Both View

When you choose this option, the display shows the Card View and the Browse View side by side, as shown in Figure 14-3.

The GeoDex Application 14

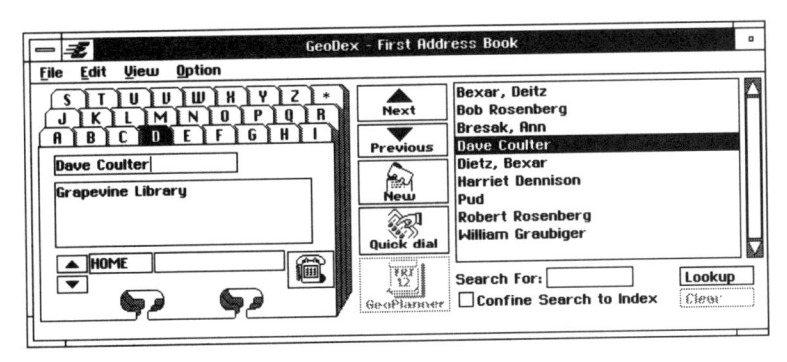

Figure 14-3 — The GeoDex Both View Display.

Note: You can double-click on a tab to change the display to the Both View option.

At the bottom right of the Both View display is a Search For box in which you can enter a text string to search for through the index cards. You must enter the text exactly as it occurs, including upper and lower case, in the card or cards you want to match.

Click the Find Next button to search for the text. If GeoDex finds an exact match, the program highlights the match in both views. When you begin a search, the GeoPlanner button on the left view becomes available. This means that you can open a GeoPlanner window and search the Events listings for the text string.

Continue clicking the Find Next button to search for more occurrences of the text string.

You can confine the search to the Index entries only and omit searching the address and phone number fields. Click on the Confine Search to Index button to select this option.

Click the Clear button to remove that text string and terminate the search request.

14 The GeoDex Application

Option

This menu has one option: Dialing. You can use this option to set a default prefix or area code for every phone number you dial in the GeoDex application. When you select the Option menu, the program displays the Dialing dialog box shown in Figure 14-4.

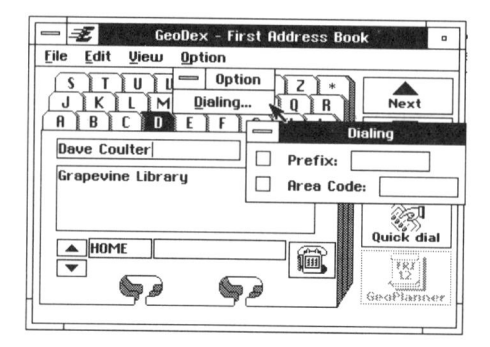

Figure 14-4 — The Dialing Dialog Box.

The Prefix and Area Code buttons are toggles — they display highlighted when they are turned on.

Prefix Option

You can enter any often-used or mandatory access code in this field. When the Prefix button is turned on, every phone call will be dialed with the prefix number.

Area Code Option

This option is handy if you take your computer on trips. Enter your area code and turn on this option to convert your otherwise local calls to long distance calls. Remember to include the number 1 with your area code.

The area code field can accept up to 10 numbers, making it easier to dial overseas numbers.

Dialing a Phone Number

Follow these steps to dial a phone number:

1. Make sure your phone is hung up correctly.

2. Flip through the index cards to display the card you want, or click the Quick dial button and scroll to the name and number you want in the Quick dial list.

3. Click the Dial button (which looks like a telephone) beside the displayed phone number. The program displays the Dialing message box to tell you that GeoDex is dialing the number. You will hear the modem dialing the number.

4. As soon as the modem finishes dialing, pick up the telephone and click the Talk button to reset the modem before it emits the loud connect tone.

Summary

You can use the GeoDex application to keep track of names, addresses, and phone numbers on separate index cards, creating more than one address book to organize your cards, if you wish. If you have a Hayes-compatible modem, you can also use GeoDex as a handy phone dialer to call local, long distance, or overseas numbers. You can move or copy text to other cards or other GeoWorks Ensemble applications. A search capability allows you to search GeoDex index cards and GeoPlanner Events lists for a string of text.

Chapter 15

America Online

GeoWorks Ensemble gives you convenient access to America Online, the bulletin board service. You must be a registered member of America Online to use it, and there is a monthly charge for the service. You can become a member of America Online directly from within GeoWorks Ensemble.

America Online offers a variety of services, including:

- Writing and receiving messages
- Receiving GeoWorks Ensemble updates and information
- Chatting online with other subscribers
- Getting answers to your computer problems
- Accessing public domain shareware programs
- Checking current stock market prices
- Making airline reservations
- Reading current news items
- Using the online encyclopedia.

15 America Online

The GeoWorks Ensemble information and support available on America Online is particularly helpful. In addition to downloading program updates from the bulletin board, you can download other useful programs. For example, the graphic screens for this book were captured with the Screen Dumper program downloaded from America Online. You can post on the bulletin board any questions about GeoWorks Ensemble and receive your answers within a day or so. The interface for accessing and using this bulletin board is similar to that for other GeoWorks Ensemble applications.

America Online Installation

America Online requires a minimum of 512K of memory, DOS 2.0 (or later), a phone line, and a Hayes (or Hayes-compatible) modem. America Online performance improves if your systems has 640K of memory, a hard drive, a mouse, and an EGA (or higher resolution) monitor. (If you have a Tandy 1000, select CGA during installation.)

Since America Online is installed as part of the GeoWorks Ensemble program, all that remains is for you to setup up your system parameters. The usual way to start the America Online application is from the GeoManager World screen. When you double-click on the America Online icon, the program displays the America Online opening window, as shown in Figure 15-1.

America Online 15

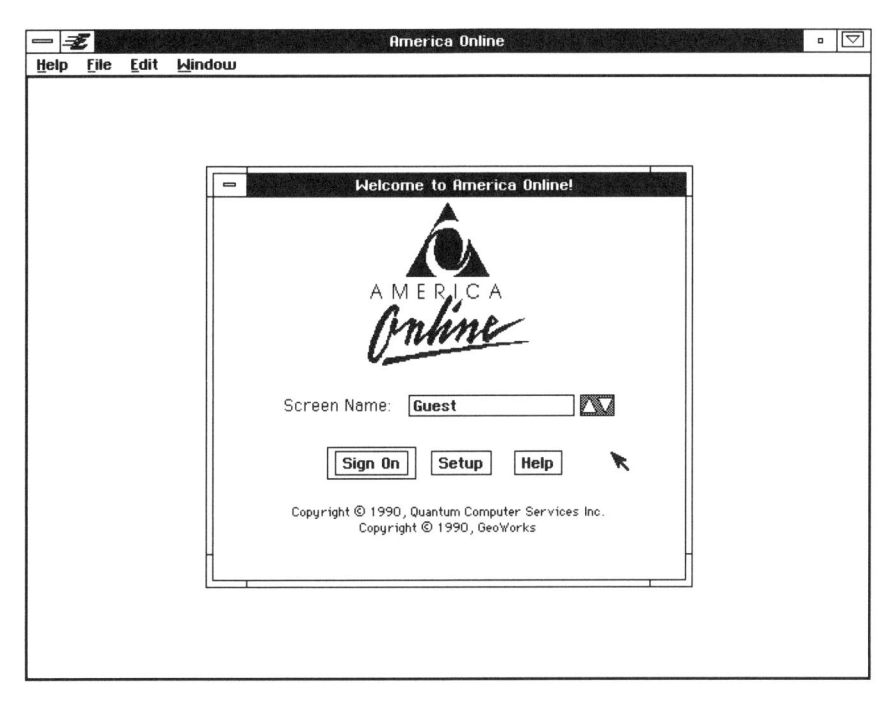

Figure 15-1 — The America Online Opening Window.

See Chapter 3 for a discussion about using the features on a GeoWorks Ensemble application window, including the Control button, Express menu, and the Minimize/Maximize button.

The Menu Bar

The offline Menu bar contains four menus: Help, File, Edit, and Window. These menus are available whether you are online or offline.

Note: Online means that you are connected to and actively communicating with the service. Offline means the connection has been terminated.

15 America Online

Help Menu

The Help menu on the Welcome screen and Help menus on other windows offer immediate help about the America Online service.

Get Help

You can select this option to display the Get Help dialog box. When you click on a topic in the Topic panel, information about the topic displays in the Description panel.

About America Online

Select this option to view copyright information and the software version number of your America Online program.

Setup

The Setup option on the Help menu is the same as the Setup button in the Welcome to America Online window. Selecting this option displays the Setup dialog box shown in Figure 15-2. You can specify the access telephone numbers and the network service to use when connecting to America Online. You can also set your system parameters.

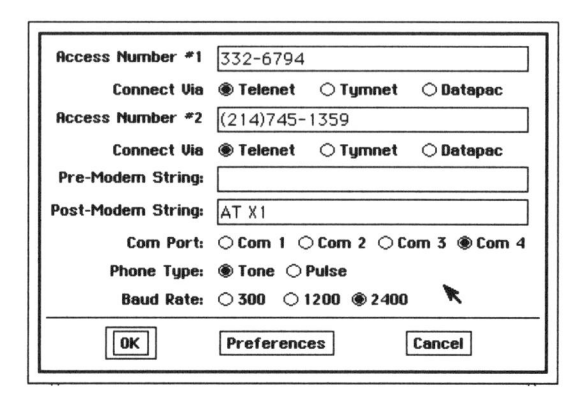

Figure 15-2 — The Setup Dialog Box.

When you click on the Preferences button in the Setup window, the program displays the Preferences dialog box shown in Figure 15-3. You can specify your modem and other parameters from the Preferences dialog box.

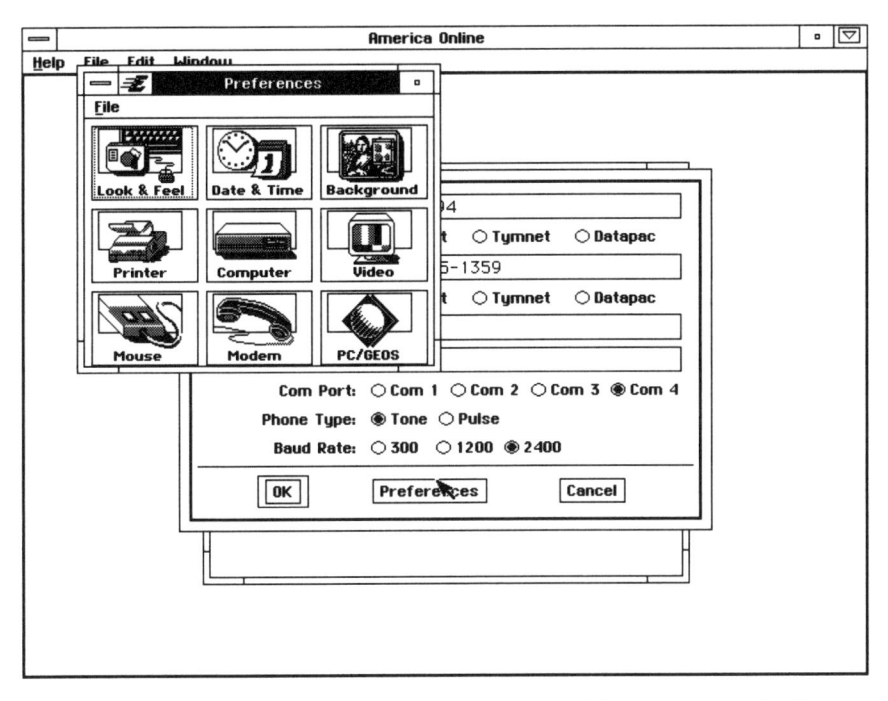

Figure 15-3 — The Preferences Menu Selected from America Online.

Options

This Help menu option allows you to change text spacing and size, automatically scroll incoming text, and change background color.

15 America Online

File Menu

The File menu, like other GeoWorks Ensemble File menus, allows you to create a new file, open, save or print an existing file, and exit the application. In addition, the America Online File menu allows you to open a communication log and cancel an action. Figure 15-4 displays the America Online File menu.

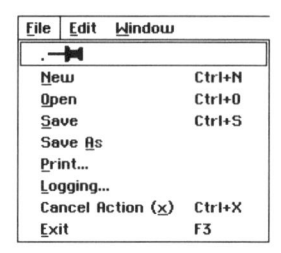

Figure 15-4 — The America Online File Menu.

Pin

See Chapter 7 for a discussion about the Pin option on the File menu.

New

When you select this option, the program opens a new blank window named Untitled, overlaying any other open window. You can type mail memos in this window while you are offline, then post the message when you are online. This can save you considerable charges for online time.

When you are online and select New from the File menu, you can type in the new document or use paste to place online text into the new document. You can then save, and/or print it. You can also attach text to a different document.

You can use the Edit menu to Cut or Copy selected text, and then use the Paste command to paste it into a window, or you can use the Quick Copy or Quick Move features. (See the Quick Copy and Quick Move section in Chapter 10 for a discussion about these features.)

Open

You can use this option to access other files (or conference logs), including those you create in America Online (using New from the File menu). You can read these while online, or, to limit connection charges, read them after you leave the service.

Save

See Chapter 7 for a discussion about the Save option on the File menu.

Save As

See Chapter 7 for a discussion about the Save As option on the File menu.

Print

This menu option allows you to print files, including those you have saved online, such as conference logs or encyclopedia articles.

See Chapter 7 for a discussion about the Print option on the File menu.

If you have not previously installed a printer or want to select a different one, you must terminate your America Online connection (if you are online) and select Setup from the offline menu. Then select Printer from the Preferences menu and select the printer you want from the list.

Logging

You can log your online activities, saving to disk a copy of the materials you read (for example, encyclopedia articles), or record your chat sessions with other America Online subscribers. You can edit the log offline, saving the portions you want as a separate document and discarding the original log. You can activate two types of logging: Conference and Session.

Conference log

The conference log saves all text from all chat areas, including classrooms, forums, conference rooms, and America Online rooms.

15 America Online

Session log

The session log saves information from all areas of America Online — except the chat areas — such as encyclopedia articles.

Opening a Log

Follow these steps to open a conference or session log:

1. Select Logging from the File menu.

2. Click the Open button in the Conference Log panel or the Session Log panel in the dialog box.

3. Select the drive and subdirectory in which you want to save the log, then name the log.

4. Click the Save button.

5. The program displays the log name in the log window. Click the OK button to accept the file name.

6. When you want to close the log, select Logging from the File menu, then click the Close button.

Note: If you exit America Online without closing the log file, the program will open the log (and start recording again) the next time you go online.

Caution: Conference and Session logs can use a great deal of disk space. If you are saving to a floppy disk, be careful to close the log before you run out of disk space. You can then replace the disk with a new floppy and open a new log.

Reading a Log

Follow these steps to read a log file:

1. Exit America Online (if you are online).

2. Select Open from the File menu.

3. In the File to open dialog box, select the drive and directory where you saved the log, then select the file you want to read.

America Online 15

Cancel (Ctrl+X)

Select this option to cancel any action in progress, such as signing off.

Exit (F3)

Select this option to exit America Online (go offline). When you select Exit, the program asks you to confirm that you want to exit. When you select Yes, you return to the Welcome to America Online window, and the program terminates the telephone connection.

Note: You can also double-click the Control button at the top left of the America Online window to go offline.

Edit Menu

The Edit menu allows you to Cut, Copy and Paste text in the same or different documents. See the Edit Menu Section in Chapter 7 for a discussion about using the Cut, Copy and Paste options on the Edit menu.

Go To Menu

The program displays the Go To menu only when you are online. Figure 15-5 shows the online Menu Bar with the Go To menu selected.

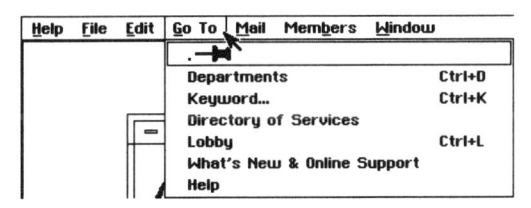

```
Help  File  Edit  Go To  Mail  Members  Window
                  .
                  Departments              Ctrl+D
                  Keyword...               Ctrl+K
                  Directory of Services
                  Lobby                    Ctrl+L
                  What's New & Online Support
                  Help
```

Figure 15-5 — The Online Go To Menu.

Compare the Online Menu Bar in Figure 15-5 with the offline Menu Bar previously shown in Figure 15-1. You can use the Go To menu to direct your online activities.

Departments (Ctrl+D)

Selecting this option displays the Browse the Service dialog box shown in Figure 15-6. The program displays icons for available departments.

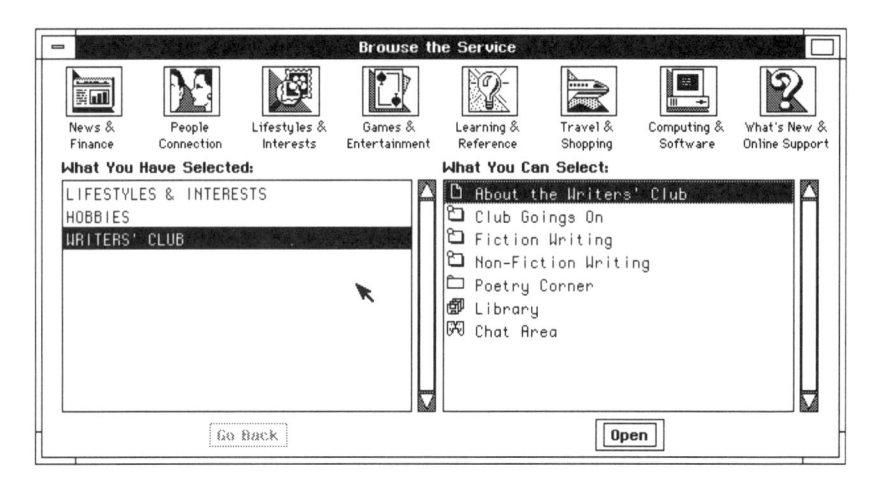

Figure 15-6 — The Browse the Service Dialog Box.

Below the row of icons are two panels. When you select a department icon, the program lists your selection in the left panel. The program displays in the right panel the contents of the highlighted option in the left panel. The symbol at the beginning of each item in the right panel indicates the item type.

Select an item in the right panel to search through the program directories (file icon) and rooms (chat areas, conference rooms) and bulletin boards for posting and reading messages). Double-click on an item in the left panel (or single-click and select Go Back) to go back to previous levels or select other options in the department.

Keyword (Ctrl+K)

You can use keywords for shortcut access to various areas of America Online. Select the Keyword option from the Go To menu, type a keyword, then click the OK button. To see a list of department-specific keywords, select Keyword Help from the Keyword window.

Directory of Services

Select this option to learn about the American Online services. The information on each service includes: the service name, keywords (if applicable), search words (if applicable), access path to the service, and a description of the service.

Search the Directory of Services

You can perform a general search (subject name) or specific search (service name) of the Directory of Services. For example, if you want to find information related to music on America Online, select Search the Directory of Services option, then type the word "music." The program displays a list of available services related to the search word. You can find additional information about a service by selecting that item from the displayed list.

Once you decide on the service you want, Select the Directory of Services option, enter the service name, then click the Go button.

Lobby (Ctrl+L)

Selecting the Lobby option is the same as selecting People Connection from the Browse the Service window. These options allow you to communicate interactively with anyone else in the room (service) you selected. Type a message, then click the Send button. Any other subscribers currently online in the same room can read your message and respond.

The following paragraphs describe the four boxes to the left of the main panel in the Lobby dialog box.

People

When you select the People icon, the program displays a list of the people currently in the room. You can learn about someone or send an instant message to someone by selecting a name from the list.

Rooms

Select this option to display a list of all America Online rooms and the number of occupants in each. To enter a room, highlight the room name, then click the Go button (or double-click the room name). If you do not want to enter a room, double-click the Control button to close the window.

You can click the Create Room button to open a public room, or click the Create Private button to open a private room for only you and invited members.

P.C. Studio

You can use this option to obtain information about online activities. What's Happening This Week lists the activities of various People Connection rooms. Center Stage Box Office provides information about Auditorium events.

Center Stage

Select this option for a variety of conferences and special events. For example, in Center Stage you can ask questions of experts, or observe special interest conferences.

What's New & Online Support

You can use this option to find the latest information about GeoWorks Ensemble, billing information, and to ask questions about your account. Normally you will receive answers within two business days.

Help

See the Menu Bar/Help Menu section previously discussed.

Mail Menu

The Mail menu is shown in Figure 15-7.

America Online 15

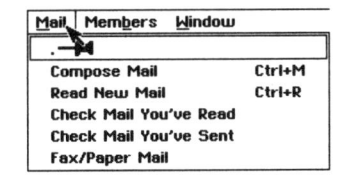

```
Mail  Members  Window
┌─────────────────────────────┐
│ Compose Mail        Ctrl+M  │
│ Read New Mail       Ctrl+R  │
│ Check Mail You've Read      │
│ Check Mail You've Sent      │
│ Fax/Paper Mail              │
└─────────────────────────────┘
```

Figure 15-7 — The Mail Menu.

You can write, read and review mail, send a fax message, or send paper mail when you select this option.

Compose Mail (Ctrl+M)

You can use this option to compose and send mail. Address the mail memo by typing in the screen name(s) of the member(s) to whom you want the mail sent. If you are addressing the mail to more than one person, separate each screen name with a comma. Use CC (Carbon Copy) to enter the screen names of any others to whom you want to send a copy of the mail.

Type the subject of your mail memo in the subject field. You must make an entry in the subject field. Type your mail message in the large panel.

You can attach files to your mail memo by clicking the Attach File button. The program displays a dialog box in which you specify the drive, subdirectory and file name of the file you want to attach, then click the Open button. The File field attaches the name of the file(s), and the Attach File button changes to Detach File.

When you are ready to send the mail (with attached files, if any) click the Send button.

Read New Mail (Ctrl+R)

When you go online, the program sounds a tone if you have mail, and the online Welcome Window mail symbol reads You Have Mail. To read your mail, select the Read New Mail option on the Mail menu (shortcut [Ctrl]-[R]), or you can click the mail symbol on the online Welcome window. The program displays the New Mail dialog box. Double-click the name of the mail you want to read.

273

Reply to Mail

You can use the Reply to Mail option to respond to someone. When you select this option, the program automatically addresses the reply to the person who sent you the currently-highlighted mail. The program inserts the name of the person who sent you the mail into the To: field, and inserts the same subject in the Subject field preceded by "Re:." You can change these fields if you wish. Type your message, attaching a file if you want to, then click the Send button.

Download Attached File

The program displays a diskette symbol next to the title of new mail that has a file attached to it. The program also displays the approximate time required to download the attached file (copy it from the America Online service to your hard disk or a floppy disk).

To download the file attached to the highlighted mail title, click the Download File button. The program displays a dialog box in which you select the drive, subdirectory and file name for the saved file. To rename the file, highlight the file name and type in the new file name. Click the Save button to save the file.

Check Mail You've Read

The program deletes any mail sent to you that is over seven days old. You can read or reread your mail anytime within the seven days. To reread your mail, select the Check Mail You've Read option from the Mail menu. The program displays the Old Mail dialog box. Double-click the title you want to reread.

Check Mail You've Sent

The program deletes any outgoing mail that is over seven days old. You can review your outgoing mail anytime within the seven days by selecting Check Mail You've Sent from the Mail menu. The program displays the Outgoing Mail dialog box. Double-click the title you want to reread.

Fax/Paper Mail

To send a fax (facsimile transmission) or send paper mail using the America Online service, select Fax/Paper Mail from the Mail menu. The program displays the Browse the Service window with the current price structure and instructions for these communications. When you are ready to proceed, click the Send Fax/Paper Mail button and follow the procedures described earlier in the Compose Mail section. You can send only one kind of message at a time: paper mail, electronic mail, or fax.

Fax

You can compose your fax in the mail window or copy a saved memo file into the mail window. You cannot attach a file to a fax transmission. If you want to send mail created with a word processor outside the GeoWorks Ensemble program, make sure to save the file as an ASCII file before opening America Online.

The To: field for a fax communication requires a name and phone number. For example: Deitz Bexar800-555-1212. You can use up to 20 characters in the name, including upper- or lower-case characters, blank spaces, and punctuation marks (except commas and parentheses).

You can fax simultaneously to any three fax machines in the U.S. (including Alaska and Hawaii) or Canada. To send a fax message to multiple fax numbers and/or to other members of America Online, enter each addressee separated by a comma in the To: and/or CC: fields. For example, Deitz Bexar800-555-1212, Preeble Deitz800-555-1213, Teddy Preeble800-555-1214.

The program formats fax messages for an 8.5" x 11" page. All lines wrap at the column 79 position. To create shorter lines, or if you do not want the lines to wrap, use a carriage return to end a line. A fax can have up to 60 lines on a page. To create a page break, type on a line by itself:

>>> PAGE BREAK <<<.

The first page of a fax displays the following information at the top:

- To: Fax names and numbers as entered in the mail window.
- CC: Carbon copy addresses, if applicable.
- From: Screen name you used to send the message.
- Date: Date and time the message was sent.
- Subj: Subject line as entered in the mail window.

15 America Online

To include your real name in a fax, you must include it in the body of the text.

Before the program transmits a fax, it displays a message stating the total charge for the fax. You can then either confirm the fax or cancel it. After you send a fax, the program posts a message in your electronic mailbox notifying you whether the fax transmission was successful or unsuccessful.

Paper mail

Paper mail allows you to send an electronic message which is subsequently converted to a paper letter and sent to the recipient by regular mail.

To address paper mail, type the name of the recipient in the To: field of the Compose Mail window. For example, to send mail to Deitz Bexar, type: Deitz Bexarusmail. You can use up to 33 characters for the name. To send paper mail to multiple addresses, separate each with a comma.

When you are ready to send the paper mail, click the Send Now button. The program displays a dialog box. Enter the RETURN address first, click the Continue button, then type the MAILING address. The America Online service mails the letter within 24 hours in a #10 business-size envelope.

A paper mail transmission can be up to four pages long. You can include up to 40 lines of text on the first page (not including the mailing address and return address). Additional pages can contain up to 53 lines. Text lines wrap at the column 70 position. The program does not include automatically this electronic mail information: To, From, CC, Date, Subject. You must include this information in the body of the message if you want to send it.

Do not use these special characters — \ , > , ^ — in paper mail. The > symbol is reserved for designating a page break. The program converts these characters to a space. You can designate a page break by typing on a line by itself:

```
>>> PAGE BREAK <<<.
```

Before the program transmits the paper mail, it displays a message stating the total charge. You can then confirm the mail or cancel it.

Members Menu

You can use the Members menu shown in Figure 15-8 to send instant messages, get member information, locate a member online, or access the member directory.

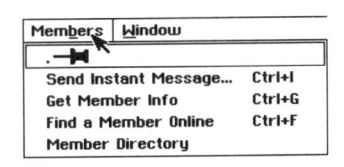

Figure 15-8 — The Members Menu.

Send Instant Message (Ctrl+I)

Select this option to send a quick message to another currently-online member. The program displays a dialog box in which you enter the recipient's screen name. You can then verify whether the member is currently online by clicking the Available button. If the member is online, type the message in the window, then click the Send button.

To respond to an instant message, click the Respond button, type your response, and then click the Send button.

Get Member Info (Ctrl+G)

This menu option displays information about other America Online members. To obtain information about a member, enter the screen name, then click the OK button. The program displays the Get Member Info window with the city and state in which the member resides. Click OK to continue. Double-click on the Control button (or select Cancel) to close the window.

Find a Member Online (Ctrl+F)

Select this option to locate a currently-online member. Type the screen name of the member you want to locate, then click the OK button. The program displays a message indicating if the member is online and in which chat area. Click OK to continue. Double-click on the Control button (or select Cancel) to close the window.

15 America Online

Member Directory

At the time this book was written, the Member Directory was under development. The Member Directory will list profiles of America Online members and allow you to search for members with specific interests.

Window Menu

The Window menu is shown in Figure 15-9.

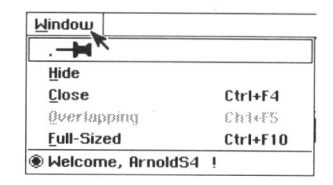

```
Window
 .-📌
 Hide
 Close          Ctrl+F4
 Overlapping    Ctrl+F5
 Full-Sized     Ctrl+F10
◉ Welcome, ArnoldS4 !
```

Figure 15-9 — The Window Menu.

Select the Window menu to hide or close windows, switch to another open window, or change the window arrangement.

It is a good idea to restrict to fewer than 10 the number of open windows in America Online.

See Chapter 4 for a discussion about window operations such as resizing, relocating, closing, and scrolling.

Hide

Select this option to hide a window (not display it) but keep it open. To display a hidden window, select the title from the list of open windows in the lower portion of the Window menu.

Close (Ctrl+F4)

Select this option from the Window menu to close a window. You can also close a window by clicking the Control button and selecting Close, or by double-clicking the Control button.

Overlapping (Ctrl+F5)

Select this option to display open windows in overlapping format. The program displays the active window (the most recently-selected window) on top. This option allows you to view more than one window at a time.

Full-Sized (Ctrl+F10)

Select this option to display the active window in full size. You can view only one window at a time when this option is active.

Bottom Section of Window Menu

The bottom section of the Window menu lists all open windows. Select a window to make it the active window.

Summary

This chapter described the services and features available in the America Online bulletin board service. If you have a modem, you can subscribe to and use the America Online service from within GeoWorks Ensemble.

Chapter 16

The GeoComm Application

In this chapter you will learn how to use the GeoComm application to communicate with bulletin boards, online services such as America Online, or other personal computers. You will learn how to:

- Create text or retrieve a file to send to the remote computer
- Retrieve text, saving it to the hard disk
- Configure GeoComm for your hardware
- Write scripts to automate repetitive communication tasks, such as logging onto a bulletin board you use frequently.

The GeoComm application allows you to communicate through a modem over telephone lines with other computers. A modem is a computer translation device. It translates information from your computer into a form that can be sent over telephone lines. At the other end of the telephone line a modem then translates the information back to a form that the other computer can understand.

16 The GeoComm Application

Accessing the GeoComm Application

You can access the GeoComm application two ways:

- Double-clicking the GeoComm icon in the GeoManager WORLD directory
- Selecting GeoComm from the Express Menu/Startup option.

Except for the Title Bar and Menu Bar, the opening GeoComm window is blank when you open the program.

See Chapters 3 and 4 for discussions about the features and functions of application windows.

Figure 16-1 shows a pinned File menu with three cascade menus displayed.

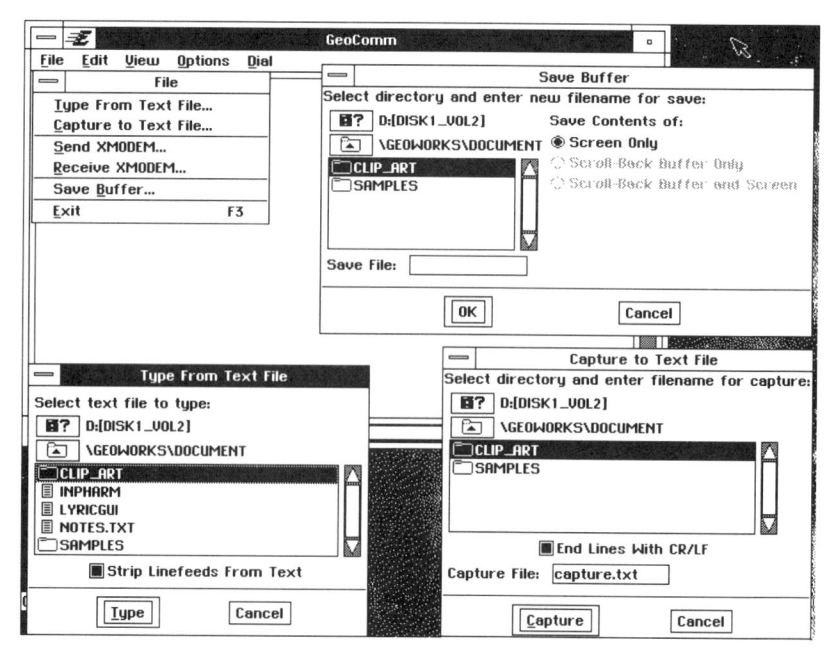

Figure 16-1 — Pinned File Menu and Three Cascade Menus.

The GeoComm Application 16

Figure 16-2 shows the same pinned File menu and the remaining two cascade menus that are accessible from the File menu.

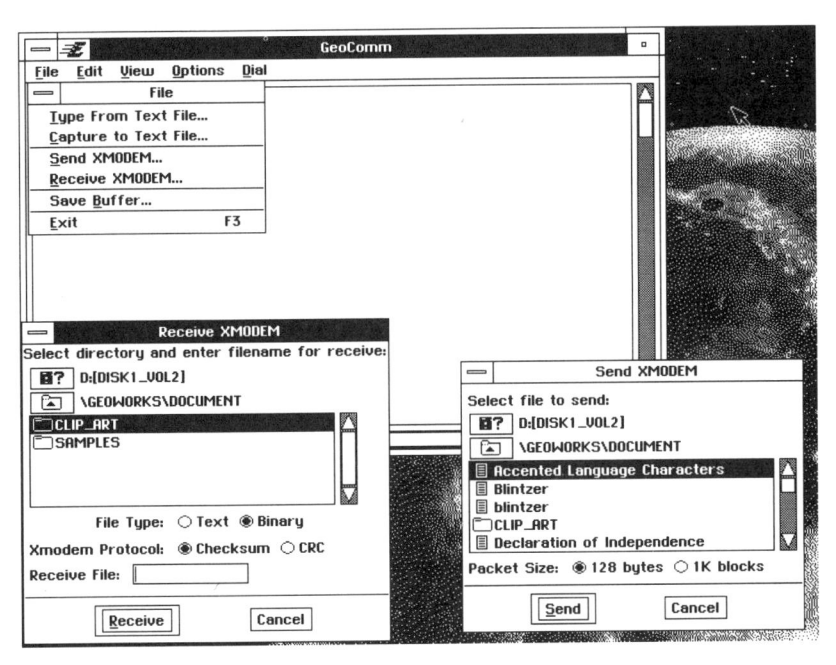

Figure 16-2 — The GeoComm File Menu and Two Cascade Menus.

When the GeoComm window is active, the cursor displays as a solid black rectangle. When the GeoComm window is not active, the cursor displays as an outline (not filled). Click on the GeoComm window to make it the active window; the cursor displays as a solid rectangle. When the GeoComm window is active, the program sends immediately to the remote computer anything you type in the GeoComm window.

The following describes the GeoComm menus.

283

16 The GeoComm Application

File Menu

You can use the File menu, as shown in Figure 16-1 and Figure 16-2, for file related functions.

Type from Text File

Once you establish communication with a remote computer (you are online), you can then exchange information. When you disconnect from the remote computer you are offline. Some bulletin boards determine your charges by the number of minutes you are online with them. When you are online, the program sends whatever you type in the GeoComm window to the remote computer (or bulletin board). The program places information you receive from the remote computer in your window at the cursor position.

You can reduce your online time by composing messages offline. You can send files from other applications, send DOS text files, or copy text from other documents into the GeoComm window. Select the Type From Text File option to copy DOS text files into GeoComm.

When you select this option, the program displays the Type From Text File dialog box. This dialog box is shown in Figure 16-1 in the lower left corner of the window. The dialog box shows drive D: is the current drive and the current directory is \GEOWORKS\DOCUMENT. See Chapter 7 for a discussion about selecting subdirectories and files.

Note: GeoComm works only with DOS files. As you move around subdirectories you will not see any GEOS-type documents listed in the subdirectory contents window when you use the Type From Text File option. For example, the program will not display any GeoWrite document file names, which are GEOS-type files.

You can, however, open a GeoWrite text window on your screen, select (highlight) text that you want to transmit, then copy it to the GeoComm window. You can use Quick Copy or Quick Move to copy the highlighted text to the GeoComm window for transmission.

The following outlines the procedure for sending (transmitting) a DOS text file.

The GeoComm Application 16

1. Select the Type From Text File option on the File menu. The program displays the Type From Text File dialog box.

2. Select the drive, subdirectory and file name of the file you want to send.

3. Click the End Lines With CR/LF option to have linefeeds after each carriage return. Normally you want this option turned On. Contact the computer service you are calling to determine whether the service requires this option.

4. Click the Type option on the Type From Text File dialog box. The program displays a status window indicating the name of the file you are transmitting and the contents of the file. Click the Stop button in the status window to stop the transfer of data.

Capture to Text File

Select this option to store data as you receive it, specifying a drive, subdirectory, and file name for the data. You can also decide when to start and stop recording data. The following steps outline the procedure for saving incoming data to a file.

1. Select the Capture to Text File option from the File menu. The program displays the Capture to Text File dialog box.

2. Select the drive and subdirectory in which you want to save the file.

3. Enter a DOS file name (1-8 characters followed by a period and an optional 1-3 character extension) for the file. The program displays the default file name CAPTURE.TXT.

4. Select the End Lines With CR/LF option to have linefeeds after each carriage return. Normally you want this option turned On.

5. Select the Capture option. The program displays the Capture Status window. Everything you send or receive is save to disk in the file you specified.

6. Click the Done button in the Capture Status window when you want to stop recording data.

16 The GeoComm Application

Send XMODEM

When you type into the GeoComm window or transmit a DOS file using the Type From Text File option, the program does not check for errors in the transmitted data. On noisy telephone lines, errors can be so severe that the received text is incomprehensible. The XMODEM technique uses error checking to assure essentially error-free transmissions, even on noisy telephone lines.

When you send or receive files using XMODEM, the program transfers the file in blocks of data. Each block is tested to make sure it transferred properly and without error. If the program detects an error, it retransmits the faulty block.

Both the local and remote computers must use the XMODEM operation. You can use XMODEM to send DOS files, or binary files such as GEOS documents. The following outlines the steps required to send a document using XMODEM.

1. Make sure the remote computer or bulletin board is set up to receive XMODEM. To do this, you must specify whether you are sending a text file or a non-text file (a binary file). Usually the instructions for setting up a remote computer to receive XMODEM are listed on the bulletin board you are calling. If not, contact the computer service.

2. Select the Send XMODEM option from the File menu. The program displays the Send XMODEM dialog box, which is shown in Figure 16-1 in the lower right corner of the window.

3. Locate the file you want to send by selecting the drive, subdirectory and file name.

4. Select a Packet Size of 1K blocks (1,000 bytes) if your telephone connection is relatively good and the remote computer accepts 1K blocks. If not, select 128 bytes.

5. Click the Send button. The program displays the Send Status window indicating the file being transmitted and any errors encountered during the transmission. Click the Cancel button if you want to stop the file transmission.

Receive XMODEM

Receiving XMODEM files is similar to sending them. The following steps outline the procedure for receiving XMODEM files. You might use this mode to download files or programs from a bulletin board.

1. Prepare the remote computer or bulletin board for XMODEM transmission. To do this, specify that you want to receive an XMODEM transmission. The instructions for setting up the remote computer to send XMODEM are usually listed on the bulletin board you are calling. If not, contact the computer service.

2. Select the Receive XMODEM option from the File menu. The program displays the Receive XMODEM dialog box, as shown in Figure 16-2 in the lower left corner of the window.

3. Specify the drive and subdirectory in which you want to save the file.

4. Enter a DOS file name (1-8 characters followed by a period and an optional 1-3 character extension) for the file.

5. Select the File Type option: Text or Binary. Select Text to receive a DOS text file. Select Binary to receive a GEOS document or a program file. (Some bulletin boards allow you to download software programs which are in the public domain.)

6. Select CRC if the remote system uses CRC checking (Cyclic Redundancy Check). Select Checksum if the remote system doesn't allow CRC. CRC is a better error-checking method than the Checksum method. Both methods, however, should produce the same results: error-free transmissions. If you are not sure which setting to use, select Checksum.

7. Click the Receive button. The program displays the Receive Status window, indicating the name of the file you are receiving and any errors occurring during the transmission. To stop receiving the file, click the Cancel button.

Note: If the program dims the Cancel button, it means you cannot interrupt the file transfer.

16 The GeoComm Application

Save Buffer

As you transmit or receive a file, the program displays the data on the screen. The program scrolls text upward as the data fills the screen. The program stores the most-recently displayed 175 lines in a special display buffer (storage device) called the scroll-back buffer.

Use the vertical scroll bar to view lines which have scrolled off the screen, up to the last 175 lines. To view the currently-active screen again, move the vertical scroll bar to the bottom.

The program stores the text in the scroll-back buffer in DOS text format. You can save the contents of the scroll-back buffer as a DOS file following these steps:

1. Select the Save Buffer option on the File menu. The program displays the Save Buffer dialog box, which was previously shown in Figure 16-1.

2. Select the drive and subdirectory in which you want to save the buffer contents.

3. Click the Save File button. Type a DOS file name for the buffer file using 1-8 characters, followed by a period and an optional 1-3 character extension.

4. Select one of the save options on the right side of the Save Buffer dialog box:

    - **Screen Only**   Use this option to save only the contents of the currently-displayed screen.

    - **Scroll-Back Buffer Only**   Use this option to save the information that has scrolled past the top of the screen.

    - **Scroll-Back Buffer and Screen**   Use this option to save both the contents of the Scroll-Back Buffer and the contents of the currently-displayed screen.

5. Click the OK button to create the file and save the text.

Exit

Select the Exit option to close all open documents and exit the application. If any documents contain unsaved changes, the program will ask if you want to save the changes before you exit.

Edit Menu

You can use the Edit menu to copy text from other applications or to other applications via the Clipboard. Figure 16-3 shows the Edit menu.

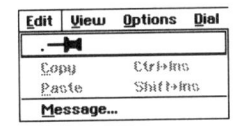

Figure 16-3 — The Edit Menu.

See Chapter 7 for a discussion about using the Edit menu to cut and paste or copy and paste text using the Clipboard.

Use the Clipboard to copy all or portions of a GEOS file (such as a GeoWrite file) into the GeoComm window.

You do not need to use the Clipboard to place DOS text files (such as files created in Notepad) in the GeoComm window, because GeoComm uses DOS files. You might consider using the Clipboard for DOS type text files, however, if you want only a portion of the DOS document.

Follow these steps to send (transmit) text copied from the Clipboard:

1. Use the Cut or Copy command (in any application) to place on the Clipboard the text you want to send.

2. Activate the GeoComm window by clicking on it, or if GeoComm is not already running, open it using the Express menu/Startup option.

3. Select Paste from the Edit menu. The program copies the contents of the Clipboard into the GeoComm window and transmits the text to the remote computer.

16 The GeoComm Application

Message

Use the Message option to edit messages before sending them. The following outlines the procedure for editing messages and then sending them.

1. Select the Message option. The program displays the Message window. Figure 16-4 shows a pinned Edit menu and a Message window.

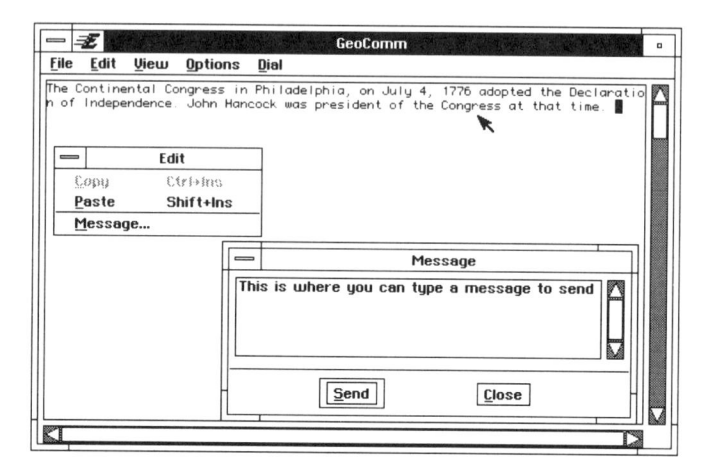

Figure 16-4 — The Edit Menu and Message Window.

2. Type the message you want to send, editing it as necessary.

3. When you are satisfied with the message, click the Send button on the Message window. The program sends the message to the remote computer. The main GeoComm window displays the portion that has been transmitted.

4. You can continue transmitting by first typing (and correcting) the message in the Message window, and then clicking the Send button when you want to transmit.

Note: Each time you click the Send button, the program transmits the entire contents of the Message window. Press [←BkSp] to delete the previous contents before typing your next message.

5. Click the Close button to return to the main GeoComm window. You can continue typing responses to incoming messages directly in the GeoComm main window, but remember that everything you type is transmitted immediately, without an opportunity to edit the message.

View Menu

You can change the appearance of the screen display using the View menu.

Figure 16-5 shows a pinned View menu and the Window Size dialog box (selected from the View menu).

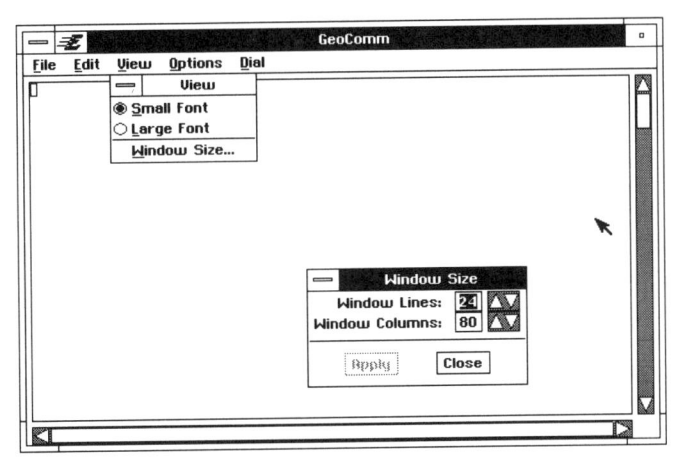

Figure 16-5 — The View Menu and the Window Size Dialog Box.

Text Large/Text Small

Select this option to change the display of text to large or small in the GeoComm window. Changing the size of the displayed font does not change the number of lines or columns displayed, unless the window becomes too large for the screen. In that case, the program reduces the number of displayed lines and columns.

16 The GeoComm Application

Window Size

When you select the Window Size option, the program displays a dialog box showing the current number of lines and columns in the display. You can click the arrow buttons to change the number of lines and the number of column in the display. After you make your selection, click the Apply button. The program changes the display to reflect your selections. When you are satisfied with the widow size, click the Close button to return to the GeoComm window.

Note: 80 columns and 24 lines are the maximums. If your screen cannot display these maximums, the program reduces them.

Options Menu

Use the Options menu to specify how you will display, store, and transfer data, matching your system with the remote system configuration.

Figure 16-6 shows a pinned Options menu in the lower left of the window. The Protocol, Terminal, and Modem dialog boxes are also shown.

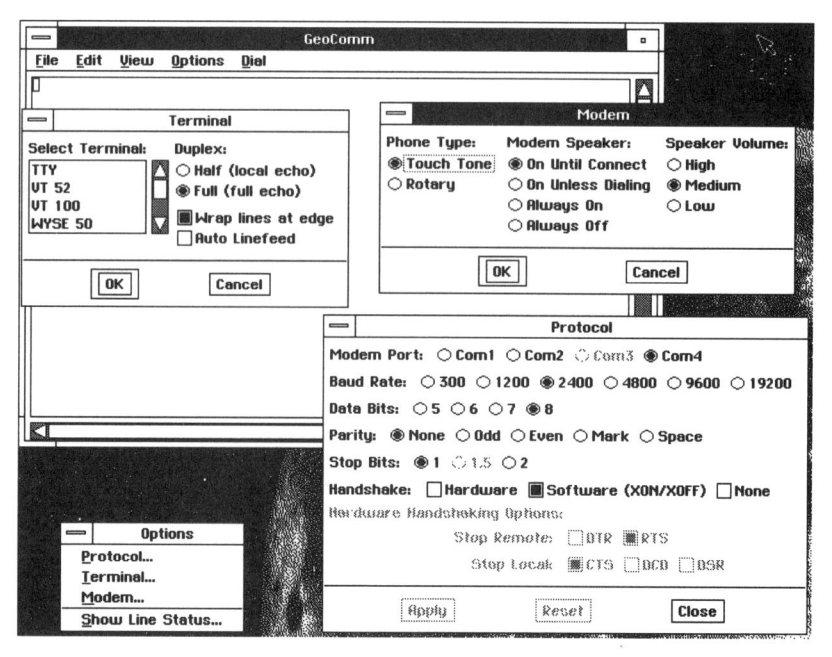

Figure 16-6 — The Options Menu, and the Protocol, Terminal, and Modem Dialog Boxes.

The GeoComm Application 16

Before you can communicate with another system, you must set certain GeoComm parameters:

- **Protocol**   The transmitting and receiving settings
- **Terminal**   The settings for displaying and decoding the data
- **Modem**   The settings required to operate your modem.

Protocol Settings

In order for your computer to communicate with a remote computer, the protocol settings of both systems must match. You set your system default settings in the Preferences application (see Chapter 4). You can change the settings for the current session by selecting Protocol. The program displays the Protocol dialog box previously shown in Figure 16-6.

Any selection you make in the Protocol dialog box will override settings in the Preferences application — for the current session only. The next time you start GeoWorks Ensemble, the program reestablishes the Preferences default settings for GeoComm. The following paragraphs describe the protocol settings:

Modem Port

Configuring your modem for your system usually involves setting switches on the modem to select the proper communication port (Com port). Each Com port has a number. The Com port number is a conventional way of telling the software where to send and receive information. Before you can make your software (GeoComm) work, you must set your modem to one of the valid Com ports, and then tell the software which Com port to use. Most modems can be set to Com1, Com2, Com3 or Com4.

Some computers have a built-in serial port (usually set as Com1). If your computer has a built-in serial port, you may need to set your modem to Com2, Com3 or Com4.

16 The GeoComm Application

The Com ports and IRQ (Interrupt Request) settings are related. The settings for these are usually determined by jumper blocks or DIP switches on the modem or serial port. Most modems can be set to use IRQ2, IRQ3, IRQ4, and IRQ5. These settings are reserved for particular devices as follows:

IRQ2 Reserved for Interrupt Controller
IRQ3 Secondary asynchronous device (Com2 and Com4)
IRQ4 Primary asynchronous device (Com1 and Com3)
IRQ5 Hard disk controller.

Communications software usually supports IRQ3 and IRQ4. This means you must be careful not to share an IRQ setting with a mouse or other device that whose software is memory resident — it stays in memory, even when the device is not active. (Often you can share an IRQ setting with a device if it is not driven by a memory resident program).

A mouse device is usually set on Com1. If so, you should not set your modem to either Com1 or Com3 (they both use IRQ4 and would interfere). In this case Com2 or Com4 would be reasonable choices.

A bus mouse does not have a Com port address, but does have an IRQ setting. You must make sure that its IRQ setting does not conflict with your modem IRQ setting.

Your transmission settings for Baud Rate, Data Bits, Parity, and Stop Bits must match those of the remote system.

Baud Rate

The Baud Rate is the number of changes per second in the electrical state of the output line from the modem. This is generally understood to be the same as the number of bits per second that can be transmitted by the modem. (2400 baud implies 2400 bits per second, which may or may not be the case. At higher speeds, the bits per second can be higher than the baud rate.)

Data Bits

This signifies the amount of data the computer can store and process at one time (word). Most PCs process eight bits at one time (8 bits = 1 byte = 1 word). However, in some cases the word length is different. Specify the number of data bits for your system.

Parity

This item specifies the type of error detection technique used to check the integrity of the binary data transmission (1 or 0 bits). In some parity systems, an extra bit is added to the block of bits (word). You can select the following types of parity:

- **None** As the name says, no bits are added.
- **Odd parity** For odd parity transmissions, the program adds an extra bit to keep the sum of the bits always odd. For example, if there are three 1 bits, the program adds a 0 bit to keep the sum of the bits at 3 (odd). If there are four 1 bits, then the program adds a 1 bit to bring the sum to 5 (odd).
- **Even parity** For even parity transmissions, the program adds an extra bit to keep the sum of all the bits always even. For example, if there are three 1 bits in the byte, the program adds a 1 bit to make the sum 4 (even). If there are an even number of 1 bits, the program adds a 0 bit.
- **Mark** Mark parity always adds an extra 1 bit to the byte.
- **Space** Space parity always adds an extra 0 bit to the byte.

Stop Bits

Use this option to set the number of stop bits to insert in the transmission to mark the end of each word.

16 The GeoComm Application

Handshake

The local and remote computers send handshake signals back and forth to establish a valid connection. You can select two handshake options: Software and None.

WARNING

Select Software (XON/XOFF) from the handshake options. If you select None, you can lose portions of your incoming data.

Accepting protocol changes

When you are satisfied with the protocol settings, click the Apply button to accept the settings, then click the Close button to return to the GeoComm window.

Terminal Settings

Some remote systems may expect your system to be a specific type of terminal, assuming your computer will be able to translate certain codes and text sequences. GeoComm provides seven terminal emulations, settings that make your computer act and respond (simulate) as a specific type of terminal so it can speak the same language as the remote computer.

Select Terminal

GeoComm emulates (simulates) the following types of terminals:

- TTY
- ANSI
- VT 522
- IBM 3101
- VT 100
- TVI 950
- WYSE 50.

Usually you use a standard TTY (teletype) terminal emulation. If you connect to a system requiring some other type of terminal, you must select the emulation from the list.

Duplex

The Duplex setting determines the direction of data flow. Full duplex allows data to flow in both directions at the same time, (to and from your computer). Half duplex allows data to flow in only one direction at a time.

- **Half (local echo)** If the characters you type do not appear on your screen, then choose Half duplex.
- **Full (full echo)** If the characters you type appear twice on your screen, select Full duplex.

Wrap lines at edge

Set this option when you want GeoComm to wrap any text lines that are too long to fit in the display window. GeoComm will automatically split long lines into shorter ones. If you do not select this option, GeoComm will not display the portions of the lines that do not fit in the window.

Auto Linefeed

This option replaces a received carriage return with a carriage return and a linefeed. Turn off this option if the lines on your display are double spaced. Turn on this option if each new line on your display overwrites the previous line.

Accepting terminal settings

When you are satisfied with the terminal settings, click the OK button to return to the GeoComm window. Click the Cancel button to return to the GeoComm window without making any changes.

Modem Settings

Your computer must have a modem in order for you to use GeoComm to communicate over telephone lines with other computers.

The term "Hayes-compatible" indicates a modem that accepts the same command language as modems made by Hayes Microcomputer Products, Inc. Hayes developed the intelligent modem for first-generation personal computers in 1978. This command language (Hayes Standard AT Command Set) for modem control is now the industry standard. Use a Hayes or Hayes-compatible modem with the GeoComm application.

The command modem has two states: command and online. In the command state the modem accepts instructions (commands). In the online state the modem can dial, answer calls, transmit, and receive data. Once a modem is connected to a remote modem, it performs the handshaking procedure. This is quite similar to someone on a phone saying, "Hello." Then the remote end responds with, "Hello, this is...." If you have the modem speaker turned on, you will hear the harsh sounds of the modem handshake.

When the handshake is complete, the two computers are online and can communicate (transmit data to each other).

Select Modem from the Options menu to change your modem settings. The program displays the Modem dialog box previously shown in Figure 16-6.

Phone Type

There are two basic types of phone systems in use today, the Touch Tone and the Rotary. Select the type of phone service you have.

- **Touch Tone** Select Touch Tone if you hear different tones as you dial your phone.
- **Rotary** Select Rotary if you hear a series of clicks as you dial your phone.

Modem speaker

Modems are constructed with a built-in speaker, allowing you to hear the telephone operations as they happen. You can select one of the following options for the modem speaker:

- **On Until Connect** Select this option to hear the dialing operation. Your speaker remains on until the other modem answers.
- **On Unless Dialing** Select this option to turn on the speaker only while you are waiting for the other modem to answer.
- **Always On** Select this option to keep the speaker turned on throughout the transmission.
- **Always Off** Select this option to keep the speaker turned off throughout the transmission.

Speaker volume

Some modems do not come with their own internal volume controls. Use the Speaker Volume option to select a comfortable volume level for your modem speaker output. The choices are High, Medium and Low.

Show Line Status

GeoComm lets you monitor the occurrence of transmission errors, allowing you to verify that your protocol settings are correct. To display the line status, select Show Line Status from the Options menu. Figure 16-7 shows the Show Line Status window.

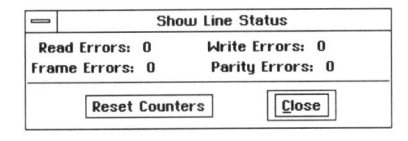

Figure 16-7 — The Show Line Status Window.

16 The GeoComm Application

GeoComm displays a count of four types of transmission errors: read, write, frame, and parity errors. Click the Reset Counters button to reset the four counters to zero. Click the Close button to close the window and return to the GeoComm window. GeoComm continues to monitor the errors. The next time you open the Show Line Status window (during the current session), GeoComm displays the updated error counts.

Dial Menu

Figure 16-8 shows a pinned Dial menu with the Quick Dial and Scripts dialog boxes displayed.

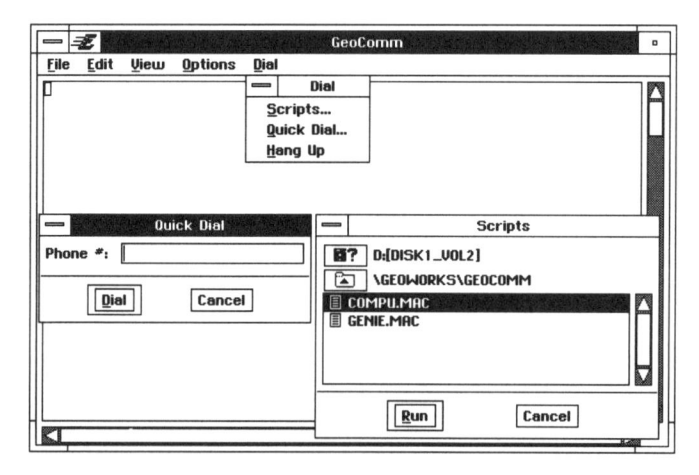

Figure 16-8 — The Dial Menu, and Quick Dial and Scripts Dialog Boxes.

Scripts

You can use the Scripts option to automate many of the repetitive communication tasks you perform regularly. For example, if you call a certain bulletin board frequently, you can set up an automatic log file so you do not have to remember the log-on sequence. GeoComm provides several script files which you can use as examples for creating you own scripts.

The GeoComm Application **16**

Creating a script file

Figure 16-9 shows the Scripts dialog box in the upper right corner. In the lower left is a Notepad display of a portion of the COMPU.MAC script file. In the lower right is another Notepad display of the GENIE.MAC script file.

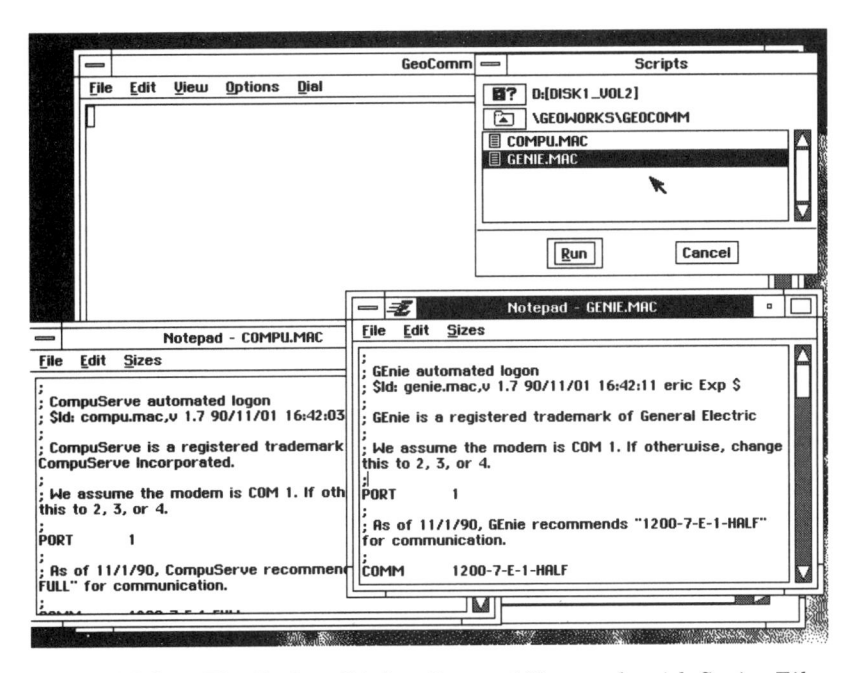

Figure 16-9 — The Scripts Dialog Box and Notepads with Script Files.

Script files are DOS files, the type of file Notepad can display and edit. You can use Notepad, or other DOS text editor, to create a new file and save it, or you can modify a supplied script file, then use the Save As option on the File menu to rename and save the file. You must use a DOS file name (1-8 characters) with the extension .MAC, or the program will not recognize the file as a script file.

It is a good idea to save all script files in the \GEOWORKS\GEOCOMM subdirectory.

See the Script Commands section later in this chapter for a discussion about writing a script.

301

16 The GeoComm Application

Running a script file

Follow these steps to run a script file:

1. Select Scripts from the Dial menu to display the Scripts dialog box previously shown in Figure 16-9.

2. Locate the script file you want to run. If the script file is not in the \GEOWORKS\GEOCOMM subdirectory, select the drive, subdirectory and file name of the file you want. You can avoid these additional steps by saving all script files in the \GEOWORKS\GEOCOMM subdirectory.

3. Click the Run button. The program displays the Script Display window, which shows you the script as it plays. Click the Stop button to stop the script.

Script commands

A script file is essentially a small program to perform repetitive tasks. For example, you can write a script to log onto a bulletin board. GeoComm provides a language of script commands for you to use when writing the script.

You must type script commands in uppercase. You can type labels in uppercase, lowercase, or a mixture of the two, although all labels must be typed consistently throughout the script. For example, GeoComm views these labels as inconsistent format:

    :Start :START :start :STarT.

In the Table 16-1, the words you must replace with text specific to your situation are enclosed in < > (angle brackets). You do not type the brackets.

The GeoComm Application 16

Table 16-1 — GeoComm Script Commands

Command	Description
:<label>	A label is a line beginning with a colon. The GOTO command (discussed later) forces the program to jump to a label to begin processing from that point.
:ABORT	:ABORT is a special label that must be in uppercase (the colon is required). If the user clicks the Stop button while the script is running, GeoComm jumps to the ABORT label and ends the script.
BELL	Sounds a beep to alert the user.
CLEAR	Clears the Script Display window.
COMM <baud-data bits-parity-stop bits-duplex>	Sets the communication settings. You can use these values in the script: 　　baud:　　300, 1200, 2400, 4800, 9600, 19200 　　data bits: 5, 6, 7, 8 　　parity:　　N, O, E, M, S 　　stop bits: 1, 1.5, 2 　　duplex:　 HALF, FULL. For example: COMM 2400-8-O-2-FULL in a script file means a 2400 baud line with eight data bits, odd parity, two stop bits, and FULL duplex.
DIAL <number>	Dials the number specified (tone or pulse does not matter here). To dial 9 for an outside line and then dial 555-1212, enter the following in the script file: `Dial 9,555-1212`
END	Stops the script and returns control to the user. It does not use the :ABORT label.

continued...

303

16 The GeoComm Application

...from previous page (Table 16-1)

Command	Description
GOTO <label>	Forces the program to jump to the line starting with :<label>. For example, when the program reaches the command GOTO ITU, the program searches for a line starting with :ITU. When the program finds the line, it jumps to the label and continues running the script program from that point.
MATCH<"text"> GOTO<label> PROMPT<number>	Use the MATCH and PROMPT commands together when you want to wait a specific length of time while the program examines incoming data for a match with the <"text"> string. You must enclose <"text"> in double quotes. If you want to match an [Enter←] keystroke, use "CR" as the text string. You can use more than one MATCH command before the PROMPT command.
	The PROMPT command pauses the script for a specific length of time while waiting for the MATCH command to be satisfied. When the program finds a match, the script uses a GOTO command to jump to a specified label. If no match is found in the specified time, then the program continues with the command following the PROMPT command.
	The MATCH command(s) must come before the PROMPT command, and you must have both the MATCH command(s) and the PROMPT command.

continued...

The GeoComm Application **16**

...from previous page (Table 16-1)

Command	Description

	You specify time in sixtieths of a second. For example, suppose you want to wait 60 seconds (60 x 60 = 3600) for a text string from the remote computer asking for your last name, or specifying that there are thunderstorms and the system is offline. Write the following in the script file.
	`MATCH "Last name?",CR GOTO ITU`
	`MATCH "Thunderstorms. System Offline!"`
	`GOTO Hqrs PROMPT 3600`

PAUSE <number>	The pause command temporarily halts the script for a specific length of time. The <number> is in sixtieths of a second. If you do not specify a number, the program pauses for one second. For example, to pause the program for one minute (60 seconds) use the following command in your script: `PAUSE 3600`
PORT<port>	Specifies the COM port to use for communicating with the remote computer. For example, to use COM port 4, use the following command in your script: `PORT 4`

continued...

305

16 The GeoComm Application

...from previous page (Table 16-1)

Command	Description
PRINT<text>	Use this command to display text on your computer screen. This text is not sent to the remote computer. For example, to display the message "Signing on" while you are signing onto the remote computer, use the following command in your script file close to where the actual sign-on command is issued: `PRINT "Signing on",CR,CR`
PULSE	Use this command if your phone uses pulse dialing, not tone dialing.
SEND<"text">	This command sends <"text"> to the remote computer. For example, to send the word "password" followed by Enter, use the following command in your script: `SEND "password",CR`
TERM <terminal type>	Use this command to make GeoComm emulate a specific terminal type. The <terminal type> must be one of the following: TTY, VT 52, VT 100, WYSE 50, ANSI, IBM 3101, TVI 950. For example, to make GeoComm emulate an ANSI terminal, use the following command in your script: `TERM ANSI`

The GeoComm Application 16

Quick Dial

You can connect your computer to a remote computer by either calling (dialing) the remote computer, or answering a call. To dial a number with your modem, select Quick Dial from the Dial menu. Figure 16-8, shown previously, shows the Quick Dial dialog box in the bottom left corner of the screen. The Quick Dial option works only with Hayes-compatible modems. If you have a different type of modem, you will probably have to dial the number manually.

Dialing a number

To dial a number, Click in the Phone # box to position the text cursor. Type the phone number you want to dial. Click the Dial button. The program dials the phone number.

Telephone number format

You can use almost any format to enter the telephone number. For example, you can use the number format 1-555-555-5555 for long distance calls. Here a 1 is placed before the area code.

If you need to use a special dialing sequence to access a long distance service, enter the sequence before the regular number. For example, the sequence `12345-1-555-555-5555` dials the long distance service access code (12345), then the long distance number.

A , (comma) briefly pauses the dialing sequence to accommodate connection delays. For example, if you use 9 to access an outside line, enter the phone number like this: 9,555-1212. The program will dial 9, pause briefly to access the outside line, and then dial 555-1212.

Hang Up

If you are on a bulletin board or connected to another computer and decide you want to quit, you should first use the log-off procedure for the remote system. (Logging off formally tells the remote computer that you are leaving.) After you log-off, select Hang Up from the Dial menu. The program displays the Hang Up dialog box asking you to confirm that you want to break the connection and hang up. Click the Yes button to terminate the connection (equivalent to hanging up your phone) and close the dialog box.

Summary

In this chapter you learned how to configure the GeoComm application for your hardware and how to use GeoComm to communicate with a remote computer, sending and receiving data. You also learned how to create scripts to automate the communication process.

Chapter 17

The Solitaire Application

The Solitaire game — Klondike — in the Professional Workspace is a more versatile version of the same game included the Appliances. You can change the settings for several aspects of the game, such as: how many cards to draw, the type of scoring to use, which game level to play, and a timer for the game.

Klondike, which is probably the most popular of all solitaire games, is known by a variety of other names, including Demon and Fascination.

The following paragraphs will refresh your memory on the rules of the games.

17 The Solitaire Application

Card Layout

The program places cards facedown in seven play stacks. The first play stack on the left contains one card, the next contains two cards, the third contains three cards and so on, with the last play stack on the right containing seven cards. When the seven stacks are made, the program turns face up the top card on each one. Above the seven stacks on the right are the four suit stacks. (A suit stack is empty until you can place an ace face up on it.) The program places the remaining undealt cards face down at the top left in the deal stack, with room for discards beside it. Figure 17-1 shows the arrangement of the cards.

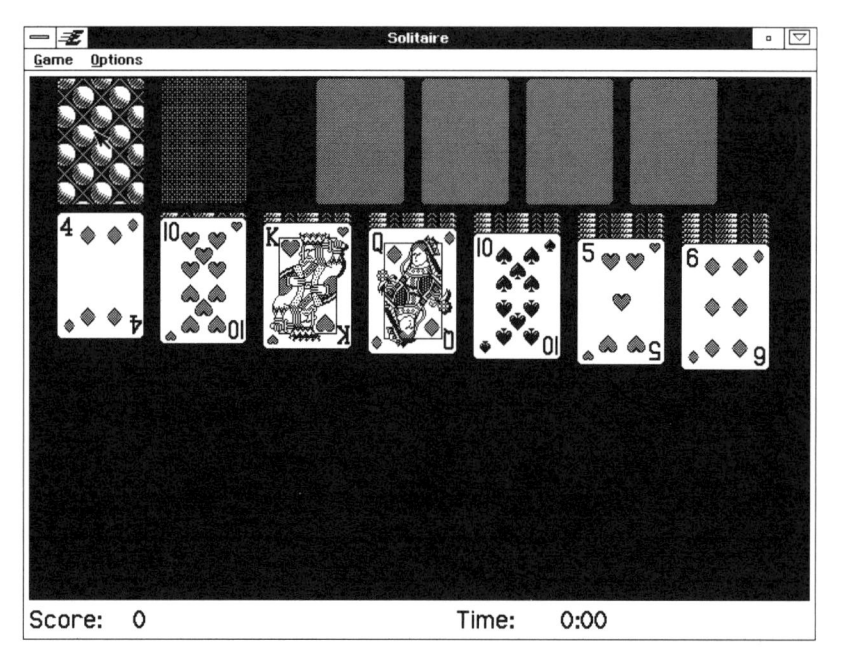

Figure 17-1 — The Solitaire Screen.

Playing the Game

The object is to build up the suit stacks with a complete sequence of cards, ace through King, of the same suit.

To play a card, position the cursor over the card, press the left mouse button, then drag the card to the new location. Release the mouse button to anchor the card.

To turn over a card, double-click on it with the left mouse button.

The top face-up card in any stack, except those in the suit stacks, can be played.

- You can move a face-up ace on a play stack to a suit stack. You can then play the two of the same suit when it becomes available by placing it on the ace. The three of that suit, when it becomes available, is placed on the two.

- You can move face-up cards on the play stacks from one stack to another following this rule: a card can be placed only on the next higher ranking card of the opposite color. For example, you can place a black 10 only on a red Jack. When you remove the last face-up card from a play stack, you then turn over the new top card of the play stack.

- You can move a sequence of face-up cards on the play stacks. For example, suppose the top card of one play stack is the 9 of diamonds. On another play stack is the face-up sequence: 8 of spades, 7 of hearts, 6 of clubs. You can move the 8-7-6 sequence onto the 9 of diamonds. You cannot move just one card of a face-up sequence on a play stack — you must move the entire face-up sequence as a group.

- If you move the last card in a play stack, leaving an empty space, you can fill the space only with a face-up King. Turn up the cards one at a time (or three at a time, depending on your Draw How Many Cards? setting) in the deal stack by clicking on the top card in the deal stack. The program places the turned up card face up on the discard stack. Play the top card in the discard stack, if possible, by placing it on the appropriate suit stack or on a play stack. When you play a card from the discard stack, the card under it becomes available for play.

When you can no longer play any face-up cards, turn up another card from the deal stack and place it face up on the discard stack.

When you have turned up all cards from the deal stack and you cannot make any other card moves, turn over the discard pile and use it as the new deal stack by double-clicking on the top card in the discard stack.

17 The Solitaire Application

The Solitaire Application

When you select Solitaire from the GeoManager window, the program displays the Solitaire window, previously shown in Figure 17-1.

The Solitaire Menu Bar contains two options: Game and Options.

Game Menu

This menu contains three options: Re-Deal, Undo, and Exit.

Re-Deal (Ctrl+R)

Select this option to re-deal the cards (begin a new game). The shortcut for Re-Deal is [Ctrl]-[R].

Undo

Select this option if you want to back out of a move, returning to the previous display. There is no shortcut for this item.

Exit (F3)

Select this option to exit the Solitaire application and return to the GeoManager window.

Options Menu

This menu contains eight items which allow you to customize the game.

Change Card Backs

You can choose from three designs for the backs of the cards. Select the one you want and then click the Apply button to see how the selection looks. When you are satisfied, click the Close button to return to the Solitaire window.

The Solitaire Application 17

Draw How Many Cards?

You can specify drawing either one card or three cards at a time from the deal stack. When you select the option you want, the program returns you to the Solitaire window.

Scoring

You can choose Standard scoring, Vegas scoring, or None.

Standard scoring

In standard scoring, the program resets the score to zero whenever you Re-Deal. The point system is:

- 10 points for playing a card on a suit stack
- 5 points for exposing (turning face up) a card in one of the seven play stacks
- 5 points for playing a card from the discard stack
- −1 point for every 10 seconds of play.

If you are turning over three cards at a time, then program penalizes you every time you reach the end of the deal stack:

- −10 points for each of the first three times. The fourth time you reach the end of the deal stack, the program penalizes you (n−3) x −10, where n is the number of times you reach the end of the deal stack.

If you are turning over one card at a time, the penalty is:

- −30 the first time you reach the end of the deal stack. From then on, the penalty is (n−1) x −30, where n is the number of times you reach the end of the deal stack.

17   The Solitaire Application

Vegas scoring

In Vegas scoring, the program follows these scoring rules:

- –52 points for redealing (score is not zeroed).
- 5 points for playing a card on a suit stack.

Level of Play

There are three levels of play: Beginner, Intermediate, and Advanced. When you select the level you want, the program returns you to the Solitaire window.

Outline Dragging

Select this option to display an outline of a card as you drag it from one pile to another.

Full Card

Select this option to display the full card as you drag it.

Fade on Deal

Select this option to determine how the program displays face-up cards following a deal or redeal. When this option is on, the program draws face-up cards from left to right. When this option is off, the program displays all face-up cards simultaneously.

Timed Game

You can set the timer to keep track of how long you take to complete a game, or how long you take for each move.

Summary

In this chapter you learned the rules for the Klondike solitaire game and how to use the options on the two Solitaire menus that set various parameters for the game.

Chapter 18

The DOS Programs Application

The DOS Programs application gives you a convenient way to run DOS programs from within GeoWorks Ensemble. From the DOS Programs application you can:

- Create, modify, and delete icons for DOS programs
- Go to the DOS prompt to enter DOS commands manually
- Create and edit DOS batch files.

Whenever you click on a DOS program icon, GeoWorks Ensemble runs the program.

18 The DOS Programs Application

Accessing the DOS Programs Application

You can access the DOS Programs application by clicking on the DOS Programs icon on the Welcome screen. When you enter the application for the first time, the program displays only one icon, as shown in Figure 18-1. The Options menu is also shown in Figure 18-1, and is discussed later in this chapter.

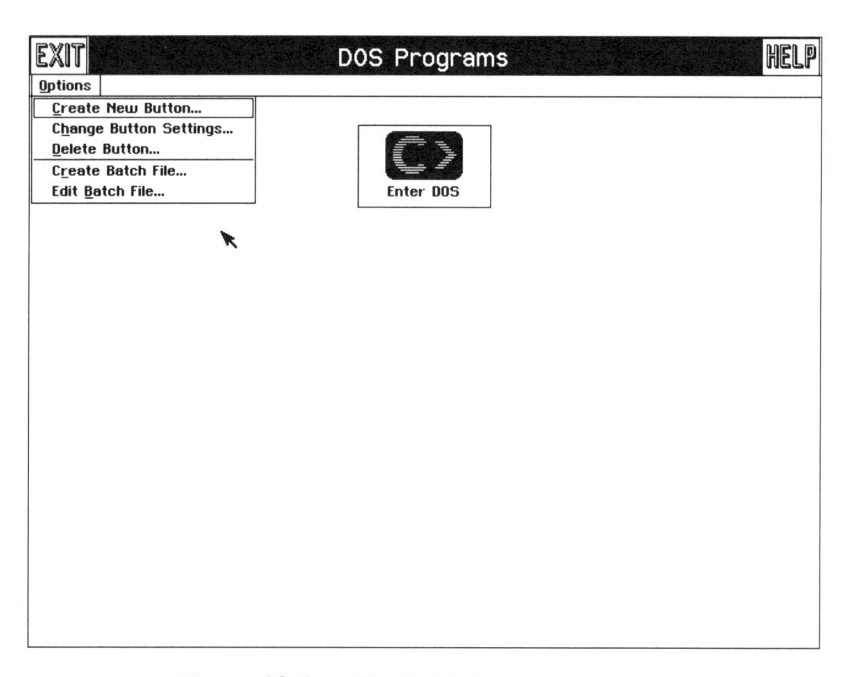

Figure 18-1 — The DOS Program Window.

The DOS Programs Window

At the top left corner of the DOS Programs window is the EXIT button. Click EXIT to return to the Welcome screen. At the top right is the HELP button. Click HELP to display information about using the DOS Programs application.

When you click the Enter DOS icon, the program takes you temporarily to the DOS prompt from which you can enter DOS commands. You can perform DOS functions such as formatting disks, checking the amount of memory available, and copying data from one disk to another. You can also run small programs. When you are ready to return to GeoWorks Ensemble, type:

Exit `Enter⏎`   Enters the DOS command to return to GeoWorks Ensemble.

Options Menu

The Options menu is the only menu available in the DOS Programs application. When you select this option, the program displays the Options menu previously shown in Figure 18-1.

The Options menu contains three sections and five items. Use the option in the top section to create a new DOS program button (icon). Use the options in the center section to change or delete buttons. Use the options in the third section to create or edit batch files.

Create New Button

You can run your DOS programs and issue DOS commands without exiting GeoWorks Ensemble. When you create a DOS program icon, you set it up to run the sequence of commands you would type directly at the DOS prompt.

When you select the Create New Button option, the program displays the Select DOS file for button dialog box shown in Figure 18-2.

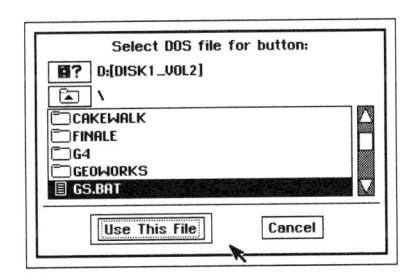

Figure 18-2 — The Select DOS File for Button Dialog Box.

In the top section are two buttons. Click the top button to change the default drive. The program displays the current (default) drive beside the drive button.

18 The DOS Programs Application

The second button is the Move Up One Directory button followed by (on the same line) the path and current directory. When you first select the Create New Button option, the program displays the root directory (\), as shown in Figure 18-2. The root directory is the top directory on the drive; you cannot move up another level.

The display box below the buttons lists the subdirectories and files in the currently-selected directory. To select a subdirectory (move down one level), double-click on a subdirectory name in the display box below the two buttons.

When the selected directory is the one you want, highlight the DOS program run file in the display box, then click the Use This File button.

For example, to create a button for the Norton program, scroll through the list of subdirectories under the root until you find the \NORTON subdirectory. Double-click on the Norton subdirectory name. The path display changes to \NORTON, and the display box lists the files and subdirectories under the \NORTON subdirectory. Only DOS files with the extensions .COM, .EXE, and .BAT display in the box. Highlight the program file that runs the program. In the case of the Norton program, the run file is NORTON.EXE. Most of the time, a DOS program run file has the extension .EXE, but some use the extension .COM.

After you highlight the NORTON.EXE file, click the Use this File button. The program displays the Button Settings dialog box shown in Figure 18-3.

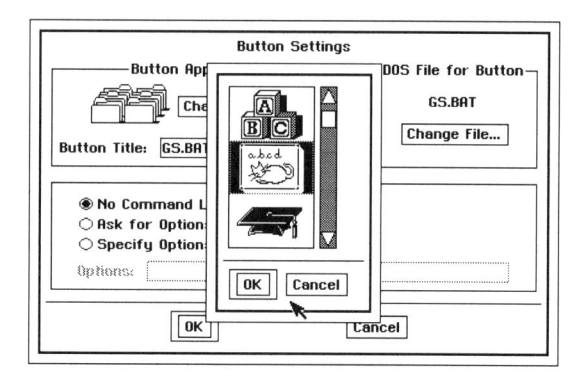

Figure 18-3 — The Button Settings Dialog Box.

Button Appearance

At the top left of the dialog box is the Button Appearance area, which includes the Button Title box. Click the mouse cursor in the Button Title box to position the text cursor. Type the title you want for the button. You can edit this text, if you want.

To change the picture for the icon you are creating, click the Change Picture button. The program displays a list of the available icons in a scroll box over the Button Settings dialog box as shown in Figure 18-3. Scroll through the list and highlight the one you want. Click the OK button to close the scroll box and accept the selection.

DOS File for Button

The name of the DOS run file you selected is displayed in the DOS File for Button area on the right. If you want to assign a different file to the button, click the Change File button under the file name. The program returns to the Select DOS file for button dialog box (see Figure 18-2). Choose the file you want and click the Use This File button. The program displays the new file name. If the Button Title you selected is the name of the run file, you should go back to the Button Title box and change the title to correspond with your new file selection. To do this, click the Button Title box to position the text cursor, then type the new button title.

Command Line Options

Some DOS programs and DOS commands accept options (switches, filespecs, or parameters) which specify something the program, or command, is to do. For example, if you were running the Norton Utilities FileFind program, you could enter a filespec such as *.* (specifies searching all files, the entire drive), and a switch such as /S (specifies including files in subdirectories). DOS commands like CHKDSK and DIR also accept options. For example, with the DIR command, you could enter the filespec *.SPR to display all files with the extension .SPR. You could also add the switch /P to pause the DOS display after each screen of files.

18 The DOS Programs Application

The Command Line Options area is located at the bottom of the Button Settings dialog box. You can choose one of three settings regarding command line options:

- **No Command Line Options**   Use this if you do not want to specify any options.
- **Ask for Options Each Time**   Select this if you want to be able to enter options each time you use that program. This is useful if you often need to change the switches you use.
- **Specify Options Now**   Select this option to use the same switches every time you use the program or command. Enter the options in the Options text box.

When you are satisfied with the Button Settings dialog box, click the OK button to accept the settings. The program displays the new button in the DOS Programs window. To run the program, click the button. The program will ask you for options if you specified Ask for Options Each Time in the Button Settings dialog box. The program will clear the screen and run the program. When you exit the DOS program or it finishes running, GeoWorks Ensemble reestablishes control and returns you to the DOS Programs window.

If you create more buttons than will fit on your screen, you can use the paging arrows at the bottom of the window to flip to the Next or Previous pages to view additional buttons.

Change Button Settings

You can change any of the settings you specified for a button. When you select the Change Button Settings option, the program displays the Select Button to Change dialog box. Highlight the name of the button you want to change, then click the Change Settings button. The program returns you to the Button Settings dialog box previously shown in Figure 18-3. Make whatever changes you wish, then click the OK button to activate the changes.

Delete Button

When you select this option to remove a button, the program displays the Select Button to Delete dialog box. Highlight the button name you want to delete, then click the Delete button. The program closes the dialog box and removes the button from the DOS Programs window.

Creating and Using Batch Files

You can create and edit batch files without leaving GeoWorks Ensemble. A batch file is collection of DOS commands contained in a text file. Rather than type the DOS commands every time you want to perform a frequent function, create a batch file which will enter the commands for you. When you run a batch file, DOS reads the commands one at a time, as if you were typing them at the DOS prompt.

Use the last two options on the Options menu to create and edit batch file.

Create Batch File

When you select this option, the program displays the Select Directory and Enter New Filename dialog box shown in Figure 18-4.

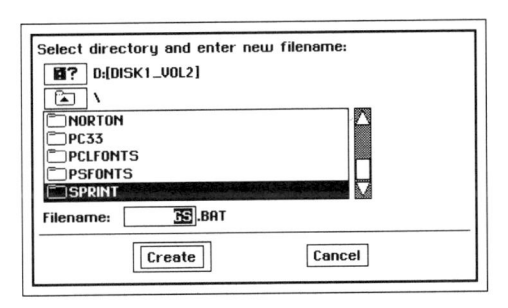

Figure 18-4 — The Select Directory and Enter New Filename Dialog Box.

This dialog box works much the same as the dialog box shown in Figure 18-2. See the Create New Button section earlier in this chapter for a discussion about moving around subdirectories.

18 The DOS Programs Application

When you have selected the subdirectory in which you want to store the new batch file, click the Filename box to position the text cursor. Enter the file name you want to use. You must use a DOS file name (1-8 characters). The program automatically gives it the .BAT extension. Click the Create button to display the Batch File Text dialog box shown in Figure 18-5.

```
Batch File Text:
d:
cd\sprint
sp
```

[Save Batch File]   [Cancel]

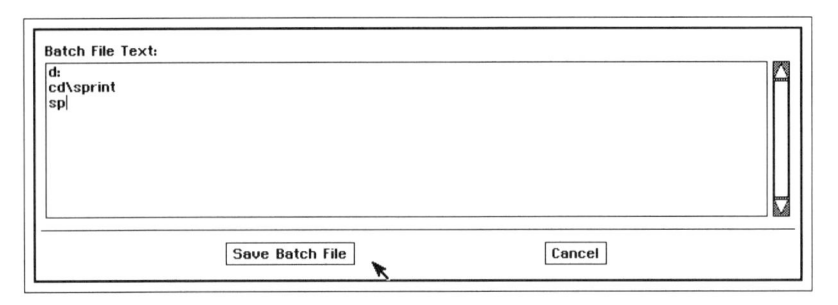

Figure 18-5 — The Batch File Text Dialog Box.

Enter your DOS commands in the box, using a new line for each command. Press [Enter] to start a new line. For example, you could enter:

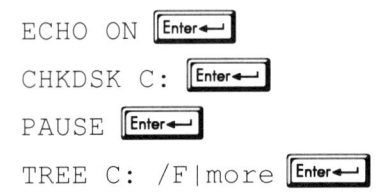

```
ECHO ON [Enter]
CHKDSK C: [Enter]
PAUSE [Enter]
TREE C: /F|more [Enter]
```

- The ECHO ON command tells DOS to display (echo to the screen) the batch file commands and results as they execute. (The echo off command tells DOS to run the batch file invisibly.)

- The CHKDSK C: command tells DOS to checks drive C: for errors. The CHKDSK program displays a status report on file integrity and memory usage.

- The PAUSE command allows you to view the report. Press any key to continue the batch file.

- The TREE command tells DOS to display the directory and file structure of drive C:, one screen at a time. (The /F switch allows you to view all the file names within each directory.)

Click the Save Batch File button to save a new batch file. To create an icon for it, select the Create New Button option and proceed as described earlier. For more information on creating batch files, refer to your DOS manual.

Edit Batch File

When you select this option to edit your batch files, the program displays the Select Batch File to Edit dialog box. Select the subdirectory which contains the batch file, and highlight the file to edit. Click the Edit File button to display the batch file in the Batch File Text dialog box as shown in Figure 18-5.

Position the text cursor on the line you want to edit. Use Backspace to delete characters. Type the characters you want. Press [Enter⏎] to start a new line.

When you are satisfied with the batch file, click the Save Batch File button to save your changes. Click the Cancel button to return to the DOS Programs screen without any changes.

Summary

The DOS Programs application allows you temporarily exit GeoWorks Ensemble to the DOS prompt to perform DOS functions. You can also create icon buttons to run DOS programs or DOS commands from the DOS Programs window. You can change or delete the icon buttons. In addition, you can create and edit batch files to execute a sequence of DOS commands. You can create icon buttons for your batch files, as well.

Appendix

Menu Map

Most GeoWorks Ensemble menus start with a pin option. When you select this option, the program pins the menu, leaving it open and displayed even after you make a selection. You can move a pinned menu, positioning it anywhere in the window, by dragging it by its Title Bar to the desired position (use the same procedure for moving any window). To close a pinned menu, double-click the Control Button (upper left corner of the menu), or single-click and select Close. Use the same procedure to close any window.

Mnemonics keys (letters you can press to access a menu or item) are underlined on the Menu Maps, as they are on the menus themselves. When an option is not available on a menu when you first open it, the program dims the option. A menu option that displays a cascade menu is indicated by a right arrow, and the cascade menu is listed next to it. A menu option which displays a dialog box is indicated by three dots (...) following the option name. Hotkeys or shortcut keys, if they exist, are listed to the right of the menu option.

Appendix

Express and Control Buttons

The express and control buttons are the available in all GeoWorks Ensemble Professional workspace applications.

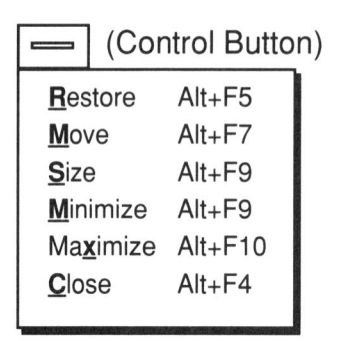

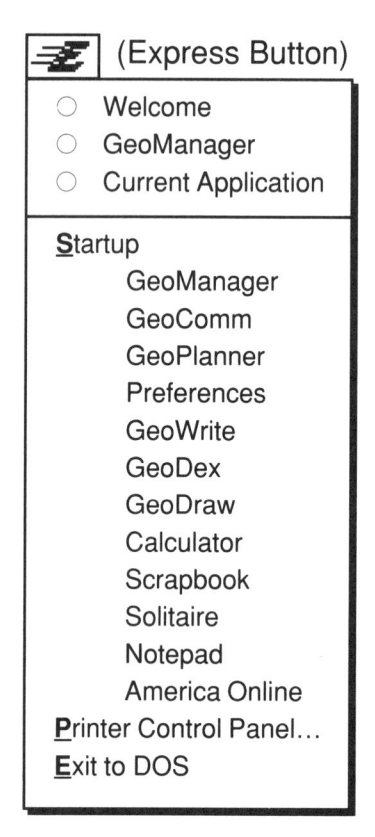

(Control Button)

Restore	Alt+F5
Move	Alt+F7
Size	Alt+F9
Minimize	Alt+F9
Ma**x**imize	Alt+F10
Close	Alt+F4

(Express Button)

○ Welcome
○ GeoManager
○ Current Application

Startup
    GeoManager
    GeoComm
    GeoPlanner
    Preferences
    GeoWrite
    GeoDex
    GeoDraw
    Calculator
    Scrapbook
    Solitaire
    Notepad
    America Online
Printer Control Panel…
Exit to DOS

Appendix

Professional Applications

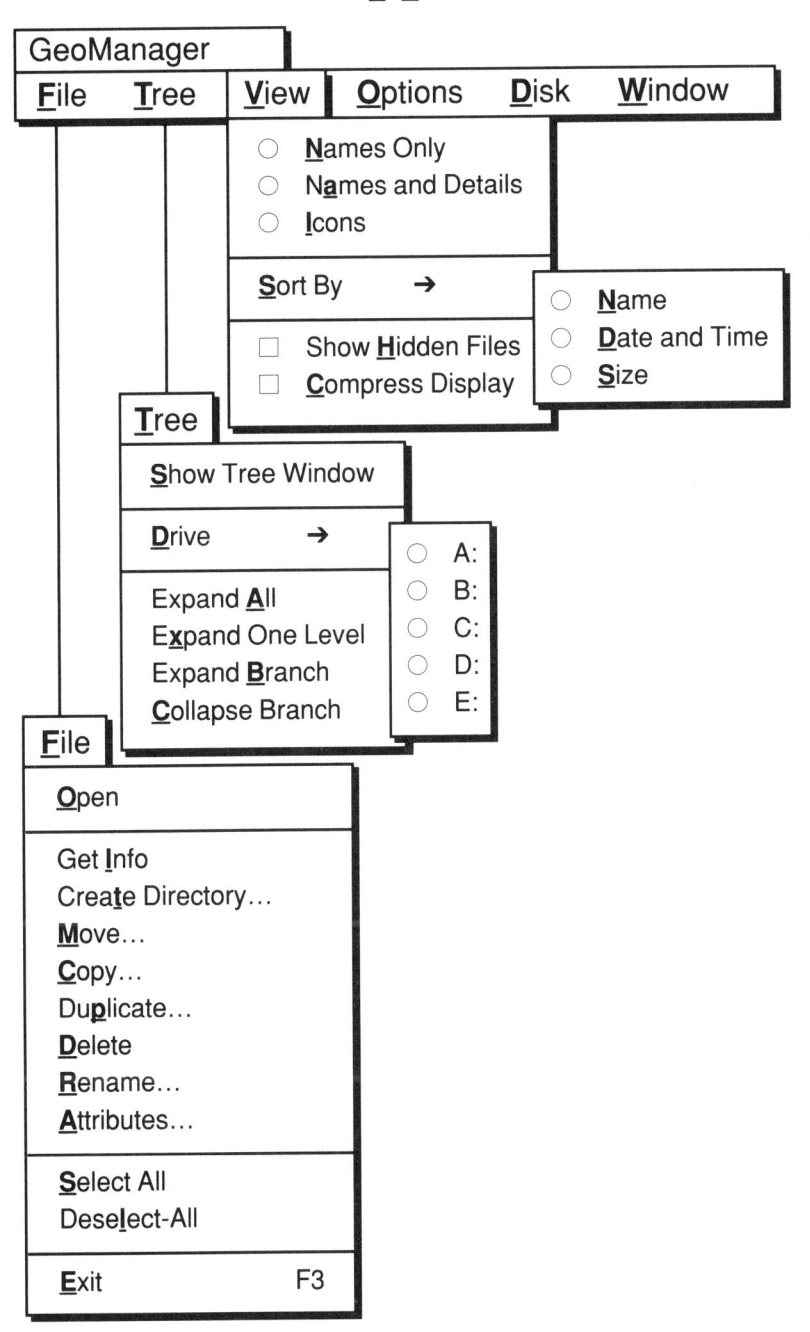

```
GeoManager
File   Tree   View   Options   Disk   Window
```

View menu:
- ○ **N**ames Only
- ○ N**a**mes and Details
- ○ **I**cons
- **S**ort By →
- ☐ Show **H**idden Files
- ☐ **C**ompress Display

Sort By submenu:
- ○ **N**ame
- ○ **D**ate and Time
- ○ **S**ize

Tree menu:
- **S**how Tree Window
- **D**rive →
- Expand **A**ll
- E**x**pand One Level
- Expand **B**ranch
- **C**ollapse Branch

Drive submenu:
- ○ A:
- ○ B:
- ○ C:
- ○ D:
- ○ E:

File menu:
- **O**pen
- Get **I**nfo
- Crea**t**e Directory…
- **M**ove…
- **C**opy…
- Du**p**licate…
- **D**elete
- **R**ename…
- **A**ttributes…
- **S**elect All
- Dese**l**ect-All
- **E**xit   F3

327

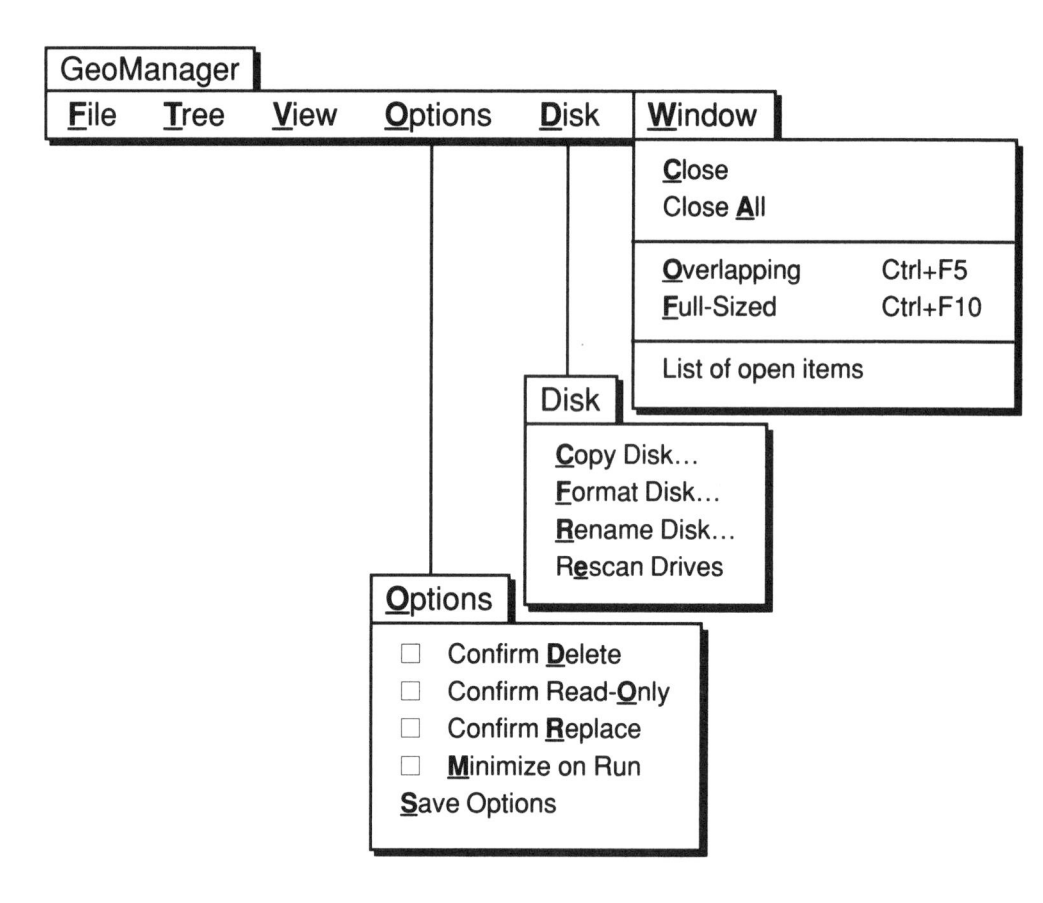

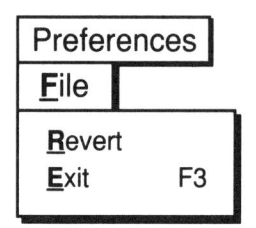

Appendix

GeoManager

| File | Tree | View | Options | Disk | Window |

Window
- Close
- Close All
- Overlapping — Ctrl+F5
- Full-Sized — Ctrl+F10
- List of open items

Disk
- Copy Disk...
- Format Disk...
- Rename Disk...
- Rescan Drives

Options
- ☐ Confirm Delete
- ☐ Confirm Read-Only
- ☐ Confirm Replace
- ☐ Minimize on Run
- Save Options

Preferences

| File |

- Revert
- Exit — F3

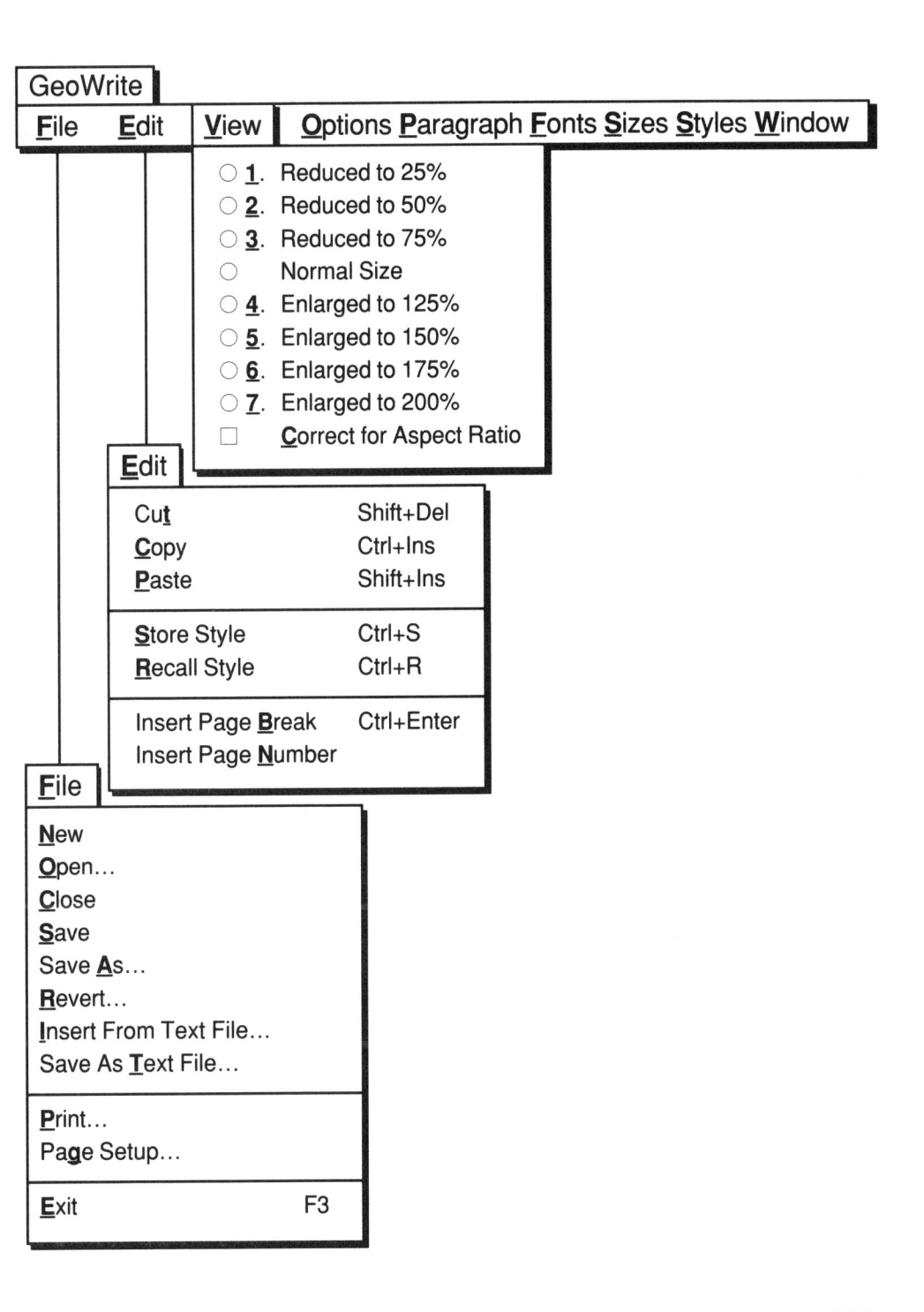

Appendix

```
GeoWrite
File    Edit    View    Options  Paragraph  Fonts  Sizes  Styles  Window
                   ○ 1. Reduced to 25%
                   ○ 2. Reduced to 50%
                   ○ 3. Reduced to 75%
                   ○    Normal Size
                   ○ 4. Enlarged to 125%
                   ○ 5. Enlarged to 150%
                   ○ 6. Enlarged to 175%
                   ○ 7. Enlarged to 200%
                   ☐    Correct for Aspect Ratio
```

```
Edit
   Cut            Shift+Del
   Copy           Ctrl+Ins
   Paste          Shift+Ins

   Store Style    Ctrl+S
   Recall Style   Ctrl+R

   Insert Page Break   Ctrl+Enter
   Insert Page Number
```

```
File
   New
   Open…
   Close
   Save
   Save As…
   Revert…
   Insert From Text File…
   Save As Text File…

   Print…
   Page Setup…

   Exit                F3
```

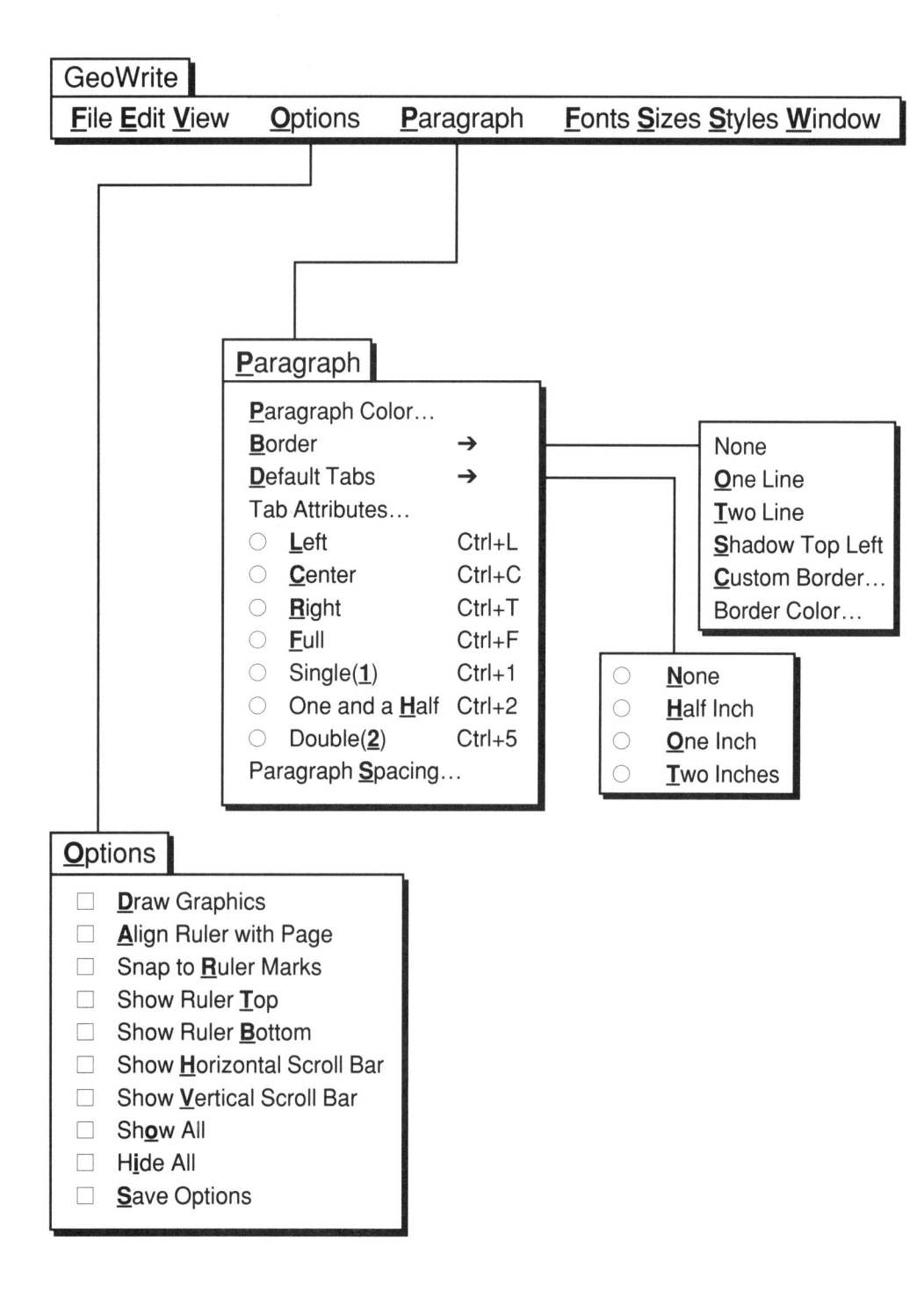

Appendix

```
┌─────────────────────────────────────────────────────────────┐
│ GeoWrite                                                    │
│  File Edit View    Options    Paragraph    Fonts Sizes Styles Window │
└─────────────────────────────────────────────────────────────┘
```

Paragraph

- Paragraph Color…
- Border →
- Default Tabs →
- Tab Attributes…
- ○ Left — Ctrl+L
- ○ Center — Ctrl+C
- ○ Right — Ctrl+T
- ○ Full — Ctrl+F
- ○ Single(1) — Ctrl+1
- ○ One and a Half — Ctrl+2
- ○ Double(2) — Ctrl+5
- Paragraph Spacing…

Border

- None
- One Line
- Two Line
- Shadow Top Left
- Custom Border…
- Border Color…

Default Tabs

- ○ None
- ○ Half Inch
- ○ One Inch
- ○ Two Inches

Options

- ☐ Draw Graphics
- ☐ Align Ruler with Page
- ☐ Snap to Ruler Marks
- ☐ Show Ruler Top
- ☐ Show Ruler Bottom
- ☐ Show Horizontal Scroll Bar
- ☐ Show Vertical Scroll Bar
- ☐ Show All
- ☐ Hide All
- ☐ Save Options

Appendix

```
GeoWrite
File  Edit  View  Options  Paragraph    Fonts    Sizes    Styles    Window
                                                 ○ 1.  10 Point
                                                 ○ 2.  12 Point
                                                 ○ 3.  14 Point
                                                 ○ 4.  18 Point
                                                 ○ 5.  24 Point
                                                 ○ 6.  36 Point
                                                 ○ 7.  54 Point
                                                 ○ 8.  72 Point
                                                 Smaller            Ctrl+9
                                                 Larger             Ctrl+0
                                                 Custom Size…
                                                 Character Spacing…

                                       Fonts
                                         ○   URW Roman
                                         ○   URW Sans
                                         ○   URW Mono
                                         ○   Cranbrook
                                         ○   Shattuck Avenue
                                         ○   Sather Gothic
                                         ○   Cooperstown
                                         ○   URW SymbolPS
                                         ○   Superb
                                       More Fonts…
```

331

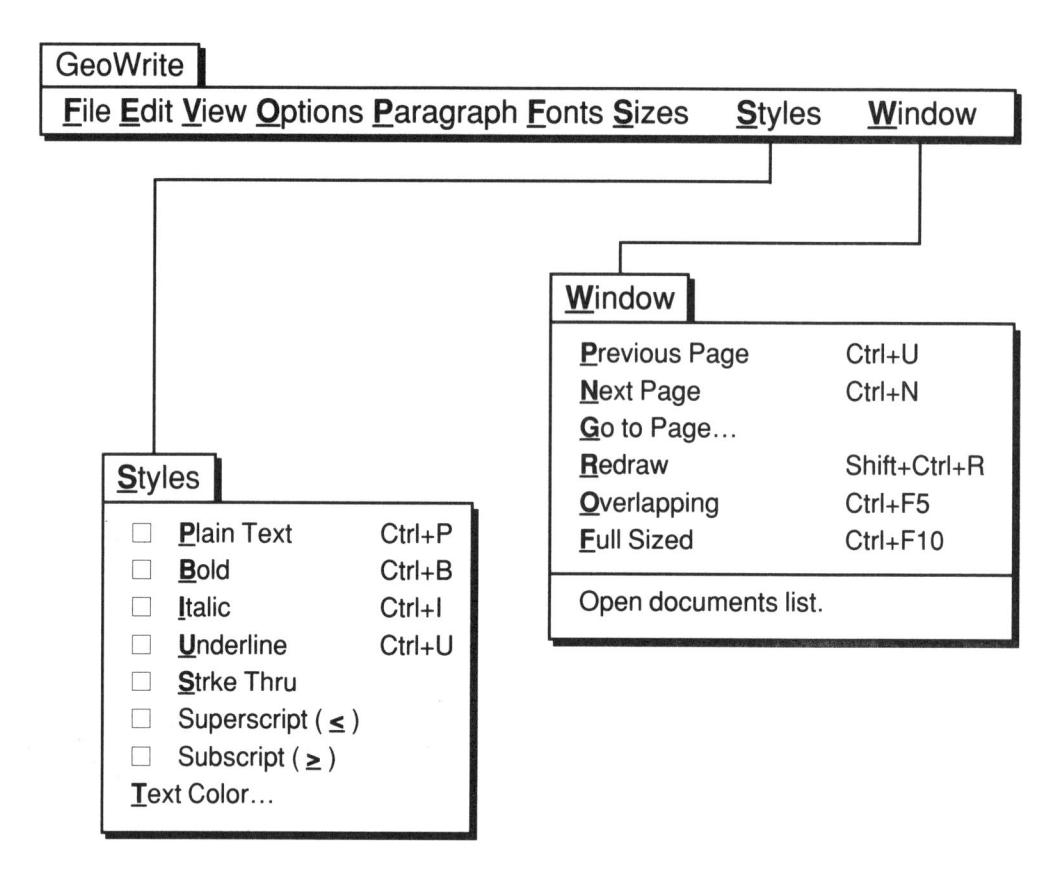

Appendix

GeoWrite
File **E**dit **V**iew **O**ptions **P**aragraph **F**onts **S**izes   **S**tyles   **W**indow

Window

Previous Page	Ctrl+U
Next Page	Ctrl+N
Go to Page…	
Redraw	Shift+Ctrl+R
Overlapping	Ctrl+F5
Full Sized	Ctrl+F10

Open documents list.

Styles

☐	**P**lain Text	Ctrl+P
☐	**B**old	Ctrl+B
☐	**I**talic	Ctrl+I
☐	**U**nderline	Ctrl+U
☐	**S**trke Thru	
☐	Superscript ($\leq$)	
☐	Subscript ($\geq$)	
	Text Color…	

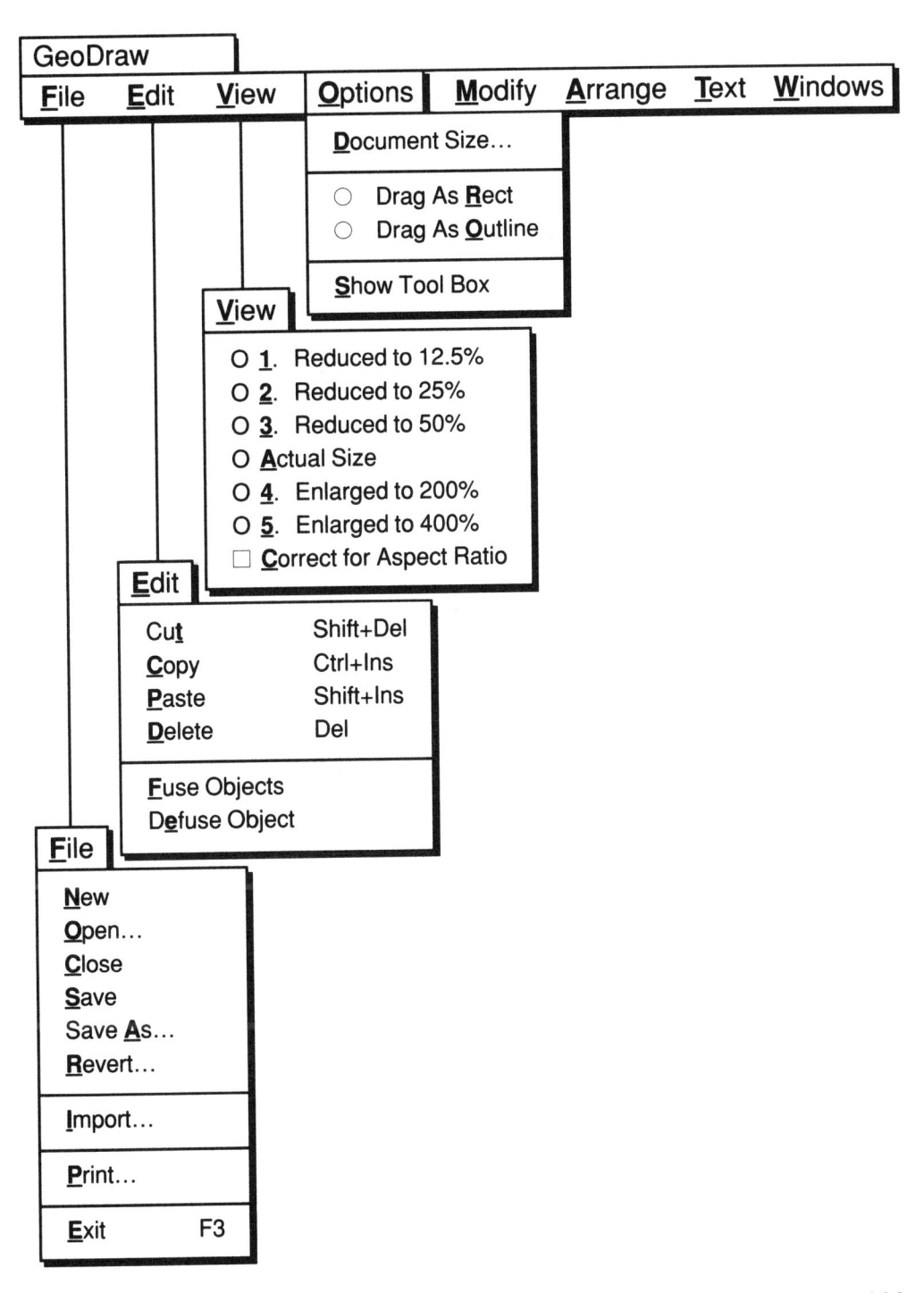

Appendix

GeoDraw							
File	**E**dit	**V**iew	**O**ptions	**M**odify	**A**rrange	**T**ext	**W**indows

Options
- **D**ocument Size…
- ○ Drag As **R**ect
- ○ Drag As **O**utline
- **S**how Tool Box

View
- ○ **1**. Reduced to 12.5%
- ○ **2**. Reduced to 25%
- ○ **3**. Reduced to 50%
- ○ **A**ctual Size
- ○ **4**. Enlarged to 200%
- ○ **5**. Enlarged to 400%
- ☐ **C**orrect for Aspect Ratio

Edit
Cu**t**	Shift+Del
Copy	Ctrl+Ins
Paste	Shift+Ins
Delete	Del

- **F**use Objects
- D**e**fuse Object

File
- **N**ew
- **O**pen…
- **C**lose
- **S**ave
- Save **A**s…
- **R**evert…
- **I**mport…
- **P**rint…
- **E**xit   F3

333

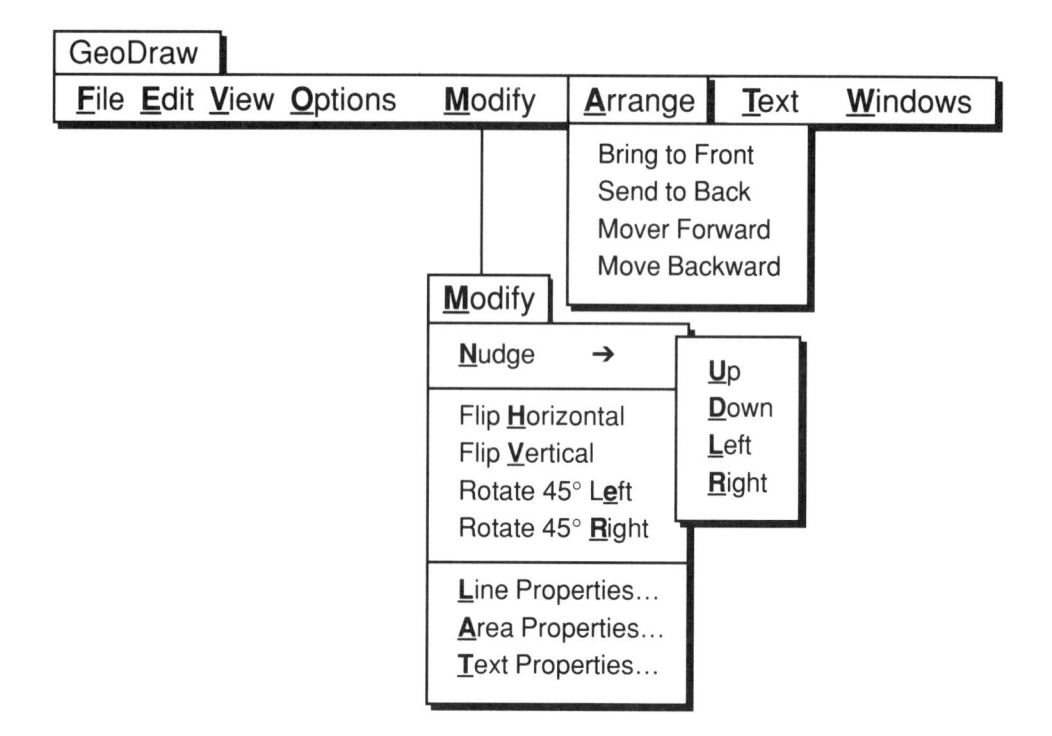

Appendix

GeoDraw							
File	**E**dit	**V**iew	**O**ptions	**M**odify	**A**rrange	**T**ext	**W**indows

Arrange:
- Bring to Front
- Send to Back
- Mover Forward
- Move Backward

Modify
- **N**udge →
- Flip **H**orizontal
- Flip **V**ertical
- Rotate 45° L**e**ft
- Rotate 45° **R**ight
- **L**ine Properties…
- **A**rea Properties…
- **T**ext Properties…

Nudge:
- **U**p
- **D**own
- **L**eft
- **R**ight

334

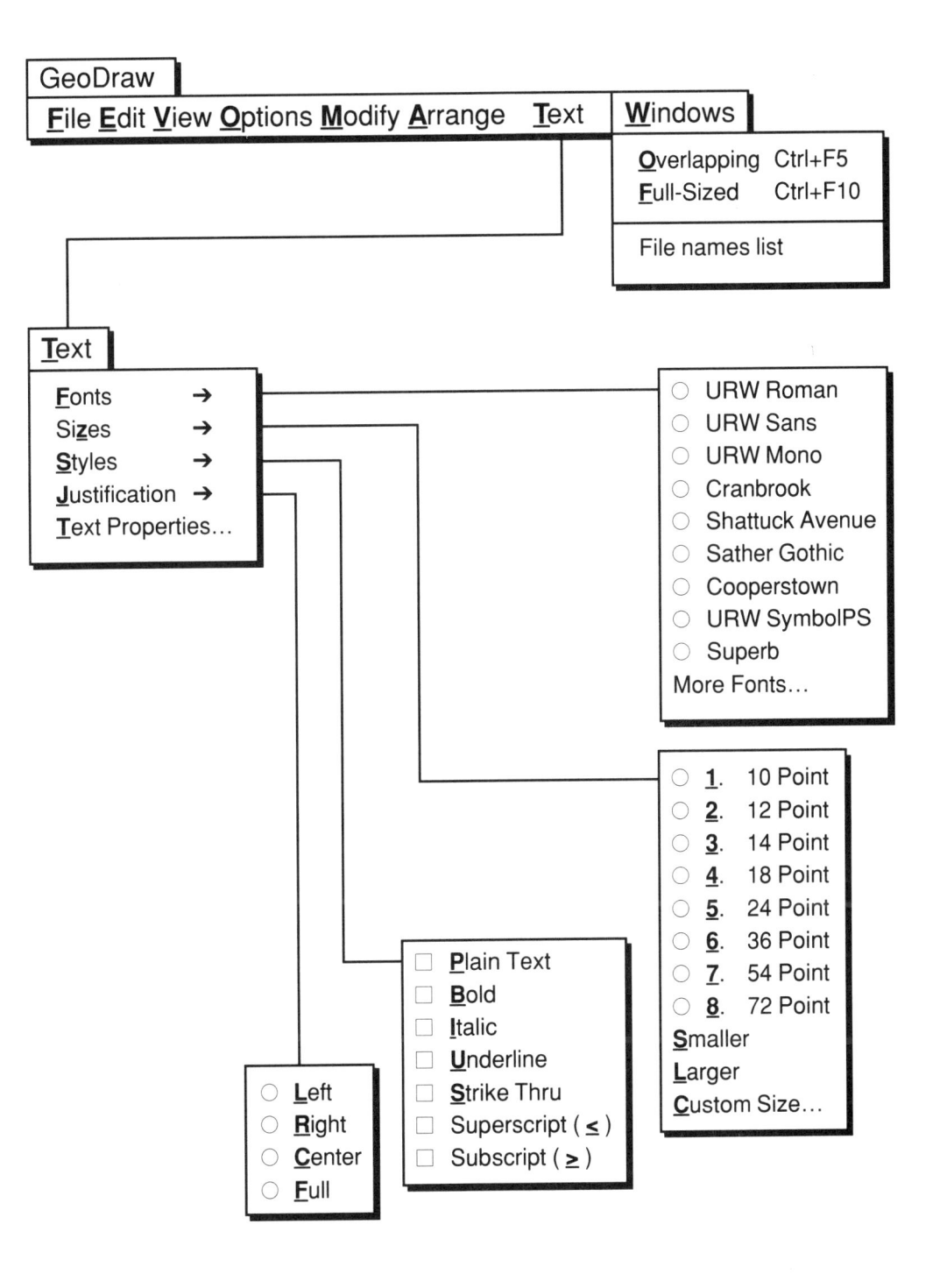

Appendix

```
GeoDraw
File  Edit  View  Options  Modify  Arrange  Text  | Windows |
                                                   Overlapping  Ctrl+F5
                                                   Full-Sized    Ctrl+F10

                                                   File names list
```

Text
- Fonts →
- Sizes →
- Styles →
- Justification →
- Text Properties…

Fonts
- ○ URW Roman
- ○ URW Sans
- ○ URW Mono
- ○ Cranbrook
- ○ Shattuck Avenue
- ○ Sather Gothic
- ○ Cooperstown
- ○ URW SymbolPS
- ○ Superb
- More Fonts…

Sizes
- ○ 1. 10 Point
- ○ 2. 12 Point
- ○ 3. 14 Point
- ○ 4. 18 Point
- ○ 5. 24 Point
- ○ 6. 36 Point
- ○ 7. 54 Point
- ○ 8. 72 Point
- Smaller
- Larger
- Custom Size…

Styles
- ☐ Plain Text
- ☐ Bold
- ☐ Italic
- ☐ Underline
- ☐ Strike Thru
- ☐ Superscript (≤)
- ☐ Subscript (≥)

Justification
- ○ Left
- ○ Right
- ○ Center
- ○ Full

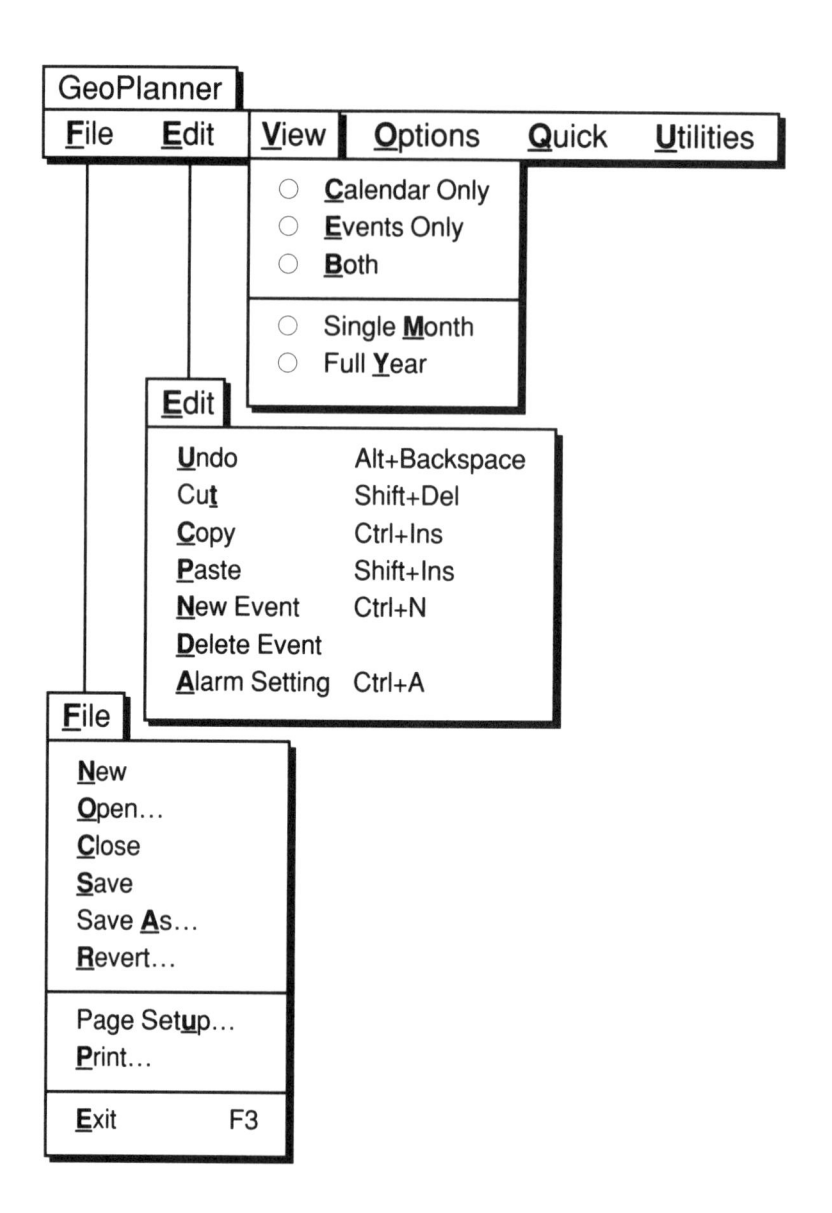

Appendix

GeoPlanner

| **F**ile | **E**dit | **V**iew | **O**ptions | **Q**uick | **U**tilities |

View
- ○ **C**alendar Only
- ○ **E**vents Only
- ○ **B**oth

- ○ Single **M**onth
- ○ Full **Y**ear

Edit

Undo	Alt+Backspace
Cu**t**	Shift+Del
Copy	Ctrl+Ins
Paste	Shift+Ins
New Event	Ctrl+N
Delete Event	
Alarm Setting	Ctrl+A

File

- **N**ew
- **O**pen…
- **C**lose
- **S**ave
- Save **A**s…
- **R**evert…

- Page Set**u**p…
- **P**rint…

- **E**xit   F3

336

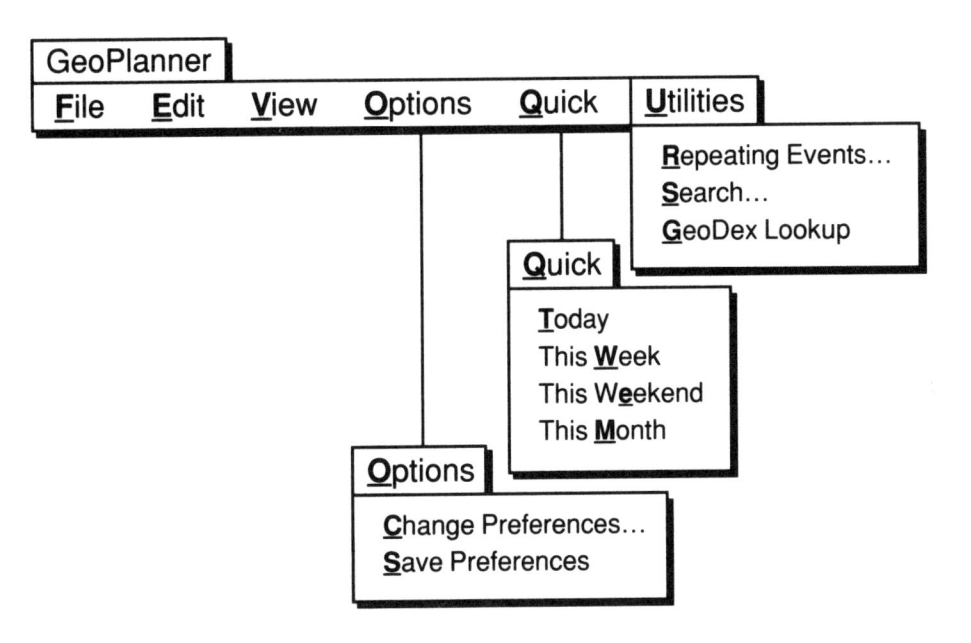

Appendix

```
┌─────────────┐
│ GeoPlanner  │
├────┬────┬────┬─────────┬───────┬──────────┐
│File│Edit│View│ Options │ Quick │ Utilities│
└────┴────┴────┴────┬────┴───┬───┴──────────┤
                                            │ Repeating Events... │
                                            │ Search...           │
                                            │ GeoDex Lookup       │
                                            └─────────────────────┘
                        ┌───────┐
                        │ Quick │
                        ├───────┴──────┐
                        │ Today        │
                        │ This Week    │
                        │ This Weekend │
                        │ This Month   │
                        └──────────────┘
            ┌─────────┐
            │ Options │
            ├─────────┴────────────┐
            │ Change Preferences...│
            │ Save Preferences     │
            └──────────────────────┘
```

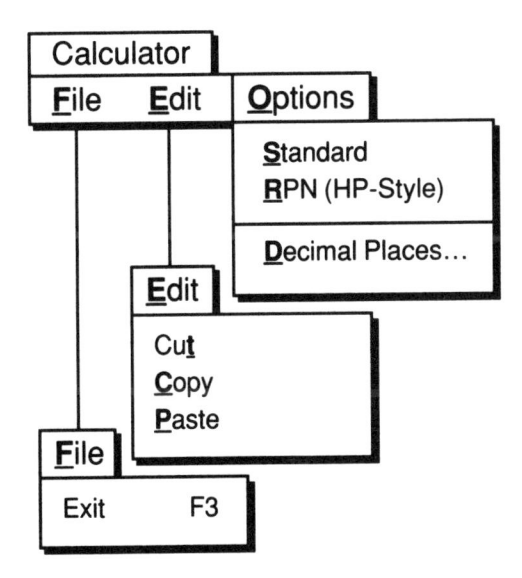

```
┌────────────┐
│ Calculator │
├──────┬──────┬─────────┐
│ File │ Edit │ Options │
└──────┴──────┴────┬────┴────────┐
                   │ Standard    │
                   │ RPN (HP-Style) │
                   │                │
                   │ Decimal Places...│
                   └──────────────────┘
          ┌──────┐
          │ Edit │
          ├──────┴──┐
          │ Cut     │
          │ Copy    │
          │ Paste   │
          └─────────┘
  ┌──────┐
  │ File │
  ├──────┴─────┐
  │ Exit    F3 │
  └────────────┘
```

337

Appendix

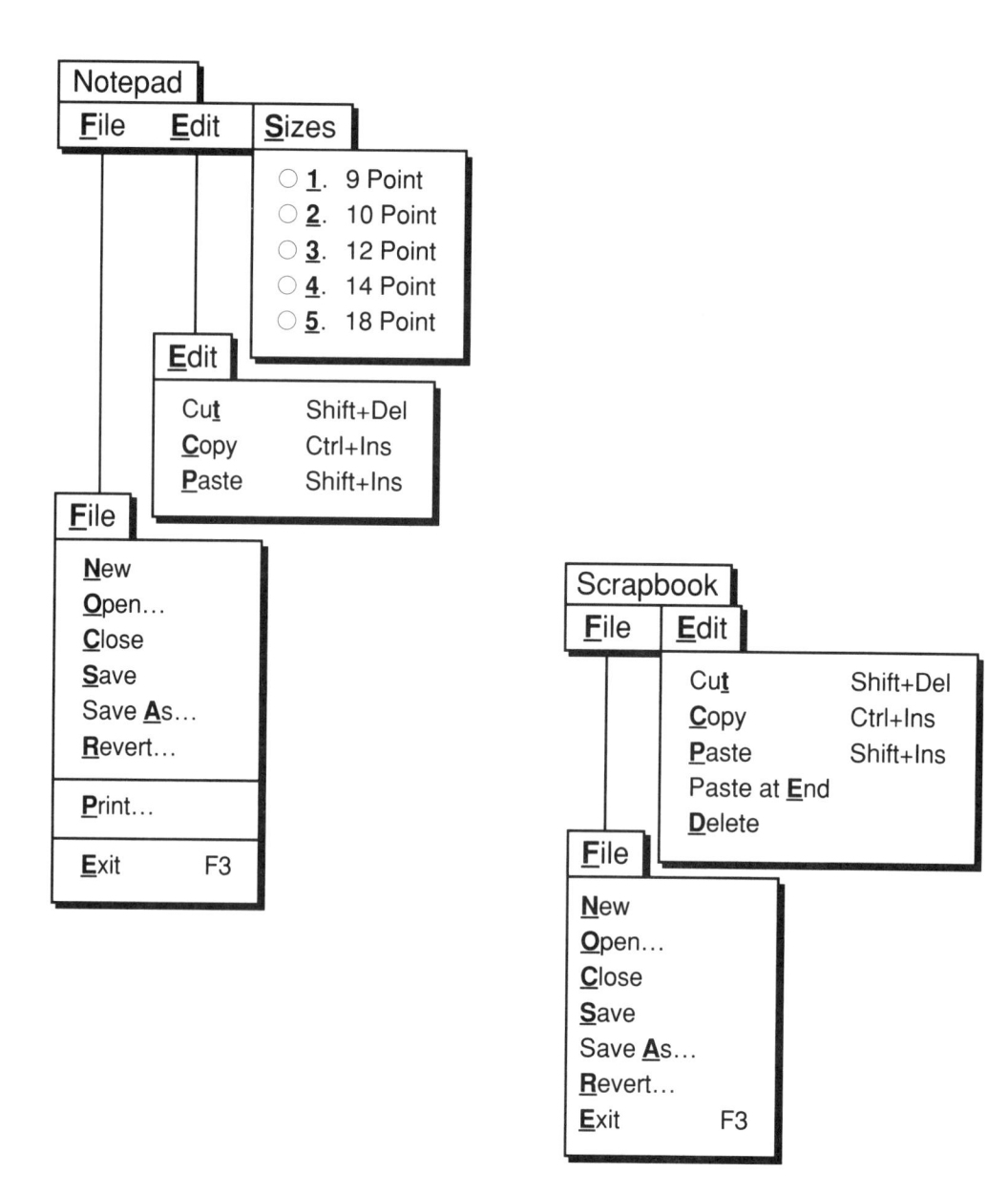

Notepad

File | **Edit** | **Sizes**

Sizes:
- ○ **1**. 9 Point
- ○ **2**. 10 Point
- ○ **3**. 12 Point
- ○ **4**. 14 Point
- ○ **5**. 18 Point

Edit
Cu**t**	Shift+Del
Copy	Ctrl+Ins
Paste	Shift+Ins

File
- **N**ew
- **O**pen…
- **C**lose
- **S**ave
- Save **A**s…
- **R**evert…
- **P**rint…
- **E**xit   F3

Scrapbook

File | **E**dit

Cu**t**	Shift+Del
Copy	Ctrl+Ins
Paste	Shift+Ins
Paste at **E**nd	
Delete	

File
- **N**ew
- **O**pen…
- **C**lose
- **S**ave
- Save **A**s…
- **R**evert…
- **E**xit   F3

Appendix

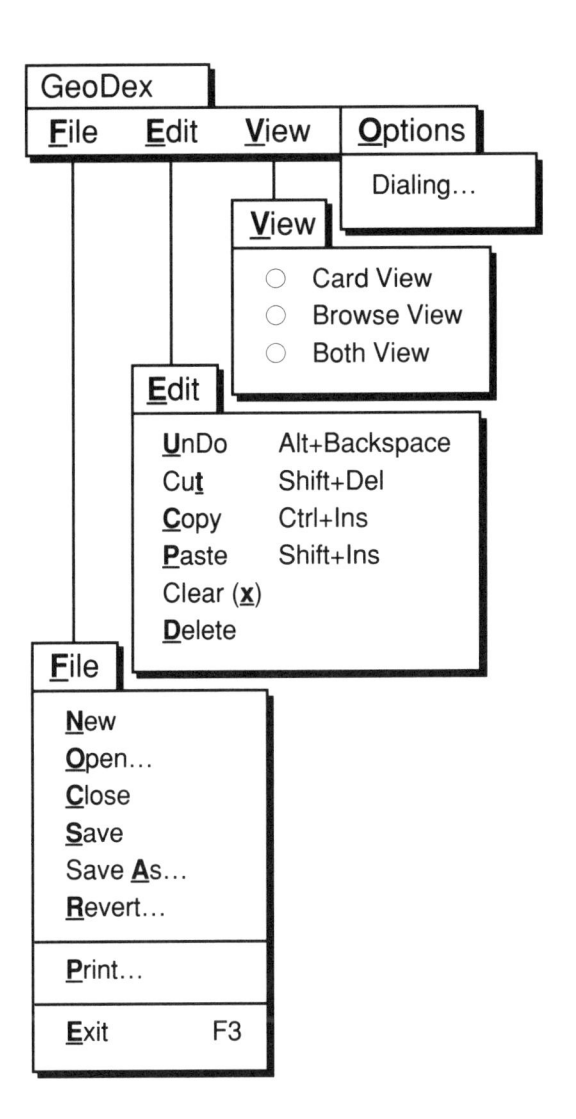

```
GeoDex
 File    Edit    View    Options
                          Dialing…
                 View
                  ○  Card View
                  ○  Browse View
                  ○  Both View

         Edit
          UnDo    Alt+Backspace
          Cut     Shift+Del
          Copy    Ctrl+Ins
          Paste   Shift+Ins
          Clear (x)
          Delete

 File
  New
  Open…
  Close
  Save
  Save As…
  Revert…

  Print…

  Exit       F3
```

339

Appendix

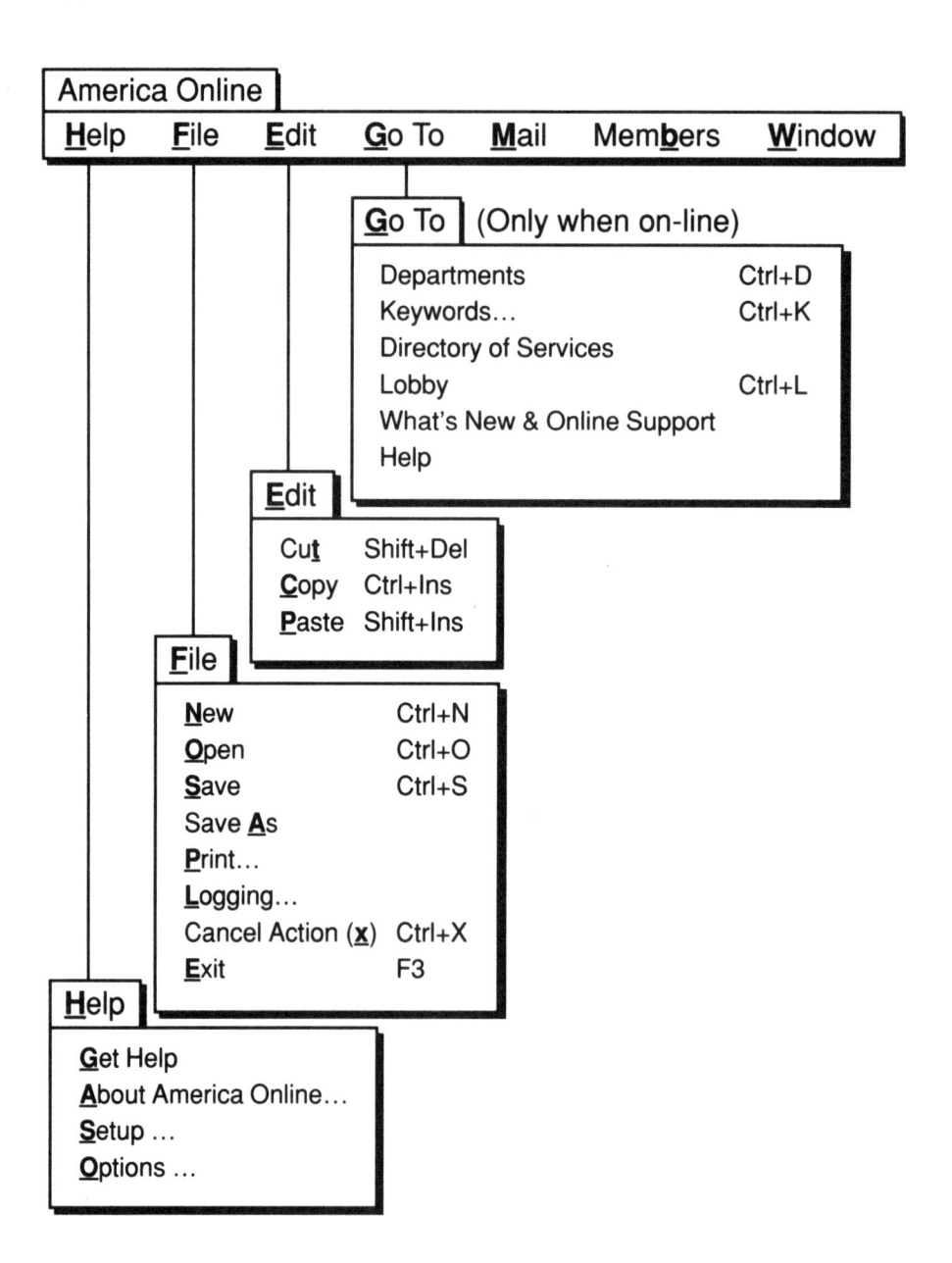

| America Online |
| Help File Edit Go To Mail Members Window |

Go To   (Only when on-line)

Departments   Ctrl+D
Keywords…   Ctrl+K
Directory of Services
Lobby   Ctrl+L
What's New & Online Support
Help

Edit

Cut   Shift+Del
Copy   Ctrl+Ins
Paste   Shift+Ins

File

New   Ctrl+N
Open   Ctrl+O
Save   Ctrl+S
Save As
Print…
Logging…
Cancel Action (x) Ctrl+X
Exit   F3

Help

Get Help
About America Online…
Setup …
Options …

340

Appendix

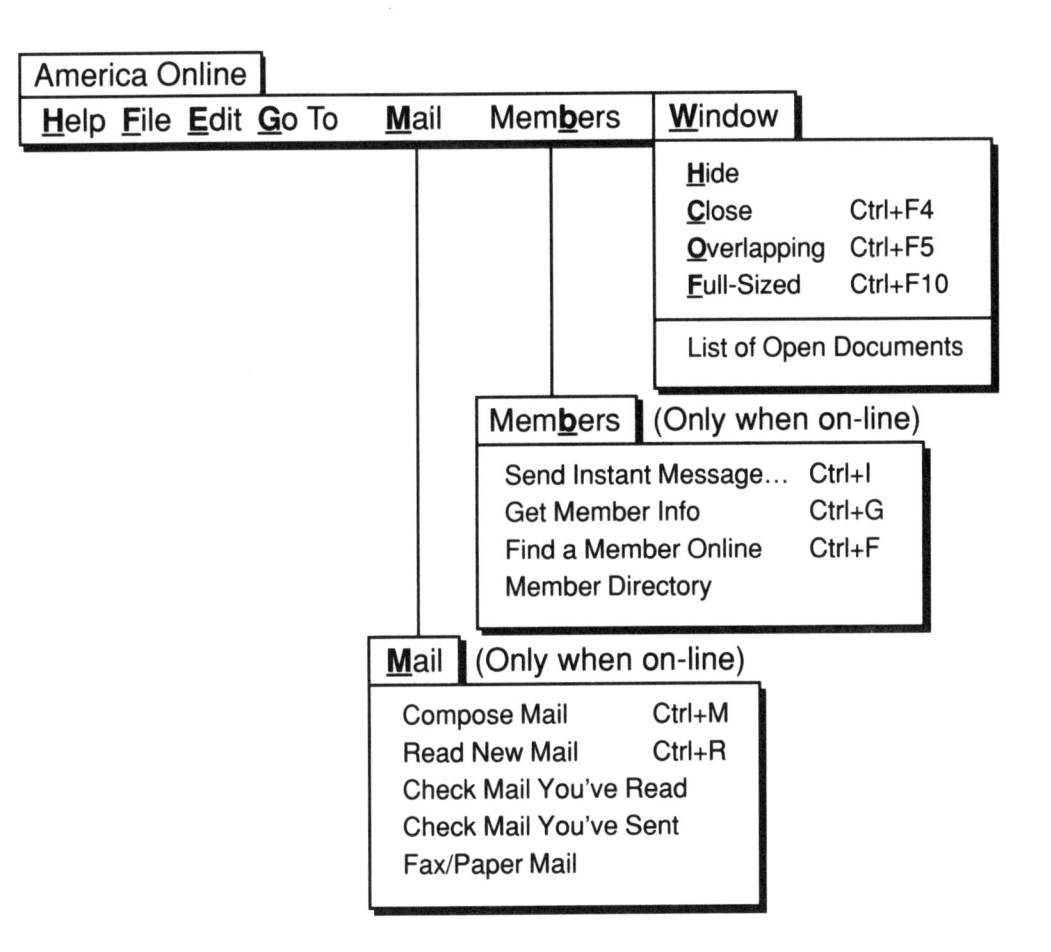

| America Online |
| Help File Edit Go To Mail Members Window |

Window
- Hide
- Close   Ctrl+F4
- Overlapping   Ctrl+F5
- Full-Sized   Ctrl+F10

List of Open Documents

Members (Only when on-line)
- Send Instant Message... Ctrl+I
- Get Member Info   Ctrl+G
- Find a Member Online   Ctrl+F
- Member Directory

Mail (Only when on-line)
- Compose Mail   Ctrl+M
- Read New Mail   Ctrl+R
- Check Mail You've Read
- Check Mail You've Sent
- Fax/Paper Mail

Appendix

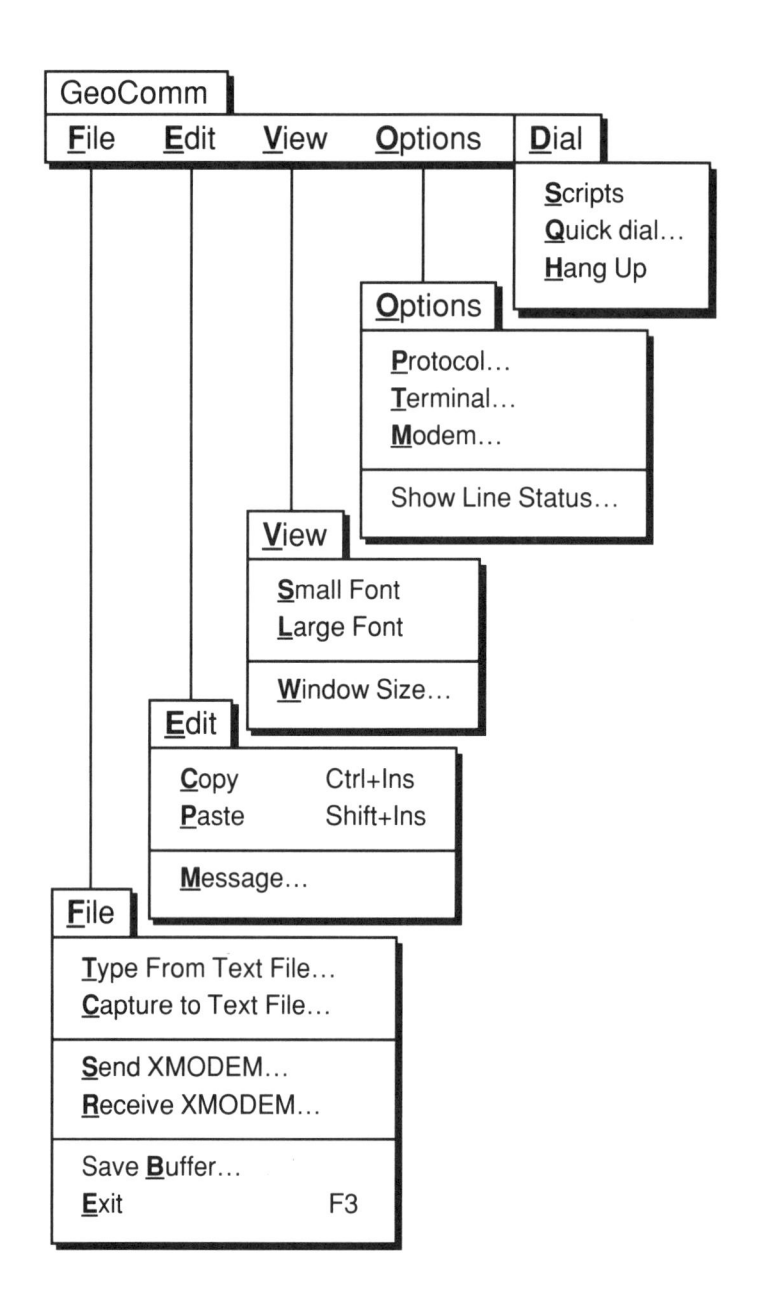

```
GeoComm
┌──────┬──────┬──────┬─────────┬──────┐
│ File │ Edit │ View │ Options │ Dial │
└──────┴──────┴──────┴─────────┴──────┘
```

Dial
- **S**cripts
- **Q**uick dial…
- **H**ang Up

Options
- **P**rotocol…
- **T**erminal…
- **M**odem…
- Show Line Status…

View
- **S**mall Font
- **L**arge Font
- **W**indow Size…

Edit
- **C**opy   Ctrl+Ins
- **P**aste   Shift+Ins
- **M**essage…

File
- **T**ype From Text File…
- **C**apture to Text File…
- **S**end XMODEM…
- **R**eceive XMODEM…
- Save **B**uffer…
- **E**xit   F3

342

Appendix

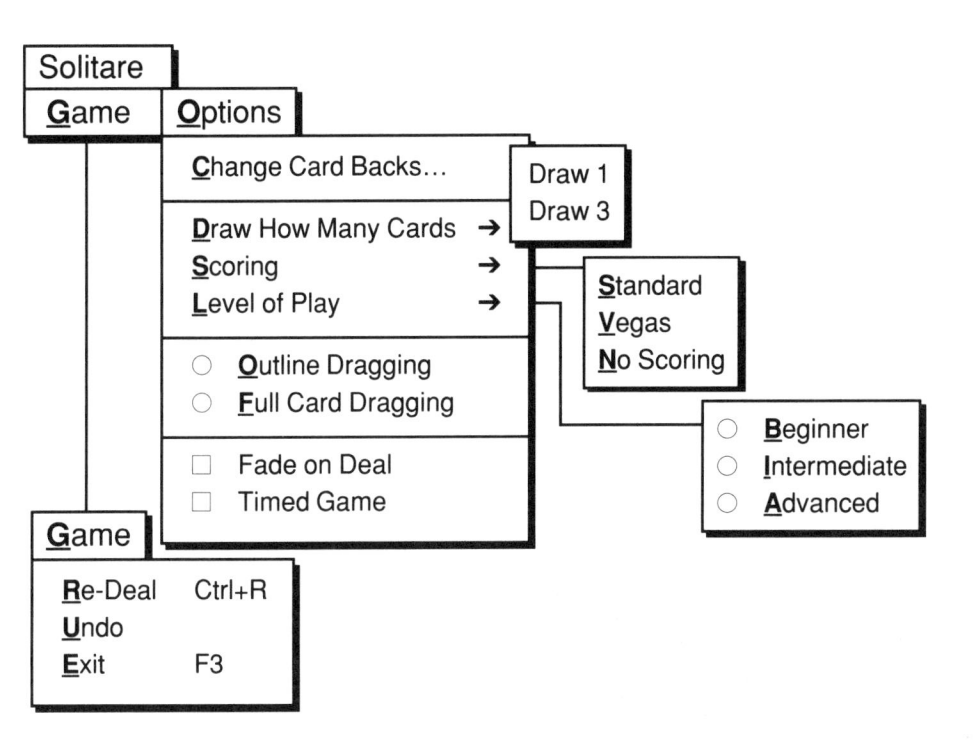

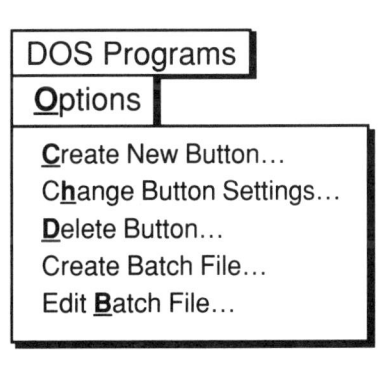

```
┌─────────┐
│ Solitare│
├─────────┼──────────┐
│ Game    │ Options  │
└────┬────┼──────────┴──────────┐
     │    │  Change Card Backs…  ┌─────────┐
     │    │                      │ Draw 1  │
     │    │  Draw How Many Cards →│ Draw 3  │
     │    │  Scoring           → └─────────┘
     │    │  Level of Play     →┌──────────────┐
     │    │                     │ ○ Standard   │
     │    │  ○ Outline Dragging │ ○ Vegas      │
     │    │  ○ Full Card Dragging│ ○ No Scoring│
     │    │                     └──────────────┘
     │    │  □ Fade on Deal    ┌──────────────┐
     │    │  □ Timed Game      │ ○ Beginner   │
┌────┴────┐                    │ ○ Intermediate│
│ Game    │                    │ ○ Advanced   │
├─────────┤                    └──────────────┘
│ Re-Deal   Ctrl+R │
│ Undo             │
│ Exit      F3     │
└──────────────────┘
```

```
┌──────────────┐
│ DOS Programs │
├──────────────┤
│ Options      │
├──────────────┴──────┐
│ Create New Button…  │
│ Change Button Settings… │
│ Delete Button…      │
│ Create Batch File…  │
│ Edit Batch File…    │
└─────────────────────┘
```

343

Index

A

Acceleration, mouse   97
Accessing GeoComm   282
Address Book   21
Adjust text selected (GeoWrite)   113
Alarm setting (GeoPlanner)   207
Align ruler with page (GeoWrite)   129
Align text (GeoWrite)
    center   108
    left   108
    right   108
America Online   261
America Online Installation   262
Appliances   13
    Accessing   15
Application, reopen   55
Archive attribute   67
Area code option (GeoDex)   258
    Color (GeoDraw)   186
    Pattern (GeoDraw)   186
Arrange menu (GeoDraw)   188
    Bring To Front   188
    Move Backward   189
    Move Forward   189
    Send To Back   189
Arrow pointer tool (GeoDraw)   193
Aspect Ratio (GeoWrite)   128
Attributes   67
    Change   68
Auto Linefeed (GeoComm)   297
Automatic screen blanking   96
Automatically switch day (GeoPlanner)   211

B

Background   90
    Inserting   91
    Selecting   90
Banner   22
    F/X   24
    Font   24
    Print out   23
    Printing   25
    Type   23
Batch file, edit (DOS Programs)   323
Batch files, creating (DOS Programs)   321
Baud rate (GeoComm)   294
Blank line, creating (GeoWrite)   155
Blanking screen   96
Bold text   144
Border (GeoWrite)   132
    Drawing   167
    Color   134
Bring to front (GeoDraw)   188
Browse View (GeoDex)   256
Buffer, save (GeoComm)   288

C

Calculator   26
    Application   217
    Functions   219
    Menu bar   222
    Using   218
Calendar (GeoPlanner)   201
Calendar only (GeoPlanner)   208
Capture text file (GeoComm)   285
Card layout (Solitare)   310
Card View (GeoDex)   256
Cascade menu   33
    Drive   71
Center-justified tab (GeoWrite)   107
Center align text (GeoWrite)   108
Center tab (GeoWrite)   151
Change attributes   68
Change button settings (DOS Programs)   320
Change drive icon   63
Changing font (GeoWrite)   153
Changing font size (GeoWrite)   141
Changing header size (GeoWrite)   158
Changing paragraph indent (GeoWrite)   170
Changing Scrapbook   244
Changing subdirectories   45

345

Index

Changing text size (Notepad)   29
Character spacing (GeoWrite)   143
Circle tool (GeoDraw)   197
Close, Control button   36
Close, File menu (GeoWrite)   119
Close, Window menu (GeoManager)   80
Close, Control Menu (GeoManager)   54
Close All, Window menu (GeoManager)   80
Closing a pinned menu   34
    (GeoWrite)   154
Collapse Branch (Tree menu)   72
COM (GeoComm)   293
COM1   98
COM2   98
Command line options (DOS Programs)   319
Commands, script   302
Compose mail (America Online)   273
Compress Display (View menu)   74
COMPU.MAC   43, 301
Computer   94
Conference log (America Online)   267
Confirm Delete (GeoManager)   66, 75
Confirm Read-Only (GeoManager)   75
Confirm Replace (GeoManager)   75
Connect line tool (GeoDraw)   196
Control Button   35
    Close   36
    (GeoManager)   52
    Maximize   36
    Minimize   36
Control line, GeoManager   52
    Control button   52
Control Menu (GeoManager)   53
    Close   54
    Maximize   53
    Minimize   53
    Move   53
    Restore   53
    Size   53
Copy, quick   206
Copy (Calculator)   222
Copy (GeoWrite)   125
Copy (Notepad)   29
Copy Disk (GeoManager)   77
Copy stop   65
Copying a table (GeoWrite)   168
Copying Scrapbooks   246
Create a document (GeoWrite)   150
Create directory (File menu)   62
Create directory dialog box   62
Create new button (DOS Programs)   317
Creating a blank line (GeoWrite)   155

Creating a card (GeoDex)   252
Creating a header (GeoWrite)   157
Creating a page break (GeoWrite)   162
Creating a table (GeoWrite)   162
Creating a text object (GeoDraw)   193
Creating Batch files (DOS Programs)   321
Ctrl+Alt+Del   3, 52
Current time (GeoPlanner)   201
Cursor movement (GeoWrite)   112
Custom border (GeoWrite)   133
Cut
    (Calculator)   222
    (GeoWrite)   125
    (Notepad)   29

D

Data Bits (GeoComm)   295
Date and Time   89
    Date   89
    OK/Reset/Cancel   89
    Time   89
Day and date, select (GeoPlanner)   201
Day template (GeoPlanner)   210
Decimal align tab (GeoWrite)   107
Decimal tabs, setting (GeoWrite)   164
Defuse Object (GeoDraw)   178
Delete by dragging (GeoManager)   67
    Confirm (GeoManager)   66
    Event (GeoPlanner)   207
Deleting text (GeoWrite)   113
Departments (America Online)   270
Deselect all (File menu)   69
Dial menu (GeoComm)   43, 300
Dialing (GeoDex)   259
    a number (GeoComm)   307
Dialog box, Scripts   43
Directory of Services (America Online)   271
Directory tree   70
Disk Copy (GeoManager)   77
Disk Format (GeoManager)   78
Disk format determination   78
Disk menu (GeoManager)   76
    Copy Disk   77
    Format Disk   78
    Pin   77
    Rename Disk   79
    Rescan Drives   79
Disk Rename (GeoManager)   79
Disk size   78
Diskcopy (DOS)   77
Document button (GeoManager)   50, 82

Index

DOCUMENT directory   38
Document extensions   43
Document saving (GeoWrite)   161, 169, 171
Document Size (GeoDraw)   179
Documents, creating   38
   File name   38
   Icons   38
   Saving   38
DOS/GEOS files   38, 39
   Exporting   40
   Importing   40
DOS Diskcopy   77
DOS files, script   43
DOS Programs Applications   315
DOS Programs Window   316
Double-click   48, 58, 60, 70, 86
Double click time, mouse   97
Drag
   As Outline (GeoDraw)   180
   As Rect (GeoDraw)   180
   Icon   58
Dragging   64
Draw graphics (GeoWrite)   128
Drawing (GeoWrite)
   Borders   167
   Vertical lines   163
Drive (Tree Menu)   71
Drive buttons   50, 83
Drive Cascade menu   71
Drives Rescan (GeoManager)   79
Duplex (GeoComm)   297

E

Edit batch file (DOS Programs)   323
Edit menu
   (Calculator)   222
      Copy   222
      Cut   222
      Paste   222
   (GeoComm)   289
   (GeoDex)   255
   (GeoDraw)   176
      Fuse Objects   177
   (GeoWrite)   125
      Copy   125
      Cut   125
      Insert Page Break   126
      Insert page number   127
      Paste   126
      Pin   125
      Recall Style   126
      Store Style   126

(Notepad)   235
End time (GeoPlanner)   210
Enter button (Calculator)   224
Entering phone numbers (GeoDex)   252
   Text (Notepad)   28
   Text in table (GeoWrite)   164
Event (GeoPlanner)   207
   Delete   207
   New   207
Event scheduling (GeoPlanner)   202
Events only (GeoPlanner)   209
Exchange button (Calculator)   224
Exit   37
   Button   15, 18
   File menu
      (GeoWrite)   124
      (GeoManager)   69
   to DOS   57
Expand all (Tree menu)   71
Expand Branch (Tree menu) 72
Expand One Level (Tree menu)   72
Expanded Memory   95
Export GEOS file   46
Export to DOS, verifying   48
Exporting DOS/GEOS files   40
Express button   42, 54
Express menu   43, 54, 86
   Button   36
   Printer Control   56
   Startup   56
   Welcome   54
   Exit to DOS   57
Extended Memory   95
Extensions, document   43

F

Fax/Paper mail (America Online)   274
File attributes   67
File menu
   (America Online)   266
   (GeoComm)   284
   (GeoDex)   255
   (GeoDraw)   174
      Import   174
   (Geomanager)   59
      Attributes   67
      Copy   65
      Create directory   62
      Delete   66
      Deselect all   69
      Duplicate   66
      Exit   69

347

Index

    Get Info   61, 62
    Move   63
    Open   60
    Pin   59
    Rename   67
    Select all   69
(GeoPlanner)   204
    Page Setup   204
    Print   205
(GeoWrite)   116
    Close   119
    Exit   124
    Insert From Text File   121
    New   117
    Open   118
    Page Setup   123
    Pin   116
    Print   122
    Printing a Document   124
    Revert   120
    Save   119
    Save As   120
    Save as Text File   121
(Notepad)   232
    Close   234
    New   233
    Open   233
    Print   235
    Revert   235
    Save   234
    Save As   235
File names   38
Find Member (America Online)   277
Font size (GeoWrite)   127
Fonts menu (GeoWrite)   139
Footers (GeoWrite)   109
Format, telephone number (GeoComm)   307
Format determination   78
Format Disk (GeoManager)   78
Full-Sized, Window menu (GeoManager)   81
Full-Sized/Overlapping buttons   50, 82
Full year (GeoPlanner)   209
Fuse Objects (GeoDraw)   177

G

Game menu (Solitare)   312
GENIE.MAC   43, 301
GeoComm   42
    Accessing   282
    Application   281
    Icon   44

GeoDex
    Application   249
    Lookup (GeoPlanner)   215
    Window   250
GeoDraw   34, 173
    Accessing   174
    Window   35
GeoManager   49
    Control line   52
    Document window   42
    Window   41
GeoPlanner
    Application   199
    (GeoDex)   254
GEOS/DOS files   38, 39
    Exporting   40
    Importing   40
GEOS file names   38
GeoWrite, Importing DOS file   46
GeoWrite, opening   44
    Import DOS file   45
GeoWrite   101
    Footers   109
    Headers   109
    Indent   105
    Justification   107
    Keyboard editing   112
    Line spacing settings   108
    Main screen   103
    Margins   105
    Menu bar   104
    Menus   115
        File menu   116
    Paging arrow   106
    Ruler bar   104
    Ruler settings   105
    Selecting text   110
    Starting   102
    Tabs   105, 106
    Text alignment   108
    Typing mode   109
Get Info (File menu)   61, 62
Get Member Info (America Online)   277

H

Halftone   131
Handshake (GeoComm)   296
Hang up (GeoComm)   308
Headers (GeoWrite)   109
    Creating   157
Help   18
    (America Online)   263

348

Index

Hidden attribute   67
Hidden Files   74
Hide all (GeoWrite)   130
Highlighting text (GeoWrite)   155
Hotkey Commands (Professional
    Workspace)   33

I

Icon   36, 55, 64
    Change drive   63
    Document   42
    GeoComm   42, 44
    Move Up One Directory level   63, 65
    Reposition   58
    Unshrinking   58
Icons, document   38
Icons (View menu)   73
Import
    DOS file/GeoWrite   45   46
    DOS/GEOS files   40
    File menu (GeoDraw)   174
Indent marker (GeoWrite)   105
Insert From Text File (GeoWrite)   44, 121
Insert page break (GeoWrite)   126
Insert page number (GeoWrite)   127
Inserting graphics in header (GeoWrite)   159
Insertion mode (GeoWrite)   109
Installation
    Geoworks   6
    Monitor   10
    Mouse   11
    Printer   11
Instant Message (America Online)   277
Interrupt Level options   95
Interrupt Request (GeoComm)   294
Interval (GeoPlanner)   211
IRQ (GeoComm)   294
Italic text   144

J

Justification
    Text (GeoDraw)   190
    (GeoWrite)   107

K

Keyboard Commands (Professional
    Workspace)   32
Keyboard editing (GeoWrite)   112
Keyword (America Online)   270

L

Label, Volume   78
Landscape (GeoDraw)   170
Leading (GeoWrite)   138
Left-justified tab (GeoWrite)   107
Line (GeoDraw)
    Color   185
    Connect   196
    Handles   195
    Pattern   185
    Style   184
    Tool   195
    Width   184
Line spacing (GeoWrite)   138
    Setting (GeoWrite)   108
Listings, Window menu (GeoManager)   81
Lobby (America Online)   271
Log (America Online)   267
    Open   268
    Read   268
Look and Feel   86
    Document Safeguarding   87
    Font Size   87
    OK/Reset/Cancel   88
    Sound   88

M

Mail menu (America Online)   272
Main Display Window   50, 81
Managed Extended Memory   95
Margins (GeoWrite)   105
Maximize, Control button   36
Maximize/Restore button   58
Maximize (Control menu)   53
Members menu (America Online)   277
Memory   95
Memory functions (Calculator)   226
Memory use (Calculator)   221
Menu
    Arrange menu (GeoDraw)   188
    Dial (GeoComm)   43, 300
    Edit
        (Calculator)   222
        (GeoComm)   289
        (GeoDex)   255
        (GeoPlanner)   206
        (Notepad)   236
    Express   43

349

Index

File
    (America Online)   266
    (GeoComm)   284
    (GeoDex)   255
    (GeoPlanner)   204
    (Notepad)   232
Fonts (GeoWrite)   139
Game (Solitare)   312
Modify (GeoDraw)   181
Option File (GeoDex)   258
Options
    (Calculator)   223
    (DOS Programs)   317
    (GeoComm)   292
    (GeoDraw)   179
    (GeoPlanner)   209
    (Solitare)   312
Pinning   34
    Moving   34
    Closing   34
Quick (GeoPlanner)   212
Sizes
    (GeoWrite)   140
    (Notepad)   236
Styles (GeoWrite)   144
Text (GeoDraw)   189
Utilities (GeoPlanner)   213
    Repeat Events   213
View
    (GeoComm)   291
    (GeoDex)   256
    (GeoDraw)   178
    (GeoPlanner)   208
    Window (GeoDraw)   191
Menu Bar   37, 59
    (America Online)   263
    (GeoPlanner)   203
    (GeoWrite)   104
Menu Control (GeoManager)   53
Menu Maps   34, Appendix
Menu Options   66, 67
Message (GeoComm)   290
Minimize Button   37, 44, 59
Minimize Control button   36
Minimize (Control menu)   53
Minimize on Run (GeoManager)   76
Minimize/Maximize Restore Button   37
Modem (GeoComm)
    Port   293
    Setting   298
    Speaker   299

Modify menu (GeoDraw)   181
    Area Properties   185
    Flip Horizontal   182
    Flip Vertical   183
    Line Properties   184
    Nudge   181
    Rotate 45° Left   183
    Rotate 45° Right   183
    Text Properties   186
Mouse operations   17
    Clicking   17
    Double-click time   97
    Dragging   18
    Scrolling   17
Mouse pointers   16
Mouse type   97
Mouse use (Professional Workspace)   32
Move
    (Control menu)   53
    (File menu)   63
    Quick   206
Move backward (GeoDraw)   189
Move by dragging   64
Move forward (GeoDraw)   189
Move Up One Directory level icon   63, 65
Moving pinned menu   34

N

Names and Details (View menu) 73
Names Only (View menu)   73
New, File menu (GeoWrite)   117
New event (GeoPlanner)   207
Notepad   28
    Changing text size   29
    Cut/Copy/Paste   29
    Entering text   28
    Printing   29
Notepad Application   229
Notes box, User   61, 62

O

One-line border (GeoWrite)   132
Open, File menu (GeoWrite)   118
Open a file   60
Open a log (America Online)   268
Opening Scrapbooks   245
Option file menu (GeoDex)   258
    Area Code option   258
    Dialing   259
    Prefix option   258

Index

Option menu
  (Calculator)   223
    Decimal Places   223
  (DOS Programs)   317
  (GeoComm)   292
  (GeoDraw)   179
    Document Size   179
    Drag As Outline   180
    Drag As Rect   180
    Show Tool Box   180
  (GeoManager)   75
    Confirm Delete   75
    Confirm Read-Only   75
    Confirm Replace   75
    Minimize on Run   76
    Pin   75
    Save Options   76
  (GeoPlanner)   209
    Change Preferences   210
  (GeoWrite)   128
    Align Ruler with page   129
    Draw Graphics   128
    Hide All   130
    Save Options   130
    Show (H/V) Scroll Bar   129
    Show All   129
    Show Ruler Bottom   129
    Show Ruler Top   129
    Snap to Ruler Marks   129
  (Solitare)   312
Options menu   66, 67
Order of operations (Calculator)   220
Overlapping, Window menu (GeoManager)   80
Overlapping/Full-Sized buttons   50, 82
Overlapping pages (GeoWrite)   147
Overwrite mode (GeoWrite)   109

P

P.C. Studio (America Online)   272
Page
  Go to (GeoWrite)   146
  Next (GeoWrite)   146
  Overlapping (GeoWrite)   147
  Previous (GeoWrite)   146
Page Setup, File menu (GeoWrite)   123
Pages, moving between (GeoWrite)   127
Paging arrows (GeoWrite)   106
Paragraph (GeoWrite)
  Changing indent   170
  Spacing   137

Paragraph menu (GeoWrite)   130
  Border   132
  Border Color   134
  Custom Border   133
  Paragraph Color   130
  Paragraph Spacing   137
  Pin   130
  Tab Attributes   135
Parallel Port   92
Parity (GeoComm)   295
Paste
  (Calculator)   222
  (GeoWrite)   126
  (Notepad)   29
Pattern, solid/see-through (GeoDraw)   186
PC/GEOS   99
People (America Online)   271
Phone type (GeoComm)   298
Pin   70
  (GeoManager)   75, 77
  (GeoWrite)   116, 125
Pin a menu   34, 59, 73, 116
Plain text   144
Planner   18
  Events   20
  Go to Month/Day   20
  Go to Year   19
  Print   20
  Screen   19
Playing Solitare   310
Pointer, quick copy   168
Polygon tool (GeoDraw)   197
Port, modem (GeoComm)   293
Portrait (GeoDraw)   179
Preferences Application   86
  Look and Feel   86
    Document Safeguarding   87
    Font Size   87
    OK/Reset/Cancel   88
    Opening Screen   88
    Sound   88
  Date and Time   89
    Date   89
    OK/Reset/Cancel   89
    Time   89
  Background   90
    Inserting   91,
    Selecting   90
  Printer   92
    Install new   92
    Test   94

351

Index

Computer 94
   Expanded Memory 95
Video 96
   Screen blanking 96
Mouse 97
   Double Click Time 97
   Acceleration 97
   Type 97
Modem 98
PC/GEOS 99
Prefix option (GeoDex) 258
Print
   Banner 25
   File menu (GeoWrite) 122
   Planner 20
Printer 92
   Control (Express menu) 56
   Install new 92
   Installation 11
   Test 94
Printing
   Banner 25
   Notepad 29
Printing a Document, File menu (GeoWrite) 124
Professional Workspace 31
   Hotkey Commands 33
   Keyboard Commands 32
   Mouse use 32
Protocol changes (GeoComm) 296
Protocol setting (GeoComm) 293

Q

Quick copy 206, 223
Quick copy pointer 168
Quick dial
   (GeoComm) 307
   (GeoDex) 253
Quick menu (GeoPlanner) 212
Quick move 206, 223

R

RAM disk 83
RCL 26
Read-only 67
   Attribute 61
   (Notepad) 233
Read a log (America Online) 268
Read mail (America Online) 273
Reboot 3, 52

Recall style (GeoWrite) 126
Receive XMODEM (GeoComm) 287
Rectangle tool (GeoDraw) 197
Redraw (GeoWrite) 147 Listing 148
Relocating a window 57
Reminder precedes event (GeoPlanner) 211
Remove tab (GeoWrite) 107
Rename (File menu) 67
Rename Disk (GeoManager) 79
Reopen an application 55
Rescan Drives (GeoManager) 79
Resizing a window 57
Respacing a table (GeoWrite) 169
Restore (Control menu) 53
Revert, File menu (GeoWrite) 120
RGB color 131
Right-justified tab (GeoWrite) 107
Right align text (GeoWrite) 108
ROM disk 83
Rooms (America Online) 272
Root directory 39, 69
Rotate any degree (GeoDraw) 183
Rotate pointer (GeoDraw) 196
RPN (Calculator) 224
RPN calculations (Calculator) 225
Ruler bar (GeoWrite) 104
Ruler setting (GeoWrite) 105

S

Save, File menu (GeoWrite) 119
Save a document (GeoWrite) 150
Save As, File menu (GeoWrite) 120
Save as Text File (GeoWrite) 46, 121
Save buffer (GeoComm) 288
Save Options (GeoManager) 76
Save options (GeoWrite) 130
Save preferences (GeoPlanner) 212
Saving a document (GeoWrite) 161, 169, 171
Saving a GEOS file as DOS file 46
Schedule of events (GeoPlanner) 202
Scoring (Solitare) 313
Scrapbook
   Application 239
   Changing 244
   Copying 246
   Menu bar 242
      Edit menu 242
      File menu 242
   Opening 245
   Window 240

Index

Screen, GeoManager   50
Screen blanking   96
Script commands (GeoComm)   302
Scripts (GeoComm)   300
Scripts   43
Search
   (GeoDex)   257
   (GeoPlanner)   214
Select all (File menu)   69
Select current time (GeoPlanner)   201
Select day and date (GeoPlanner)   201
Select year (GeoPlanner)   201
Selecting text (GeoWrite)   110, 112, 152
Send to back (GeoDraw)   189
Send XMODEM (GeoComm)   286
Serial Port   93, 98
Setting options (GeoWrite)   151
Setting table margins (GeoWrite)   163
Settings, alarm (GeoPlanner)   207
Setup (America Online)   264
Shadow border (GeoWrite)   132
Show (H/V) scroll bar (GeoWrite)   129
Show all (GeoWrite)   129
Show empty days (GeoPlanner)   210
Show Hidden Files (View menu)   74
Show ruler bottom (GeoWrite)   129
Show ruler top (GeoWrite)   129
Show Tool Box (GeoDraw)   180
Show Tree Window (Tree menu)   70
Single month (GeoPlanner)   209
Size (Control menu)   53
Sizes menu
   (GeoWrite)   140
   (Notepad)   236
Snap to ruler marks (GeoWrite)   129
Solid/see-through pattern (GeoDraw)   186
Solitaire   25
   Application   309
   Scoring   313
Sort By (View menu)   73
Spacing (GeoWrite)
   Character   143
   Paragraph   137
Speaker volume (GeoComm)   299
Start time (GeoPlanner)   210
Startup   86
   (Express menu)   56
Status line (GeoComm)   299
STO+   26
STO   26
Stop Bits (GeoComm)   295

Stop button (copy)   65
Store style (GeoWrite)   126
Strike thru text   145
Styles menu (GeoWrite)   144
Subdirectories   39, 45
Subscript text   145
Superscript text   145
Switch day automatically (GeoPlanner)   211
System attribute   67

T

Tab
   Attributes (GeoWrite)   135
   Copy (GeoWrite)   107
   Markers, removing (GeoWrite)   166
   Remove (GeoWrite)   107
   Type (GeoWrite)   107, 135
Table
   Entries, underlining (GeoWrite)   166
   Margins, setting (GeoWrite)   163
   Respacing (GeoWrite)   169
Tabs (GeoWrite)   105, 106
Telephone number format (GeoComm)   307
Template day (GeoPlanner)   210
Terminal
   Emulation (GeoComm)   296
   Settings (GeoComm)   296
Text
   Alignment (GeoWrite)   108
   Bold   144
   Color   145
   Creating (GeoDraw)   193
   File (GeoComm)   284
   Highlighting (GeoWrite)   155
   Italic   144
   Justification (GeoDraw)   190
   Large/small (GeoComm)   291
   Menu (GeoDraw)   189
   Plain   144
   Delecting (GeoWrite)   152
   Size (Notepad)   29
   Strike thru   145
   Subscript   145
   Superscript   145
   Tool (GeoDraw)   193
   Underline   144
Tiled   90
Title Bar   36, 57
   Relocating a window   57
   Resizing a window   57

Index

Tool Box (GeoDraw)   192
   Show   180
Tree, directory   70
Tree menu (GeoManager)   69
   Collapse Branch   72
   Drive   71
   Expand all   71
   Expand Branch   72
   Expand One Level   72
   Pin   70
   Show Tree Window   70
Tutorial (GeoWrite)   149
Two line border (GeoWrite)   132
Typing mode (GeoWrite)   109
Typing text (GeoWrite)   156

U

Underline text   144
Underlining table entries (GeoWrite)   166
User Notes box   61, 62
Using Notepad   231

V

Verifying DOS export   48
Vertical line, drawing (GeoWrite)   163
View menu
   (GeoComm)   291
   (GeoDex)   256
      Browse View   256
      Card View   256
   (GeoDraw)   178
   (GeoManager)   72
      Compress Display   74
      Icons   73
      Names and Details   73
      Names Only   73
      Pin   73
      Show Hidden Files   74
      Sort By   73
   (GeoPlanner)   208
      Calendar only   208
      Events Only   209
      Full Year   209
      Single Month   209
   (GeoWrite)   127
      Correct for Aspect Ratio   128
Viewing events (GeoPlanner)   203
Volume label   78

W

Wastebasket   50, 82
Welcome (Express menu)   54
Welcome Screen   14
Welcome screen Exit to DOS   57
Welcome window   40
Window (GeoDraw)   35
   Welcome   40
   (GeoWrite)   146
      Full-Sized   148
      Go to Page   146
      Next Page   146
      Overlapping   147
      Page Listing   148
      Pin   146
      Previous Page   146
      Redraw   147
   Size (GeoComm)   292
Window menu
   (America Online)   278
   (GeoDraw)   191
      Full-Sized   192
      Listing   192
      Overlapping   192
   (GeoManager)   79
      Close   80
      Close All   80
      Full-Sized   81
      Listing and Selections   81
      Overlapping   80
      Pin   80
World button   50, 82
WORLD directory   38
World display   41
Wrap lines (GeoComm)   297

Y

Year, select (GeoPlanner)   201